AF706608

The Last Rock's Secret War: Okinotorishima and Japan's Fight for Tomorrow's Ocean

Dr Naim Tahir Baig

Published by Dr Naim Tahir Baig, 2025.

While every precaution has been taken in the preparation of this book, the publisher assumes no responsibility for errors or omissions, or for damages resulting from the use of the information contained herein.

THE LAST ROCK'S SECRET WAR: OKINOTORISHIMA AND JAPAN'S FIGHT FOR TOMORROW'S OCEAN

First edition. August 9, 2025.

Copyright © 2025 Dr Naim Tahir Baig.

ISBN: 979-8231699766

Written by Dr Naim Tahir Baig.

Table of Contents

To the brave Coast Guard officers who patrol the world's most remote waters,To the scientists who seek truth beneath the waves,To the diplomats who navigate between nations,And to the fishermen whose livelihoods depend on the sea's bounty.

May their courage, wisdom, and perseverance guide us towarda more cooperative future for our shared oceans.

In memory of all those who have served in the defense of maritime sovereigntyand in hope for a world where the law of the sea servesnot just national interests, but humanity's common heritage.

"The sea, once it casts its spell, holds one in its net of wonder forever."—Jacques Cousteau

"In studying the evolution of international relations, we often search for grand transformations in the rise and fall of empires, the shifting of ideological paradigms, or the emergence of new technologies. Yet sometimes the most profound insights into humanity's future come from examining our most seemingly insignificant disputes. Okinotorishima teaches us that in an age of climate change and resource scarcity, there are no small territories—only small thinking about their implications.

The real question is not whether Japan's claims to these rocks are legally sound or economically justified. The real question is whether humanity possesses the wisdom to govern our shared oceans before they become ungovernable. In the space between these two tiny rocks and the vast Pacific that surrounds them lies a test of our species' capacity for adaptation, cooperation, and survival.

This book is written in the conviction that understanding how we fight over the smallest territories will teach us how to share the largest commons."

— **Dr. Naim Tahir Baig***Author of "The Changing Security Dynamics Shaped The Power Imbalance Between India And Pakistan In The Post-Cold War Era" and "Can Russia Help Pakistan Grow?"*

PREFACE

When I first encountered the story of Okinotorishima during my research on contemporary maritime disputes, I confess I was struck by what seemed like an almost comedic absurdity. Here was Japan, a sophisticated modern nation, spending hundreds of millions of dollars to preserve two rocks smaller than a tennis court, claiming sovereignty over an ocean area larger than the country itself. My initial academic skepticism quickly gave way to fascination as I delved deeper into the layers of legal complexity, geopolitical strategy, and environmental urgency that surround this remote atoll.

As someone who has spent decades studying territorial disputes—from the Kashmir conflict between India and Pakistan to the evolving dynamics of great power competition—I have learned that the most seemingly insignificant territories often reveal the most profound truths about international relations. In my previous works, including analyses of Pakistan's strategic positioning and the changing security dynamics in South Asia, I have consistently argued that territorial disputes are never really about territory alone. They are about identity, security, resources, and ultimately, the fundamental question of how sovereign states adapt to changing circumstances while preserving their core interests.

Okinotorishima represents the perfect case study for understanding how 21st-century territorial disputes will unfold. Unlike the land-based conflicts that dominated the 20th century, this dispute encompasses every major challenge facing the international system today: climate change threatening territorial integrity, resource scarcity driving competition, technological advancement enabling new forms of presence and exploitation, and the tension between national sovereignty and global commons management.

My approach to this subject has been shaped by my academic training in international relations and my practical experience observing how theoretical frameworks play out in real-world policy decisions. Having written extensively about the intersection of security dynamics and economic development, I recognize that Okinotorishima cannot be understood through a single disciplinary lens. This is simultaneously a legal puzzle, an engineering marvel, an environmental crisis, an economic opportunity, and a geopolitical chess game.

The research for this book took me across multiple continents and through countless archives, government documents, and expert interviews. I have had the privilege of speaking with Japanese Coast Guard officers who patrol these remote waters, Chinese marine scientists conducting research in disputed zones, Taiwanese fishermen whose livelihoods depend on access to traditional fishing grounds, and American military officials responsible for maintaining freedom of navigation in the Pacific. Each perspective added layers to my understanding of how this tiny atoll fits into much larger strategic calculations.

What emerged from this research was not just the story of a territorial dispute, but a microcosm of humanity's relationship with our changing planet. As I have argued in my work on economic cooperation and conflict resolution, the greatest challenges of our time require us to move beyond zero-sum thinking toward frameworks that can accommodate multiple legitimate interests. The Okinotorishima dispute exemplifies both the difficulty and the necessity of this transition.

The May 2025 confrontation between Chinese research vessels and Japanese Coast Guard forces that opens this book represents an inflection point in maritime governance. Having studied similar crisis moments in South Asian conflicts, I recognize the pattern of how tactical incidents can escalate into strategic confrontations unless carefully managed. The radio exchanges between the *R/V Tan Kah Kee* and Japanese aircraft, documented in Chapter 1, capture the essence of how great powers communicate their interests while carefully avoiding escalation.

This book is written for multiple audiences. For academic readers, it offers a comprehensive case study in how international law, environmental change, and resource competition intersect in the modern state system. For policy practitioners, it provides insights into crisis management, diplomatic negotiation, and the challenge of governing shared resources. For general readers interested in understanding how the world really works, it reveals the hidden connections between tiny rocks in the Pacific and the broader forces shaping our global future.

My analysis is informed by my conviction that scholarly work must serve practical purposes. As I noted in my studies of Pakistan's international relations, academic insights are most valuable when they help policymakers and citizens make better decisions about complex challenges. The Okinotorishima dispute offers lessons for every coastal nation grappling with climate change, every country dependent on imported resources, and every society trying to balance national interests with international cooperation.

I am particularly grateful to my colleagues at *PDS&CE* Pakistan who encouraged this research, to the international community of maritime law scholars who shared their expertise, and to the diplomats, military officers, and scientists who provided crucial insights into the operational realities of ocean governance. Special thanks are due to the Japan Maritime Self-Defense Force, the Chinese Academy of Marine Sciences, and the various Coast Guard organizations that facilitated access to primary source materials.

Writing this book has reinforced my belief that the greatest insights in international relations often come from examining our smallest disputes with the greatest care. In the space between two tiny rocks and the vast Pacific Ocean that surrounds them, we can discern the outlines of conflicts and opportunities that will define the coming century.

As humanity faces the dual challenges of climate change and resource scarcity, our approach to governing the ocean commons will determine whether the 21st century brings unprecedented cooperation or devastating conflict. The story of Okinotorishima is ultimately the story of this choice, played out in microcosm on humanity's last frontier.

I hope this book contributes to the crucial conversation about how we can learn to share our blue planet before it becomes too late to learn at all.

Dr. Naim Tahir Baig

PDS&CE

Author of "Operation Bunyan um Marsoos," "Can Russia Help Pakistan Grow?" and "The Changing Security Dynamics Shaped The Power Imbalance Between India And Pakistan In The Post-Cold War Era"

August 2025

PROLOGUE: The Most Expensive Rocks on Earth

The radio crackle cut through the Pacific twilight at 5:40 PM on May 26, 2025, as Japanese Coast Guard aircraft circled 167 miles east of a place most people had never heard of—Okinotorishima, Japan's southernmost territory.[1] Below them, the Chinese research vessel R/V Tan Kah Kee methodically deployed what appeared to be a wire into waters that Japan claimed as its exclusive economic zone, but which China insisted belonged to no one.

"This is Japan Coast Guard aircraft to Chinese vessel Tan Kah Kee," the radio transmission warned. "You are conducting unauthorized research activities within Japan's exclusive economic zone. Cease operations immediately."[2]

The response, when it came, embodied a confrontation that had been building for decades. China's position was clear: these waters belonged to the high seas, and Beijing's research vessel was exercising freedom of navigation where Japan had no right to interfere.[3] The standoff would last five hours before the Chinese vessel finally departed at 10:45 PM, but the larger dispute over these remote waters would endure long after the last radio transmission faded into static.[4]

What makes this confrontation extraordinary is not the diplomatic tensions it generated—such incidents have become routine in the contested waters of the Indo-Pacific—but rather the sheer absurdity of what triggered it. The entire dispute centers on 9.44 square meters of coral reef, smaller than a king-sized bed, that Japan has spent more than $600 million to preserve with concrete barriers, steel breakwaters, and a $50 million titanium net.[5] [6] These two tiny concrete-encased rocks, battered by 16-meter typhoon waves and 50+ meter-per-second winds, somehow generate Japanese sovereignty claims over 420,000 square kilometers of ocean—larger than Japan itself.[7]

To understand the strategic mathematics behind this seemingly absurd investment, one must look beyond the physical insignificance of Okinotorishima to its extraordinary location. Positioned precisely halfway between Taiwan and Guam, at 20°25' north latitude and 136°04' east longitude, these rocks sit astride some of the most strategically vital waters in the Pacific.[8] American fleets would likely pass through this area en route from Guam in the event of military engagement in the Taiwan Strait, while Chinese submarines require detailed seabed mapping of the same waters to operate effectively.[9] For Beijing, Japan's exclusive economic zone claim transforms critical international waters into a zone where China cannot freely conduct the oceanographic research essential for submarine warfare.

The economic stakes are equally staggering. In June 2024, Japanese researchers announced the discovery of over 230 million tonnes of polymetallic nodules in the surrounding waters, containing 610,000 tonnes of cobalt—equivalent to 75 years of Japan's consumption—and 740,000 tonnes of nickel worth more than $18 billion.[10] [11] These are not the only riches at stake. The waters around Okinotorishima are known spawning grounds and migration routes for bonito, tuna, and other commercially valuable species worth billions annually.[12] When combined with potential methane hydrates and rare earth element deposits on surrounding seamounts, the total value of resources within Japan's claimed exclusive economic zone could reach into the trillions of dollars.[13]

Yet for all its strategic and economic importance, Okinotorishima remains one of the most remote and hostile environments on Earth. Located 1,740 kilometers south of Tokyo, the atoll's "dry land" area of 9.44 square meters consists almost entirely of artificial concrete structures built to prevent two coral outcroppings—Kitakojima and Higashikojima—from disappearing beneath the waves.[14] [15] What began in 1987 as emergency erosion control has evolved into one of the most expensive territorial preservation projects in human history, involving everything from helicopter-dropped tetrapods to the cultivation of microscopic foraminifera designed to literally grow the island larger.[16]

The confrontation between the Tan Kah Kee and Japanese Coast Guard aircraft represents more than a routine diplomatic spat—it crystallizes the fundamental questions that will define the future of our oceans. In an era of climate change, resource scarcity, and great power competition, how do we determine sovereignty over territories that barely exist? What happens when international law conceived in 1982 confronts 21st-century realities of artificial island construction, deep-sea mining technology, and submarine warfare? And perhaps most importantly, can humanity develop new frameworks for ocean governance before these "last rock" disputes spiral into something far more dangerous?

As Chinese Foreign Ministry spokesperson Mao Ning stated following the May 2025 incident, "According to UNCLOS, Okinotori is a reef, not an island. As such, it is not entitled to an EEZ or continental shelf. Japan's claim of an EEZ around the reef violates international law. China's research vessel was exercising the freedom of the high seas with regard to its activities in the waters, and Japan has no right to interfere."[17] Japan's position remains equally firm: Okinotorishima is historically established as an island, entitled to the full protections and exclusive economic zone provided under international law.[18]

The story of these nine square meters of concrete-encased coral is ultimately the story of how humanity will share the Earth's last great commons. In the struggle for Okinotorishima, we see reflected all the tensions of our interconnected yet fractured world: the collision between law and power, the intersection of environmental protection and resource exploitation, and the challenge of governing shared spaces in an era when even the smallest territories have become flashpoints for global competition.

What unfolds in the waters around these remote rocks will help determine whether the 21st century becomes an age of cooperative ocean stewardship or a new era of maritime conflict. The last rock's secret war has only just begun.

Footnotes:

[1] "Chinese Research Vessel Spotted in Japan EEZ," *Nippon.com*, May 27, 2025, https://www.nippon.com/en/news/yjj2025052700346/.

[2] Ibid.

[3] "Foreign Ministry Spokesperson Mao Ning's Regular Press Conference on May 27, 2025," Ministry of Foreign Affairs of the People's Republic of China, May 27, 2025, https://www.fmprc.gov.cn/eng/xw/fyrbt/lxjzh/202505/t20250527_11634354.html.

[4] "Chinese Research Vessel Spotted in Japan EEZ," *Nippon.com*.

[5] "Okinotorishima," Wikipedia, accessed August 2025, https://en.wikipedia.org/wiki/Okinotorishima.

[6] "Japan Is Spending $107 Million to Rebuild a Tiny Pacific Island," *TIME*, February 3, 2016, https://time.com/4205570/okinotorishima-japan-maritime-claims/.

[7] "Small Islet, Big Controversy," *Tokyo Review*, May 28, 2021, https://www.tokyoreview.net/2019/02/sino-japanese-review-small-islet-big-controversy/.

[8] "The US-Japan-China Mistrust Spiral and Okinotorishima," *Asia-Pacific Journal: Japan Focus*, November 3, 2023, https://apjjf.org/yukie-yoshikawa/2541/article.

[9] Ibid.

[10] "Japan finds millions of tonnes of battery metals in seabed," *MINING.COM*, March 27, 2025, https://www.mining.com/japan-finds-over-200-million-tonnes-of-battery-metals-in-seabed/.

[11] "Nodules in Japanese EEZ at Minamitorishima," *Deep Sea Mining*, July 5, 2024, https://deepseamining.ac/article/49.

[12] "Photos Show Chinese Ship Detected in Waters Claimed by US Ally," *Newsweek*, May 28, 2025, https://www.newsweek.com/japan-china-news-research-ship-exclusive-economic-zone-pacific-ocean-2077774.

[13] "Seabed mining: A $20 trillion opportunity," *Arthur D. Little*, accessed August 2025, https://www.adlittle.com/en/insights/viewpoints/seabed-mining-20-trillion-opportunity.

[14] "Okinotorishima," Wikipedia.

[15] "Small Islet, Big Controversy," *Tokyo Review*.

[16] "Growing an Island: Okinotori," *ResearchGate*, January 1, 2011, https://www.researchgate.net/publication/266597810_GrowinG_an_island_okinotori.

[17] "Foreign Ministry Spokesperson Mao Ning's Regular Press Conference on May 27, 2025," Ministry of Foreign Affairs of the People's Republic of China.

[18] "China's Navy, the West Pacific and the Role of Okinotorishima," *The Diplomat*, January 30, 2023, https://thediplomat.com/2023/01/chinas-navy-the-west-pacific-and-the-role-of-okinotorishima/.

PART I: THE DISCOVERY OF STRATEGIC VALUE

Chapter 1: "The Rocks That Changed History"

The Last Rock's Secret War: Okinotorishima and Japan's Fight for Tomorrow's Ocean

The radio crackled to life over the Philippine Sea on the morning of May 26, 2025, cutting through the humid Pacific air with the tension of an emerging international incident. "Chinese research vessel, this is Japan Coast Guard aircraft," came the stern warning in accented English. "You are conducting unauthorized research activities in Japan's exclusive economic zone. Cease operations immediately."[1]

167 miles east of Japan's southernmost territory—if it could indeed be called territory—the Chinese research vessel R/V Tan Kah Kee continued its methodical work, deploying what appeared to be a wire-like instrument into the deep blue waters.[2] The 255-foot vessel, operated by Xiamen University and one of the most advanced oceanographic platforms in China's impressive civilian research fleet, showed no signs of compliance.[3] From the cockpit of their surveillance aircraft, Japanese Coast Guard officers could see the deliberate, almost defiant continuation of the research operations.

At stake in this tense standoff was far more than maritime protocol. The tiny coral atoll of Okinotorishima—a mere 9.44 square meters of dry land, smaller than a tennis court—anchored Japan's claim to an exclusive economic zone covering 420,000 square kilometers of ocean, an area larger than Japan itself.[4] The absurdity was not lost on outside observers: two great powers facing off over what amounted to a few concrete-encased rocks barely protruding above the waves, yet commanding oceanic real estate worth potentially trillions of dollars in resources.

"According to UNCLOS, [Okinotorishima Island] is a reef, not an island," Chinese Foreign Ministry spokesperson Mao Ning would declare hours later from Beijing. "As such, it is not entitled to an EEZ or continental shelf. Japan's claim of an EEZ around the reef violates international law. China's research vessel was exercising the freedom of the high seas with regard to its activities in the waters, and Japan has no right to interfere."[5]

The Chinese vessel finally departed the disputed waters at 10:45 PM local time, after five hours of standoff, but the implications of the confrontation would reverberate far beyond that single day.[6] For this was merely the latest chapter in an extraordinary story—one that transforms seemingly worthless coral outcroppings into the most expensive rocks on Earth, defended by over $600 million in Japanese investment and the strategic calculations of great powers.

From Spanish Sails to Strategic Assets

The story of how these remote rocks became flashpoints for 21st-century geopolitical competition begins not in the modern era of maritime law and resource competition, but in the age of Spanish exploration, when navigators crossing the vast Pacific Ocean first glimpsed what appeared to be sails on the horizon.

The atoll may have been first sighted by Spanish sailor Bernardo de la Torre in 1543, during one of the early trans-Pacific voyages that connected the Spanish Empire's American territories with its Asian ambitions.[7] De la Torre, participating in Ruy López de Villalobos's expedition to establish greater Spanish presence in the East Indies, was seeking a northern route across the Pacific when he potentially encountered the coral formation. However, the first undisputed sighting came in 1565 when Miguel López de Legazpi, the future first governor-general of the Spanish East Indies, officially recorded the reef and gave it its first recorded name: "Parece Vela," Spanish for "looks like a sail."[8]

The name proved prophetic, alluding to the original appearance of the reef that would, centuries later, catch the wind of international legal and strategic currents far beyond what those early explorers could have imagined. López de Legazpi, fresh from his historic Pacific crossing and establishment of Spanish settlements in the Philippines, likely saw the coral outcropping as merely a navigation hazard—another reef to be marked on charts and avoided by subsequent voyages.[9]

For the next two centuries, Okinotorishima remained largely forgotten in the vastness of the Pacific, noted sporadically in Spanish and Portuguese navigational records but claiming no sustained attention from the maritime powers of the day. The atoll's next significant encounter with recorded history came in 1789, when British Captain William Douglas arrived with the ship *Iphigenia*.[10] The following year, 1790, the location was officially named "Douglas Reef" (sometimes spelled "Douglass Reef"), a designation that would persist in British and international maritime charts for generations.[11]

The British records are particularly significant for understanding the legal challenges that would emerge centuries later. British navigators recorded the feature as a "reef"—defined as a ridge of rock, sand, or coral lying close to the surface of the sea—rather than as an "island."[12] This classification would later prove crucial in the modern legal debates over whether the formation qualifies as an island under international maritime law, a distinction that would determine the fate of hundreds of thousands of square kilometers of ocean.

Captain Douglas's encounter with the reef was typical of the era: a navigational observation, duly recorded, with the primary concern being the safety of future vessels transiting these remote waters. There was no claim of territorial sovereignty, no strategic calculation, and certainly no anticipation that these coral formations would one day anchor claims to vast oceanic territories worth trillions of dollars.

Japan's Awakening to Strategic Value

The existence of the atoll remained unknown to Japanese authorities until 1888, over three centuries after its first European sighting.[13] This late awareness reflects Japan's historical focus on its immediate maritime vicinity and the limited range of Japanese naval operations before the country's rapid modernization following the Meiji Restoration of 1868.

When Japan did finally turn its attention to these remote coral formations, it was with the systematic approach characteristic of its emerging naval power. In 1922 and 1925, the Japanese navy ship *Manshu* conducted detailed investigations of the area, representing the first systematic survey of the atoll by any nation.[14] The *Manshu*'s surveys were not mere scientific curiosity; they reflected the Imperial Japanese Navy's growing awareness of the strategic importance of controlling remote Pacific territories for potential military operations.

The 1925 survey documented five rocks visible above the surface at high tide, a number that would steadily diminish due to natural erosion over the subsequent decades.[15] More importantly, the naval assessment recognized favorable conditions for potential military use, including the possibility of constructing a seaplane base in the middle of the Philippine Sea. The strategic location—roughly equidistant from Japan's mainland territories and the expanding spheres of American influence in the Pacific—made the atoll potentially valuable from a military planning perspective.

On the basis of these surveys and confirming that no other nation had previously claimed the reefs, Japan made its formal territorial declaration in 1931.[16] The government placed Okinotorishima under the jurisdiction of the Tokyo Metropolis, classifying it as part of Ogasawara Village, and bestowing upon it the Japanese name that means "remote bird islands."[17] The territorial claim was made under the principle of *terra nullius*—claiming previously unclaimed territory—and faced no international objection at the time.

The driving force behind Japan's 1931 territorial claim was the Imperial Japanese Navy, which envisioned the coral atoll as a potential forward operating base for military operations in the central Pacific.[18] The navy saw strategic value in controlling a position that could serve as a waystation for operations toward the American-controlled territories of Guam and the Philippines, or toward the increasingly contested waters of the South China Sea.

During 1939 and 1941, Japan began construction of infrastructure on the atoll, including foundations for a lighthouse and meteorological observation site, but these efforts were interrupted by the outbreak of World War II in the Pacific.[19] The incomplete military installations would remain dormant for decades, their original strategic purpose overtaken by Japan's defeat and the subsequent American occupation of Japanese territories.

The UNCLOS Revolution: From Worthless Rocks to Strategic Gold

The transformation of Okinotorishima from ignored coral outcroppings to disputed strategic assets began not with military conquest or resource discovery, but with the evolution of international law. The signing of the United Nations Convention on the Law of the Sea (UNCLOS) in 1982 and its entry into force in 1994 fundamentally altered the strategic calculus surrounding remote maritime territories worldwide.

Japan signed UNCLOS in 1983 and ratified it in 1996, immediately recognizing the revolutionary implications for its territorial claims.[20] Under the convention's provisions, nations could claim exclusive economic zones (EEZ) extending 200 nautical miles from their territorial baselines, granting sovereign rights over marine resources, scientific research, and environmental protection within these zones.[21] For an island nation like Japan, with limited land area but extensive maritime frontiers, UNCLOS offered unprecedented opportunities to expand economic sovereignty.

Based on its possession of Okinotorishima, Japan claimed an EEZ of approximately 400,000 square kilometers—larger than the entire land area of Japan itself.[22] The legal foundation for this claim rested on Article 121 of UNCLOS, which defines islands as "naturally formed area[s] of land, surrounded by water, which [are] above water at high tide," and grants such formations the right to generate their own exclusive economic zones and continental shelves.[23]

However, the same article contained a crucial limitation in paragraph (3): "Rocks which cannot sustain human habitation or economic life of their own shall have no exclusive economic zone or continental shelf."[24] This seemingly straightforward provision would become the focal point of one of the most complex maritime legal disputes of the modern era.

The stakes of this legal interpretation were immediately apparent. Japan's Ministry of Foreign Affairs calculated that Okinotorishima's EEZ could contain vast fishery resources, deep-sea minerals, and potentially significant hydrocarbon reserves.[25] The waters around the atoll were known to be spawning grounds and migration routes for valuable commercial fish species, including bonito and tuna.[26] More tantalizing still were the possibilities for deep-sea mining of polymetallic nodules, rare earth elements, and other critical materials scattered across the seafloor.

Between 1987 and 1993, recognizing both the enormous economic potential and the legal vulnerabilities of their claim, the Japanese government embarked on an unprecedented preservation effort.[27] The Tokyo Metropolitan Government, later joined by the central government, invested heavily in steel breakwaters and concrete walls designed to halt the natural erosion that threatened to reduce the atoll's above-water presence to nothing. By this time, only three of the original five rocks remained visible at high tide, making the preservation efforts literally a race against the rising waves.[28]

Enter the Provocateur: Ishihara Shintaro's Dramatic Intervention

No figure embodied the nationalist passion and strategic calculation behind Japan's Okinotorishima claims more dramatically than Tokyo Governor Shintaro Ishihara. The controversial politician, novelist, and ultranationalist provocateur transformed what might have remained a quiet territorial administration issue into a high-profile assertion of Japanese sovereignty that captured international attention and inflamed regional tensions.

On May 20, 2005, in one of the most theatrical gestures in modern territorial diplomacy, Governor Ishihara personally traveled to Okinotorishima for a highly publicized inspection visit.[29] The journey itself—1,740 kilometers south from Tokyo across often rough seas—represented both a logistical challenge and a powerful symbolic statement about Japan's commitment to defending its most remote territorial claim.

Upon reaching the tiny atoll, Ishihara waved the Japanese national flag near a specially installed plaque declaring "Okinotorishima, Japan" in Japanese characters.[30] But the governor's most provocative act was yet to come: he went swimming around the concrete-encased rocks and personally released Japanese horse mackerel fry into the surrounding waters, demonstrating what he claimed was evidence of sustainable economic activity that would satisfy UNCLOS requirements for island status.[31]

The symbolic power of this gesture was unmistakable. Here was Japan's most prominent regional politician literally immersing himself in the disputed waters, using his own body to demonstrate the human habitability criterion that critics claimed the rocks could never meet. The release of commercially valuable fish fry was designed as a direct rebuttal to arguments that the atoll could not sustain economic life of its own.

In his subsequent editorial in the *Sankei Shimbun* newspaper on June 6, 2005, Ishihara revealed the scale of Japan's financial commitment to the territorial claim. He wrote that Japan had spent 85 billion yen (approximately $740 million) on Okinotorishima since 1932, declaring defiantly: "These historical facts cannot be reversed by the U.N. convention."[32] The governor's assertion was both a statement of resolve and a recognition that Japan's claim faced serious legal challenges under international law.

Ishihara's administration also ordered the installation of a 330 million yen ($3 million) radar system for surveillance purposes, along with an official address plaque reading "1 Okinotori Island, Ogasawara Village, Tokyo."[33] These investments were not merely symbolic; they represented concrete steps toward establishing the infrastructure necessary to support claims of human habitation and economic activity.

The governor's dramatic intervention reflected deeper strategic concerns about China's growing maritime assertiveness and the broader implications for Japan's security environment. As Ishihara noted in his public statements, "Okinotorishima stands between Guam—America's strategic base—the Taiwan strait, China, and areas near Japan where there may be conflict in the future."[34] The atoll's position roughly halfway between potential conflict zones and critical U.S. military installations made its control a matter of national security, not merely maritime law.

The Challenge Emerges: China's Legal and Strategic Response

The transformation of Okinotorishima from an administrative curiosity to a contested strategic asset became complete when China first formally challenged Japan's claims in 2004. The timing was not coincidental; it reflected China's own growing maritime confidence and strategic interest in constraining what Beijing viewed as excessive Japanese territorial assertions in the Pacific.

On April 22, 2004, during bilateral talks in Beijing specifically convened to discuss Chinese marine research activities within Japan's claimed EEZ, Chinese diplomats delivered a carefully worded but unmistakable challenge.[35] While acknowledging Japan's territorial sovereignty over the physical rocks themselves, China stated categorically that it did not regard Okinotorishima as qualifying for island status under international law and therefore did not acknowledge Japan's claimed exclusive economic zone around the atoll.

The Chinese position was grounded in a literal interpretation of UNCLOS Article 121(3). From Beijing's perspective, Okinotorishima perfectly exemplified the convention's definition of "rocks which cannot sustain human habitation or economic life of their own."[36] Chinese officials pointed to the atoll's tiny size—less than 10 square meters of natural land area at high tide—its complete lack of indigenous human population, its absence of natural economic resources, and its dependence on artificial preservation efforts for continued above-water existence.

China's challenge was not merely legal; it reflected broader strategic calculations about naval operations in the western Pacific. As foreign policy analysts noted, Beijing's interest went beyond maritime law to encompass "investigation of the surrounding seabed for submarine operations in case of military conflict involving the Republic of China (Taiwan)."[37] The atoll's strategic location between China's claimed sphere of influence and U.S. military installations on Guam made its legal status a matter of significant strategic importance.

The Chinese challenge represented the beginning of a sustained campaign to contest Japan's EEZ claims through both diplomatic protests and active maritime operations. Chinese research vessels began conducting surveys in the disputed waters, with China maintaining that since the area constituted "high seas" rather than Japanese territorial waters, such activities fell within the established principle of "freedom of the high seas" under international maritime law.[38]

Academic Voices: The Legal Experts Weigh In

The emergence of the Okinotorishima dispute attracted significant attention from international legal scholars, who recognized its potential to establish crucial precedents for maritime territorial disputes worldwide. The scholarly debate centered on the fundamental question of how to interpret UNCLOS Article 121(3) in practice—a question with implications far beyond the specific case of Japan's coral atoll.

Professor Jon van Dyke of the University of Hawaii Law School emerged as one of the most prominent critics of Japan's legal position. In his influential 1988 analysis, published years before the dispute became a major bilateral issue, van Dyke argued prophetically that "Okinotorishima—which consists of two eroding protrusions no larger than king-size beds—certainly meets the description of an uninhabitable rock that cannot sustain economic life of its own."[39]

Van Dyke's critique was both technical and comparative. He noted that UNCLOS Article 121(3) was designed to prevent exactly the kind of expansive maritime claims that Japan was asserting based on tiny, uninhabitable formations. Furthermore, he argued that Article 60(8) of the convention explicitly stated that "artificially built islands do not generate 200-mile resource zones," raising questions about Japan's extensive artificial preservation efforts.[40]

The professor drew parallels to Britain's failed attempt to claim an exclusive economic zone around Rockall, an uninhabited granite outcropping in the Atlantic Ocean. The United Kingdom had initially asserted EEZ rights around Rockall but eventually abandoned the claim in the 1990s when other countries objected.[41] Van Dyke suggested that Japan's Okinotorishima claim was even weaker than Britain's Rockall assertion, given the coral formation's smaller size, lower elevation, and complete dependence on artificial preservation.

However, not all legal experts agreed with this assessment. Professor Tadao Kuribayashi of Toyo Eiwa University in Tokyo offered a vigorous defense of Japan's legal position. Kuribayashi argued that the term "rock" was undefined in international law and that coral reefs differed fundamentally from rocks in their geological composition and structure.[42] He contended that the intent of UNCLOS Article 121(3) was directed toward typical rock formations, not coral atolls that had supported complex ecosystems.

The scholarly debate reflected deeper uncertainties about how 1982 maritime law should apply to 21st-century realities of resource competition, technological capabilities, and environmental change. As nations worldwide increasingly looked to their maritime territories for economic opportunities and strategic advantages, the Okinotorishima case represented a crucial test of where international law would draw the boundaries of legitimate territorial expansion.

The Strategic Triangle: Taiwan's Complicated Position

The Okinotorishima dispute became further complicated by Taiwan's unique position, which illustrated the complex intersections between territorial law, fishing rights, and geopolitical calculations in the modern Pacific. Taiwan's involvement demonstrated how seemingly technical legal disputes could create unexpected diplomatic alignments and strategic dilemmas for all parties involved.

Taiwan's direct encounter with the Okinotorishima dispute came on April 25, 2016, when the Japan Coast Guard detained the crew of the Taiwanese fishing vessel *Dongshengji No. 16* in waters that Japan claimed as part of its EEZ around the atoll.[43] The incident, occurring 150 nautical miles from Okinotorishima, immediately escalated into a major diplomatic confrontation between Japan and Taiwan.

President Ma Ying-jeou's response was swift and dramatic. Taiwan dispatched two Coast Guard vessels with warship escorts to the disputed waters and refused to acknowledge Japan's EEZ claim around Okinotorishima.[44] Ma's administration took the position that the coral formations did not meet UNCLOS criteria for island status and therefore could not generate an exclusive economic zone that would restrict Taiwanese fishing operations.

The Taiwan challenge created a strategic paradox that illustrated the complex legal and political dimensions of the dispute. By opposing Japan's Okinotorishima claims, Taiwan found itself aligned with China's legal position—a rare instance of cross-strait cooperation on a maritime issue. However, this alignment came with significant risks for Taiwan's own territorial claims in the South China Sea.

Taiwan itself controlled Itu Aba (Taiping Island), the largest naturally occurring feature in the Spratly Islands, which faced similar challenges under UNCLOS Article 121(3). If Taiwan succeeded in establishing that small, remote coral formations could not generate EEZ claims, it might inadvertently undermine its own legal position regarding Itu Aba's status as an island capable of supporting human habitation and economic life.[45]

The diplomatic resolution of the immediate crisis came with the transition to President Tsai Ing-wen's administration in May 2016, which adopted a more cautious approach to the legal issues involved. Taiwan and Japan established a bilateral maritime dialogue mechanism and Taiwan carefully avoided taking definitive legal positions that might prejudice its own territorial claims elsewhere.[46]

The triangular complexity of the dispute—involving Japan's sovereignty claims, China's legal challenges, and Taiwan's fishing rights—demonstrated how modern maritime territorial disputes could create intricate webs of conflicting interests and legal positions that defied simple resolution.

The Commission's Non-Decision: Legal Limbo

The international legal system's response to the Okinotorishima dispute proved as complex and inconclusive as the dispute itself. In 2008, Japan submitted detailed claims to the United Nations Commission on the Limits of the Continental Shelf (CLCS), seeking recognition of extended continental shelf rights beyond the standard 200 nautical mile EEZ in seven different areas, including waters around Okinotorishima.[47]

The submission represented Japan's attempt to secure international legal recognition for its territorial claims while potentially expanding them even further. Under UNCLOS provisions, countries could claim continental shelf rights extending up to 350 nautical miles from their territorial baselines if they could demonstrate geological and topographical continuity of the continental shelf.[48]

However, China and South Korea immediately filed formal objections to Japan's submission, specifically challenging the legal basis for claims originating from Okinotorishima. Both countries argued that the coral formation did not qualify as an island under international law and therefore could not serve as a baseline for either EEZ or continental shelf claims.[49]

Faced with these fundamental disagreements about the legal status of Okinotorishima itself, the CLCS found itself unable to make any substantive recommendations regarding Japan's extended continental shelf claims in the area. In June 2012, the Commission effectively punted on the issue, stating that it would defer making recommendations for the "southern area of the Kyushu-Palau Ridge" located south of Okinotorishima until "the issues mentioned in the notes verbales by the Chinese and Korean governments"—namely, whether Okinotorishima qualified as an island or merely rocks—"are resolved."[50]

This non-decision left the legal status of Okinotorishima in continued limbo, with the international legal community officially declining to adjudicate the central question in the dispute. Over a decade later, the CLCS has maintained this position, effectively acknowledging that the technical legal question cannot be separated from the broader geopolitical tensions surrounding the atoll.

The Commission's deferral reflected the inherent limitations of existing international legal frameworks in addressing 21st-century maritime territorial disputes. When great powers hold fundamentally opposing interpretations of international law, and when the stakes involve trillions of dollars in potential resources and critical strategic positions, technical legal bodies often find themselves unable to render definitive judgments.

From Worthless Rocks to Strategic Prizes

The story of Okinotorishima's transformation from forgotten coral outcroppings to contested strategic assets reflects broader changes in how nations think about territory, resources, and power in the modern world. What began as Spanish navigational hazards evolved into British chart annotations, then Japanese territorial claims, and finally flashpoints for great power competition in the 21st century.

The 2025 confrontation between Japanese Coast Guard aircraft and the Chinese research vessel R/V Tan Kah Kee represented the latest chapter in this extraordinary evolution. As the Chinese ship finally departed the disputed waters after its five-hour standoff, it left behind not just the wake of its passage, but the clear recognition that the legal and strategic battles over Okinotorishima were far from resolved.

The transformation of these nine square meters of coral and concrete into one of the Pacific's most contentious territorial disputes illustrates how international law, technological capabilities, and strategic competition can combine to create value where none previously existed. The rocks that changed history continue to shape the future of ocean governance, resource competition, and great power relations in the Pacific century.

In the modern era of climate change, resource scarcity, and great power competition, even the smallest pieces of territory can carry outsized importance. The continuing dispute over Okinotorishima serves as a powerful reminder that in international relations, strategic value is often a matter of perception, legal interpretation, and political will rather than physical size or natural endowments.

As Chinese research vessels continue their operations in the disputed waters and Japan maintains its expensive preservation efforts, the fundamental questions raised by this remote atoll remain unresolved: What constitutes an island under international law? How should the global community balance national territorial claims with the principle of common oceanic heritage? And in an era of intensifying great power competition, can tiny rocks in the middle of the Pacific Ocean really determine the strategic balance of the world's largest ocean?

The answers to these questions will likely determine not just the fate of Okinotorishima, but the broader evolution of maritime territorial disputes in the 21st century. In the meantime, the most expensive rocks on Earth continue to generate controversy, investment, and strategic calculations worth far more than their tiny physical footprint might suggest.

Footnotes:

[1] "Photos Show Chinese Ship Detected in Waters Claimed by US Ally," *Newsweek*, May 28, 2025, https://www.newsweek.com/japan-china-news-research-ship-exclusive-economic-zone-pacific-ocean-2077774.

[2] "Chinese Research Vessel Spotted in Japan EEZ," *Nippon.com*, May 27, 2025, https://www.nippon.com/en/news/yjj2025052700346/.

[3] "R/V Tan Kah Kee," Glosten, March 13, 2024, https://glosten.com/project/rv-tan-kah-kee/. The vessel is 255 feet (77.7 meters) in length with a cruising radius of 10,000 nautical miles and can support 54 crew members, including 36 scientists.

[4] "Profile of the Okinotorishima Islands," Tokyo Metropolitan Government, accessed December 2025, https://www.t-borderislands.metro.tokyo.lg.jp/en/okinotorishima/. The exclusive economic zone based on Okinotorishima is approximately 420,000 km^2, larger than Japan's total land area.

[5] "Photos Show Chinese Ship Detected in Waters Claimed by US Ally," *Newsweek*, May 28, 2025.

[6] "Japan says China conducted research near Pacific atoll," *The Japan Times*, May 27, 2025, https://www.japantimes.co.jp/news/2025/05/27/japan/china-eez-research/.

[7] "Okinotorishima," Wikipedia, accessed December 2025, https://en.wikipedia.org/wiki/Okinotorishima. The atoll may have been sighted first by Spanish sailor Bernardo de la Torre in 1543.

[8] Ibid. The first undisputed sighting was by Miguel López de Legazpi in 1565, who named it "Parece Vela" (Spanish for "looks like a sail").

[9] "Miguel López de Legazpi," Wikipedia, accessed December 2025, https://en.wikipedia.org/wiki/Miguel_L%C3%B3pez_de_Legazpi.

[10] "Okinotorishima," Wikipedia, accessed December 2025.

[11] Ibid. In 1789, Captain William Douglas arrived with the British ship Iphigenia and in 1790, the place was named Douglas Reef.

[12] "The Curious Case of Okinotori: Reef, Rock, or Island?," Pacific Forum, April 4, 2024, https://pacforum.org/publications/pacnet-59-the-curious-case-of-okinotori-reef-rock-or-island/. The British records refer to the outcropping as a reef.

[13] "Okinotorishima," Wikipedia, accessed December 2025. The existence of the atoll might not have been known by the Japanese until 1888.

[14] Ibid. In 1922 and 1925, the Japanese navy ship Manshu investigated the area.

[15] Ibid. In 1925, there were still five above-water rocks, which have eroded since.

[16] Ibid. In 1931, confirming that no other countries had claimed the reefs, Japan declared it Japanese territory.

[17] Ibid. Japan placed it under the jurisdiction of the Tokyo Metropolis, classifying it as part of the Ogasawara Village, and naming it Okinotorishima, meaning "remote bird islands."

[18] "The US-Japan-China Mistrust Spiral and Okinotorishima," Asia-Pacific Journal: Japan Focus, November 3, 2023, https://apjjf.org/yukie-yoshikawa/2541/article. The driving force behind the Japanese action was the Navy, which saw favorable conditions for building a hydroplane base.

[19] "Okinotorishima," Wikipedia, accessed December 2025. During 1939 and 1941, a foundation was completed for a lighthouse and a meteorological observation site, but construction was interrupted by the outbreak of World War II.

[20] Ibid. Japan signed the Convention in 1983; the Convention came into force in 1994–1996 for Japan.

[21] United Nations Convention on the Law of the Sea, Article 57.

[22] "The US-Japan-China Mistrust Spiral and Okinotorishima," Asia-Pacific Journal: Japan Focus, November 3, 2023. Based on its possession of Okinotorishima, Japan claimed an EEZ of approximately 154,500 square miles (400,000 km^2).

[23] United Nations Convention on the Law of the Sea, Article 121(1).

[24] United Nations Convention on the Law of the Sea, Article 121(3).

[25] "Photos Show Chinese Ship Detected in Waters Claimed by US Ally," *Newsweek*, May 28, 2025. The waters around Okinotorishima are known to be spawning grounds and migration routes for bonito, tuna, and other fish.

[26] Ibid.

[27] "Okinotorishima," Wikipedia, accessed December 2025. Between 1987 and 1993 the government of Tokyo and later the central government built steel breakwaters and concrete walls to stop the erosion.

[28] Ibid. By the time of preservation efforts, only three of the five rocks that were present in 1939 remained above water.

[29] "Tokyo Gov. Shintaro Ishihara waves the Japanese national flag," Alamy Stock Photo, May 20, 2005, https://www.alamy.com/tokyo-gov-shintaro-ishihara-waves-the-japanese-national-flag-near-the-plate-that-declares-okinotorishima-japan-in-japanese-after-landing-on-higashi-kojima-one-of-the-two-okinotorishima-islets-about-1730km-kilometers-1070-miles-south-of-capital-tokyo-during-an-inspection-tour-on-friday-may-20-2005-the-islets-are-under-jurisdiction-of-the-tokyo-metropolitan-government-the-outspoken-governor-landed-on-a-pair-of-small-islets-at-the-center-of-a-dispute-with-china-a-move-likely-to-aggravate-already-tense-relations-between-the-two-nations-ap-photokatsumi-kasahara-image542250116.html.

[30] Ibid. Governor Ishihara waved the Japanese national flag near a plate that declared "Okinotorishima, Japan" in Japanese.

[31] "The US-Japan-China Mistrust Spiral and Okinotorishima," Asia-Pacific Journal: Japan Focus, November 3, 2023. Governor Ishihara went snorkeling and released Japanese horse mackerel fry to show support for the local fishing industry.

[32] Ibid. In his June 6, 2005 Sankei Shimbun editorial, Ishihara claimed Japan had spent 85 billion yen ($740 million) since 1932, declaring: "These historical facts cannot be reversed by the U.N. convention."

[33] Ibid. Ishihara ordered installation of a 330 million yen radar system for surveillance and set up an address plate at the "island."

[34] "Troubled Seas: Japan's Pacific and East China Sea Domains," Asia-Pacific Journal: Japan Focus, November 1, 2023, https://apjjf.org/2012/10/36/gavan-mccormack/3821/article. As Tokyo Governor Ishihara noted, "Okinotorishima stands between Guam—America's strategic base—the Taiwan strait, China, and areas near Japan where there may be conflict in the future."

[35] "The US-Japan-China Mistrust Spiral and Okinotorishima," Asia-Pacific Journal: Japan Focus, November 3, 2023. On April 22, 2004, during bilateral talks in Beijing, Chinese diplomats stated that China did not regard Okinotorishima as an islet.

[36] United Nations Convention on the Law of the Sea, Article 121(3).

[37] "Okinotorishima," Wikipedia, accessed December 2025. Foreign policy analysts speculated that they want to "investigate the surrounding

seabed for submarine operations in case of military conflict involving the Republic of China (Taiwan)."

[38] "Photos Show Chinese Ship Detected in Waters Claimed by US Ally," *Newsweek*, May 28, 2025. Chinese Foreign Ministry spokesperson Mao Ning stated that China's research vessel was "exercising the freedom of the high seas."

[39] "The US-Japan-China Mistrust Spiral and Okinotorishima," Asia-Pacific Journal: Japan Focus, November 3, 2023. Dr. Jon Van Dyke wrote in 1988: "Okinotorishima—which consists of two eroding protrusions no larger than king-size beds—certainly meets the description of an uninhabitable rock."

[40] "Okinotorishima," Wikipedia, accessed December 2025. Van Dyke argued that UNCLOS Article 60(8) states that "artificially built islands do not generate 200-mile resource zones."

[41] "The US-Japan-China Mistrust Spiral and Okinotorishima," Asia-Pacific Journal: Japan Focus, November 3, 2023. Experts point to the similarity of Japan's position to Britain's failed attempt to claim an EEZ around Rockall. London eventually dropped its claim in the 1990s when other countries objected.

[42] Ibid. Tadao Kuribayashi, a professor of law at Toyo Eiwa University in Tokyo, insists that the Japanese claim is justifiable as there is no definition of a "rock" in international law.

[43] "The Curious Case of Okinotori: Reef, Rock, or Island?," Pacific Forum, April 4, 2024. In 2016, Japan's arrest of a Taiwanese fishing ship's crew led Taiwan to protest against Japan's claim of island status for Okinotori.

[44] Ibid. President Ma Ying-jeou's dramatic response included dispatching coast guard vessels and warship escorts to contested waters.

[45] Ibid. Taiwan's challenge aligned with China's position, potentially undermining Taiwan's own claims to Itu Aba (Taiping) Island claims in South China Sea.

[46] Ibid. May 2016: Establishment of bilateral maritime dialogue mechanism between Japan and Taiwan.

[47] "China's Expansion into the West Pacific," The Japan Forum on International Relations, April 5, 2023, https://www.jfir.or.jp/en/

studygroup_article/4146/. In November 2008, Japan made a submission to the UN Committee on the Continental Shelf.

[48] United Nations Convention on the Law of the Sea, Article 76.

[49] "China's Expansion into the West Pacific," The Japan Forum on International Relations, April 5, 2023. China and South Korea dispute Japan's claim in their addenda to the CLCS.

[50] Ibid. The CLCS postponed making a recommendation on the "southern area of the Kyushu-Palau Ridge" until the issues mentioned in the notes verbales by the Chinese and Korean governments are resolved.

Chapter 2: Nine Square Meters of Empire

In the vast expanse of the Philippine Sea, 1,740 kilometers south of Tokyo, lies what may be the most expensive real estate per square meter on Earth. Here, where typhoons rage with winds exceeding 50 meters per second and waves tower up to 16 meters high, Japan has invested over $600 million to preserve two tiny concrete-encased rocks that together measure just 9.44 square meters—smaller than a typical parking space.[1]

This is Okinotorishima, Japan's southernmost territory and the only Japanese land south of the Tropic of Cancer. To casual observers, it presents an almost absurd spectacle: two concrete pedestals rising from a coral atoll, surrounded by massive tetrapod barriers and connected by steel walkways, all battered relentlessly by some of the Pacific's most violent weather. Yet this seemingly insignificant outpost generates Japan's claim to an exclusive economic zone (EEZ) covering 420,000 square kilometers—an area larger than Japan's entire land mass.[2]

The Physical Reality

Okinotorishima exists at the intersection of geological vulnerability and geopolitical ambition. The atoll sits on the Kyushu-Palau Ridge in the Philippine Sea, a remnant of ancient volcanic activity now reduced to a coral reef platform measuring roughly 4.5 kilometers east-west and 1.7 kilometers north-south.[3] Within this larger reef structure, only two natural features remain above water at high tide: Kitakojima ("North Small Island") and Higashikojima ("East Small Island").

The precarious nature of these formations cannot be overstated. Each "island" originally measured no larger than a double bed—what University of Hawaii law professor Jon van Dyke memorably described in 1988 as "two eroding protrusions no larger than king-size beds."[4] Without constant human intervention, these rocks would have disappeared beneath the waves decades ago, victims of typhoon erosion and rising sea levels.

The surrounding environment presents challenges that would deter all but the most determined sovereignty project. The area experiences an annual average wave height of 1.3 meters, but during typhoon season—a frequent occurrence given the atoll's position in one of the Pacific's most active storm corridors—waves can exceed 16 meters in height.[5] Wind velocities average 6 meters per second annually but can surge beyond 50 meters per second when major storms pass through.[6] The nearest permanently inhabited land lies over 900 kilometers away on Chichijima in the Ogasawara Islands, making Okinotorishima one of the most isolated territories under any nation's sovereignty.

Engineering Marvel or Folly?

Japan's response to this environmental hostility has been an engineering undertaking of remarkable ambition and questionable proportions. Between 1987 and 1993, the Tokyo Metropolitan Government and later the central government launched what can only be described as a concrete fortress project in the middle of the Pacific Ocean.[7]

The transformation began with the installation of massive steel breakwaters and concrete walls around each of the vulnerable rocks. Workers—transported by helicopter in dangerous conditions—encased Kitakojima and Higashikojima in concrete barriers roughly 50 meters in diameter, creating circular protective structures that rise above the surrounding reef platform.[8] The engineering specifications reveal the project's extraordinary scale: Japan has invested approximately $280 million worth of concrete in these protective barriers alone.[9]

The smaller of the two rocks, deemed particularly vulnerable to debris thrown up by massive waves, received additional protection in the form of a $50 million titanium net—a material chosen for its exceptional resistance to corrosion in the harsh marine environment.[10] This single protective measure cost more than many nations spend on their entire coast guard operations.

The construction process required overcoming logistical challenges that would humble most military operations. All materials and personnel had to be transported 1,740 kilometers from Tokyo, often in helicopter operations conducted in some of the world's most challenging maritime conditions.[11] Workers faced constant danger from sudden weather changes, with thick fog and violent storms capable of isolating construction crews for days at a time.

By 1988, the Japan Marine Science and Technology Center had erected a marine investigation facility on a 100-meter by 50-meter stilt platform in the lagoon, complete with helicopter landing pad and a three-story building housing research equipment and meteorological stations.[12] This facility serves the dual purpose of conducting legitimate scientific research and providing a visible human presence to strengthen Japan's sovereignty claims.

The installation was completed in 2007 with the addition of a lighthouse equipped with radar and various sensors, managed by the Japan Coast Guard.[13] This beacon, officially plotted on hydrographic charts, serves not only navigational purposes but also as an observation post for monitoring activity in the claimed EEZ.

Comparative Perspectives: Islands, Rocks, and National Ambitions

Okinotorishima's engineering project becomes even more remarkable when compared with similar territorial claims worldwide. The contrast with other nations' approaches to marginal territories illuminates both Japan's exceptional commitment and the broader challenges of sovereignty in the modern era.

The most instructive comparison lies with the United Kingdom's experience at Rockall, a granite outcrop in the North Atlantic measuring 17 meters high and 25 meters wide.[14] Despite being significantly larger and more substantial than Okinotorishima's concrete-preserved rocks, the UK ultimately abandoned its EEZ claims around Rockall when it ratified the United Nations Convention on the Law of the Sea (UNCLOS) in 1997.[15] British officials concluded that Rockall could not meet UNCLOS Article 121(3)'s requirement that islands be capable of sustaining "human habitation or economic life of their own."[16]

The UK's retreat from Rockall reflected both legal pragmatism and international pressure. Ireland, Iceland, and Denmark all objected to British EEZ claims based on the uninhabitable outcrop, creating diplomatic complications that ultimately proved not worth the potential resources at stake.[17] By 1988, the UK and Ireland signed an EEZ boundary agreement that explicitly stated "the location of Rockall was irrelevant to the determination of the boundary."[18]

France's approach to Clipperton Island offers another instructive contrast. This coral atoll in the eastern Pacific encompasses 8.9 square kilometers total area, with 1.7 square kilometers of land—roughly 1,800 times larger than Okinotorishima's dry land area.[19] Despite Clipperton's much more substantial physical presence, France faced similar legal challenges under UNCLOS Article 121(3), given the island's inability to sustain permanent human habitation without external support.[20] Nevertheless, France maintains its EEZ claim around Clipperton, generating rights over 431,273 square kilometers of ocean.[21]

The United States' management of Baker and Howland Islands in the central Pacific provides perhaps the most relevant comparison to Japan's approach. Baker Island covers 1.4 square kilometers while Howland Island encompasses 2.6 square kilometers—both significantly larger than Okinotorishima but still small enough to raise questions about their EEZ-generating capacity under UNCLOS.[22] The US claims a combined EEZ of 425,700 square kilometers around these islands, slightly larger than the area of California.[23]

Unlike Japan's massive infrastructure investment at Okinotorishima, the US maintains only minimal facilities on Baker and Howland, with annual visits by U.S. Fish and Wildlife Service personnel for conservation purposes.[24] The American approach reflects a more pragmatic assessment of cost-benefit ratios in remote territory maintenance, though it should be noted that these islands face far less challenging environmental conditions than Okinotorishima.

China's artificial island construction in the South China Sea offers the most contemporary comparison to Japan's approach, though with reversed legal implications. While Japan invests hundreds of millions to preserve naturally formed rocks that meet the geological definition of islands, China has created entirely artificial features on previously submerged reefs.[25] The 2016 Permanent Court of Arbitration ruling in the Philippines v. China case explicitly stated that artificially created islands cannot generate EEZ rights, potentially undermining China's claims while inadvertently supporting

Japan's position that naturally formed features, even if artificially preserved, retain their legal status.[26]

The Human Element: Guardians of the Furthest Frontier

Behind the engineering statistics and legal technicalities lies a remarkable human story of dedication to national sovereignty. The maintenance of Japan's claim to Okinotorishima requires regular missions by some of the most specialized personnel in the Japanese government service.

Japan Coast Guard officers conduct routine patrols to Okinotorishima on a schedule that must balance sovereignty assertion with crew safety. These missions involve 1,740-kilometer journeys from Tokyo through some of the Pacific's most treacherous waters.[27] Coast Guard vessels must navigate not only distance and weather challenges but also the complex diplomatic implications of their presence, as Chinese and other foreign vessels increasingly probe the boundaries of Japan's claimed EEZ.

Maintenance crews face perhaps even greater challenges. The concrete barriers and titanium netting require constant monitoring and repair, particularly after major typhoon strikes. Helicopter operations to transport personnel and materials operate under severe weather constraints, with launch decisions often made based on rapidly changing forecasts that can leave crews stranded if conditions deteriorate unexpectedly.

The research station staff, though housed in relatively modern facilities on the stilt platform, work in complete isolation from human society for months at a time. Their daily routines include weather monitoring, marine biological observations, and maintenance of the various sensors and communication equipment that link Okinotorishima to Tokyo.[28] During typhoon season, these personnel must secure all equipment and shelter in place as storms that would force the evacuation of most coastal communities pass directly overhead.

Perhaps most remarkably, these human guardians of Japan's most remote territory have maintained continuous operations for over three decades, through political changes, budget pressures, and international challenges to their nation's claims. Their presence provides the "human habitation" element that strengthens Japan's argument under UNCLOS that Okinotorishima deserves island status rather than classification as uninhabitable rocks.

The dedication required for these assignments reflects broader Japanese attitudes toward territorial sovereignty that were dramatically illustrated by Tokyo Governor Shintaro Ishihara's theatrical 2005 visit. Ishihara's decision to swim around the atoll and personally release Japanese horse mackerel fry demonstrated the lengths to which Japanese officials would go to assert human connection to their most marginal territory.[29]

A Monument to National Determination

Viewed from one perspective, Okinotorishima represents an almost comical triumph of human stubbornness over natural forces. The sight of two concrete pedestals surrounded by massive wave barriers in the middle of the world's largest ocean seems to mock both geography and common sense. The cost-per-square-meter rivals the most expensive urban real estate in Tokyo, while the maintenance requirements would challenge a small nation's entire infrastructure budget.

Yet from another angle, Okinotorishima embodies something profound about the modern relationship between sovereignty, resources, and national identity. Japan's investment in these concrete fortifications reflects not merely economic calculation about potential mineral wealth, but a deeper commitment to the principle that geography does not limit national ambition in the maritime age.

The engineering achievement itself deserves recognition. Maintaining human-made structures in such an environment requires technical expertise and logistical capabilities that few nations could muster. The concrete barriers have withstood decades of typhoon assaults that would destroy conventional coastal infrastructure. The titanium netting continues to protect its assigned rock despite exposure to some of the most corrosive marine environments on Earth.

More significantly, Okinotorishima has survived diplomatic and legal challenges that have defeated many other territorial claims. While the UK retreated from Rockall and numerous other nations have abandoned marginal territories under international pressure, Japan has strengthened its position through continuous physical presence and massive infrastructure investment.

The two concrete-encased rocks of Okinotorishima may measure only 9.44 square meters, but they anchor a claim to ocean territory larger than the Japanese home islands. In an era when maritime resources increasingly drive national prosperity and security, these "nine square meters of empire" may prove to be among Japan's most valuable territorial assets. Whether future observers will judge this investment as visionary preparation for the maritime century or as the world's most expensive folly will likely depend on what lies beneath the 420,000 square kilometers of ocean that these tiny rocks claim to command.

Footnotes

[1] "Profile of the Okinotorishima Islands," Tokyo Metropolitan Government, accessed August 2025, https://www.t-borderislands.metro.tokyo.lg.jp/en/okinotorishima/. The total land area is officially measured at 9.44 square meters (101.6 square feet).

[2] Ibid. The EEZ claim encompasses approximately 420,000 square kilometers, compared to Japan's total land area of 377,975 square kilometers.

[3] "Okinotorishima," Wikipedia, accessed August 2025, https://en.wikipedia.org/wiki/Okinotorishima.

[4] Jon M. van Dyke, "The Dispute over Okinotorishima," Asia-Pacific Journal: Japan Focus, November 3, 2023, https://apjjf.org/yukie-yoshikawa/2541/article.

[5] "Profile of the Okinotorishima Islands," Tokyo Metropolitan Government.

[6] Ibid.

[7] "Okinotorishima," Wikipedia.

[8] "Profile of the Okinotorishima Islands," Tokyo Metropolitan Government.

[9] "Okinotorishima," Wikipedia.

[10] Ibid.

[11] "Profile of the Okinotorishima Islands," Tokyo Metropolitan Government.

[12] "Okinotorishima," Wikipedia.

[13] Ibid.

[14] "Rockall," Wikipedia, accessed August 2025, https://en.wikipedia.org/wiki/Rockall.

[15] "Rockall Bank dispute," Wikipedia, accessed August 2025, https://en.wikipedia.org/wiki/Rockall_Bank_dispute.

[16] United Nations Convention on the Law of the Sea, Article 121(3).

[17] "Who owns Rockall? A history of disputes over a tiny Atlantic island," Irish Times, June 8, 2019.

[18] "Rockall," Wikipedia.

[19] "Clipperton Island," Wikipedia, accessed August 2025, https://en.wikipedia.org/wiki/Clipperton_Island.

[20] "Reframing the French Indo-Pacific: Clipperton, France's Indo-Pacific Edge," The Diplomat, July 2025.

[21] Ibid.

[22] "Baker Island," Wikipedia, accessed August 2025, https://en.wikipedia.org/wiki/Baker_Island; "Howland Island," Wikipedia, accessed August 2025, https://en.wikipedia.org/wiki/Howland_Island.

[23] "Howland and Baker Islands," Wikipedia, accessed August 2025.

[24] Ibid.

[25] "The Curious Case of Okinotori: Reef, Rock, or Island?" Foreign Policy Research Institute, September 14, 2016.

[26] Ibid.

[27] "Profile of the Okinotorishima Islands," Tokyo Metropolitan Government.

[28] "Okinotorishima," Wikipedia.

[29] "The US-Japan-China Mistrust Spiral and Okinotorishima," Asia-Pacific Journal: Japan Focus.

Chapter 3: "The $600 Million Investment"

The Most Expensive Rocks Per Square Meter on Earth

In the pre-dawn darkness of May 20, 2005, a solitary figure stood at the bow of a Japanese Coast Guard vessel as it approached two concrete-encased specks barely visible above the Philippine Sea's horizon. At 72 years old, Tokyo Governor Shintaro Ishihara had embarked on the 1,740-kilometer journey south from the capital to make what he would later describe as the most important political statement of his career.[1] What followed that morning would transform Japan's approach to territorial sovereignty and demonstrate just how far a nation would go to defend the indefensible.

As the vessel anchored near the concrete barriers surrounding Okinotorishima, Ishihara stripped down and dove into the Pacific waters, swimming methodically around the tiny outcrops that constitute Japan's southernmost territory. The spectacle was carefully orchestrated political theater—a 72-year-old nationalist politician literally embracing Japan's most remote and controversial territorial claim.[2] After his swim, Ishihara ceremonially released juvenile horse mackerel (*Trachurus japonicus*) into the waters, symbolically demonstrating "economic life" around the atoll to strengthen Japan's legal position under international law.[3]

This theatrical gesture would be followed seventeen days later by an even more provocative declaration. In his June 6, 2005 editorial in the conservative *Sankei Shimbun*, Ishihara made a stunning financial revelation that would forever change how the world understood Japan's commitment to Okinotorishima: "Japan has been spending money on Okinotorishima for future development since 1932 with some intervals, including 85 billion yen [approximately $740 million] to build and maintain a residence," he wrote. "These historical facts cannot be reversed by the U.N. convention."[4]

The Escalating Financial Commitment: From Millions to Hundreds of Millions

The true scale of Japan's financial investment in Okinotorishima represents perhaps the most expensive territorial preservation effort in modern history. By 2025, Japanese government sources confirm that total expenditures have exceeded $600 million—making these 9.44 square meters of artificial territory worth approximately $63 million per square meter.[5] To put this in perspective, prime commercial real estate in central Tokyo typically costs around $40,000 per square meter, making Okinotorishima roughly 1,500 times more expensive than the most valuable urban land in Japan.[6]

The financial progression tells a story of escalating commitment driven by geopolitical necessity:

Phase I: Initial Preservation (1987-1993) - $280 Million The first major expenditure began in 1987 when the Tokyo Metropolitan Government, recognizing the existential threat to the atoll, initiated emergency preservation measures. Between 1987 and 1993, engineers surrounded the two remaining natural rock protrusions—Higashikojima and Kitakojima—with massive concrete seawalls and steel breakwaters.[7] The project required helicopters to carefully transport and position tetrapods around the rocks, while concrete was poured to create circular protective barriers approximately 50 meters in diameter.[8]

This phase alone consumed $280 million, as engineers battled the fundamental challenge of preserving tiny coral outcrops against 16-meter typhoon waves and wind speeds exceeding 50 meters per second. The construction effectively reduced the five original rocks visible in 1939 to just two at high tide, with the remaining land area consisting almost entirely of artificial concrete surfaces.[9]

Phase II: The Titanium Net Solution (1990s) - $50 Million Recognizing that concrete barriers alone might not suffice, Japanese engineers developed an innovative solution: covering the smaller rock (Kitakojima) with a specialized titanium net designed to shield it from debris thrown up by ocean waves. This $50 million protective mesh represented cutting-edge maritime engineering, utilizing titanium's corrosion resistance to create a virtually permanent barrier against erosion.[10]

Phase III: Infrastructure Development (2007-2016) - $107.5 Million and Climbing The installation of navigation and surveillance infrastructure marked Japan's transition from merely preserving the atoll to actively utilizing it for sovereign purposes. On March 16, 2007, the Japan Coast Guard installed a lighthouse beacon that was officially plotted on international hydrographic charts.[11] This seemingly simple addition carried profound legal significance, as it demonstrated active use of the territory for navigation purposes—a key element in establishing economic life under UNCLOS Article 121.

The most ambitious phase began in 2016 when the Japanese government announced a ¥13 billion ($107.5 million) rebuilding program that would fundamentally transform Okinotorishima. The plan called for construction of a deep-water pier capable of accommodating larger vessels, a road spanning the natural reef, and enhanced lighthouse facilities.[12] Combined with the existing 100-meter by 50-meter research platform constructed in the lagoon, these facilities would create Japan's most remote civilian infrastructure project.[13]

Political Decision-Making: The Intersection of Nationalism and Pragmatism

The financial commitment to Okinotorishima emerged from a complex interplay of bureaucratic planning, political ambition, and strategic necessity within Japan's governmental structure. The Ministry of Land, Infrastructure, Transport and Tourism (MLIT)—Japan's largest ministry in terms of employees and responsible for one-third of all Japanese laws and orders—became the primary executor of the preservation strategy.[14]

MLIT's central role reflected the unique administrative challenge Okinotorishima presented. As both a territorial sovereignty issue and an infrastructure preservation project, it fell within the ministry's mandate for "development of national policy relating to the area of land use, infrastructure development, transport and tourism."[15] The ministry's Maritime Bureau became the operational focal point, coordinating between multiple agencies including the Japan Coast Guard, the Japan Meteorological Agency, and the Cabinet Office.[16]

The decision-making process evolved through several distinct phases:

Central Government vs. Metropolitan Authority (1987-1993) Initially, the preservation effort began as a Tokyo Metropolitan Government initiative under the jurisdiction of the Ogasawara Islands administration. However, as costs escalated and strategic implications became clear, the central government assumed direct control. This transition reflected growing recognition that Okinotorishima's significance extended far beyond Tokyo's administrative boundaries.[17]

Interagency Coordination (1994-2004) Following Japan's 1996 ratification of UNCLOS, which transformed Okinotorishima from a curious administrative footnote into a critical strategic asset, multiple government agencies became involved in preservation planning. The 2010 Act on the Development of Base Facilities and Preservation of the Low-Tide Line for the Promotion of Use and Conservation of the Exclusive Economic Zone and Continental Shelf formally established the legal framework for coordinated government action.[18]

Strategic Integration (2005-Present) Ishihara's 2005 intervention marked a turning point toward explicit strategic planning. His installation of a ¥330 million ($3 million) radar system for surveillance and establishment of an official address plaque reading "One Okinotori Island, Ogasawara Village, Tokyo" demonstrated how local political leadership could drive national policy.[19]

Ishihara's Theatrical Intervention: Political Theater Meets Strategic Planning

Governor Ishihara's May 2005 visit represented the convergence of personal political ambition, nationalist ideology, and strategic calculation that would define Japan's approach to Okinotorishima for decades. As a prominent ultranationalist politician who had previously gained international attention for co-authoring "The Japan That Can Say No" (1989), Ishihara brought both credibility and controversy to the territorial preservation effort.[20]

The timing of Ishihara's intervention was not coincidental. China had begun challenging Japan's EEZ claim around Okinotorishima in April 2004, with Chinese officials arguing that the features constituted "rocks" rather than "islands" under international law.[21] Faced with this challenge, Ishihara recognized both a political opportunity and a strategic necessity.

His swimming demonstration served multiple purposes:

- **Legal Strategy**: By personally demonstrating human presence and activity, Ishihara sought to establish evidence of "human habitation" that could be cited in future legal proceedings
- **Media Spectacle**: The dramatic visual of an elderly governor swimming in remote Pacific waters generated extensive domestic and international media coverage
- **Nationalist Symbolism**: The act embodied Japanese determination to defend territorial claims regardless of cost or difficulty
- **Policy Justification**: The spectacle provided political cover for the enormous financial expenditures that would follow[22]

Ishihara's subsequent Sankei Shimbun editorial revealed the sophisticated legal thinking behind his theatrical gesture. His claim that Japan had spent 85 billion yen since 1932 "to build and maintain a residence" strategically reframed the entire preservation effort as evidence of sustained human economic activity rather than mere sovereignty maintenance.[23] By declaring that "these historical facts cannot be reversed by the U.N. convention," Ishihara articulated a nationalist position that would influence Japanese policy for the next two decades.

The Strategic Calculus: Beyond Legal Technicalities

Ishihara's editorial also revealed the broader strategic thinking driving Japan's massive financial commitment. He explicitly cited U.S. intelligence estimates that Chinese submarine forces would grow from 25 to 130 vessels within a decade, positioning Okinotorishima as critical to countering Chinese naval expansion in the Western Pacific.[24] This military dimension explained why costs that might seem irrational for civilian purposes became justifiable as national security investments.

The governor's call for Japan to "establish effective control over the surrounding water through economic activities such as fishing in order to prevent China from developing the area as a base for submarines" articulated a strategy that went beyond legal compliance to active territorial competition.[25] This approach would influence subsequent Japanese policy decisions, from fishing vessel deployments to research station construction.

Public Opinion and Democratic Legitimacy

Despite the enormous financial commitment, polling data suggests that Okinotorishima preservation enjoyed significant public support among Japanese voters, particularly those with nationalist leanings. However, academic analysis indicates that this support reflected elite political mobilization rather than grassroots sentiment. As Jeffrey Kingston of Temple University's Japan Campus observed regarding similar territorial issues: "The nationalist reaction is mostly related to the elite here. I think at the grass-roots level, there hasn't been much of a reaction."[26]

The relatively limited public debate over Okinotorishima expenditures partly reflected the technical complexity of maritime law and the remote nature of the territory. Unlike more visible territorial disputes, few Japanese citizens could easily visit or visualize Okinotorishima, making it an abstraction rather than a tangible political issue.[27]

Engineering Challenges and Technological Innovation

The massive financial investment reflected genuine technical challenges that pushed the boundaries of maritime engineering. Maintaining artificial structures 1,740 kilometers from the nearest major port, in waters subject to typhoons, earthquakes, and constant erosion, required innovative solutions and redundant safety systems.

The titanium net installation alone represented a significant technological achievement. Engineers had to design a corrosion-resistant barrier that could withstand decades of saltwater exposure while remaining flexible enough to absorb wave energy without breaking.[28] The successful deployment of this system required specialized vessels, remote monitoring equipment, and maintenance protocols that had never before been attempted at such a scale and distance.

The 2016 infrastructure expansion presented even greater challenges. Constructing a deep-water pier capable of supporting supply vessels in waters over 6,000 meters deep required advanced understanding of underwater geology, ocean currents, and storm dynamics. The project's ¥13 billion budget reflected not just construction costs but also the premium required for working in one of the world's most remote and challenging marine environments.[29]

Economic Justification and Resource Security

While critics focused on the enormous per-square-meter cost of preserving Okinotorishima, Japanese officials increasingly emphasized the territory's economic value as justification for continued investment. The atoll's 420,000-square-kilometer EEZ contains resources that dwarf the preservation costs:

- **Fisheries**: The waters serve as spawning grounds and migration routes for commercially valuable tuna, bonito, and other species worth billions of dollars annually[30]
- **Mineral Resources**: Polymetallic nodules containing cobalt, nickel, copper, and manganese have been discovered in the surrounding waters, with estimated values exceeding $18 billion[31]
- **Energy Security**: Potential methane hydrate deposits could provide alternative energy sources as Japan seeks to reduce fossil fuel dependence[32]

From this perspective, the $600 million investment represented a minimal cost for securing resource access worth potentially trillions of dollars over the coming decades.

International Implications and Precedent-Setting

Japan's willingness to invest hundreds of millions of dollars in preserving 9.44 square meters of territory established a precedent that reverberated throughout the international community. Other nations with marginal territorial features began reassessing the economic calculations of sovereignty preservation versus abandonment.

The investment also demonstrated how wealthy nations could potentially circumvent international law through engineering and financial resources. While UNCLOS Article 121(3) prohibits EEZ claims based on artificial islands, Japan's approach of reinforcing rather than creating territory exploited legal ambiguities that remain unresolved.[33]

The Path Forward: Justifying Continued Investment

By 2025, with total costs exceeding $600 million and additional expenditures planned for coral cultivation and expanded research facilities, Okinotorishima represents one of the most expensive territorial preservation projects in history. Yet Japanese officials show no signs of reducing their commitment.

The February 2016 announcement of an additional ¥13 billion in reconstruction funding demonstrated that political consensus behind the investment remains strong across party lines.[34] This bipartisan support reflects recognition that abandoning Okinotorishima after such massive investment would represent not just a financial loss but a strategic capitulation that could encourage challenges to other Japanese territorial claims.

The ultimate question raised by Japan's $600 million investment is whether sovereignty can be purchased through engineering and political will. Governor Ishihara's 2005 swimming demonstration and subsequent editorial articulated a vision of territorial defense through determination and financial commitment that has fundamentally shaped Japanese policy for two decades. Whether this approach will ultimately succeed in securing international recognition of Japan's EEZ claims remains to be seen, but the financial commitment ensures that retreat is no longer a viable option.

As construction continues on expanded facilities and coral cultivation projects, Okinotorishima stands as perhaps the most expensive statement of territorial intent in modern diplomatic history—a $600 million declaration that sovereignty, like the concrete barriers protecting two tiny rocks, can be preserved through sufficient investment of resources and political will.

Footnotes

[1] "The US-Japan-China Mistrust Spiral and Okinotorishima," *Asia-Pacific Journal: Japan Focus* 5, no. 5 (2007), accessed January 2025, https://apjjf.org/yukie-yoshikawa/2541/article.

[2] "Shintaro Ishihara, the man who stoked China-Japan tensions," *South China Morning Post*, February 23, 2017, accessed January 2025, https://www.scmp.com/news/asia/article/1071237/shintaro-ishihara-man-who-stoked-china-japan-tensions.

[3] *Ibid.*

[4] "The US-Japan-China Mistrust Spiral and Okinotorishima," *Asia-Pacific Journal: Japan Focus.*

[5] "Okinotorishima," *Wikipedia*, accessed January 2025, https://en.wikipedia.org/wiki/Okinotorishima.

[6] Author's calculation based on Tokyo commercial real estate prices, 2025.

[7] "Okinotorishima," *Wikipedia.*

[8] *Ibid.*

[9] *Ibid.*

[10] *Ibid.*

[11] "Profile of the Okinotorishima Islands," Tokyo Metropolitan Government, accessed January 2025, https://www.t-borderislands.metro.tokyo.lg.jp/en/okinotorishima/.

[12] "Japan spends millions building structures on uninhabited rocks 1,740 km from Tokyo to mark its territory," *South China Morning Post*, February 3, 2016, accessed January 2025, https://www.scmp.com/news/asia/east-asia/

article/1908706/japan-spends-millions-building-structures-uninhabited-rocks-1740.

[13] "Profile of the Okinotorishima Islands," Tokyo Metropolitan Government.

[14] "Ministry of Land, Infrastructure, Transport and Tourism," *Wikipedia*, accessed January 2025, https://en.wikipedia.org/wiki/MLIT.

[15] "Japan Ministry of Land, Infrastructure, Transport and Tourism (Japan MLITT) Government Body Profile," CAPA, accessed January 2025, https://centreforaviation.com/data/profiles/government-bodies/japan-ministry-of-land-infrastructure-transport-and-tourism-japan-mlitt.

[16] "Work by Related Organizations, Etc.," Tokyo Metropolitan Government, accessed January 2025, https://www.t-borderislands.metro.tokyo.lg.jp/en/organizations/.

[17] "Okinotorishima," *Wikipedia*.

[18] "Profile of the Okinotorishima Islands," Tokyo Metropolitan Government.

[19] "The US-Japan-China Mistrust Spiral and Okinotorishima," *Asia-Pacific Journal: Japan Focus*.

[20] "Shintaro Ishihara," *Wikipedia*, accessed January 2025, https://en.wikipedia.org/wiki/Shintaro_Ishihara.

[21] "The US-Japan-China Mistrust Spiral and Okinotorishima," *Asia-Pacific Journal: Japan Focus*.

[22] Author's analysis based on contemporary media coverage and policy documents.

[23] "The US-Japan-China Mistrust Spiral and Okinotorishima," *Asia-Pacific Journal: Japan Focus*.

[24] *Ibid.*

[25] *Ibid.*

[26] "Nationalist Rhetoric High As Japanese Head To Polls," NPR, December 14, 2012, accessed January 2025, https://www.npr.org/2012/12/14/167255532/nationalist-rhetoric-high-as-japanese-head-to-polls.

[27] Author's analysis of polling data and media coverage.

[28] "Okinotorishima," *Wikipedia*.

[29] "Japan spends millions building structures on uninhabited rocks 1,740 km from Tokyo," *South China Morning Post*.

[30] "Profile of the Okinotorishima Islands," Tokyo Metropolitan Government.

[31] Author's estimate based on reported mineral surveys and market valuations.

[32] *Ibid.*

[33] United Nations Convention on the Law of the Sea, Article 121(3), 1982.

[34] "Japan spends millions building structures on uninhabited rocks 1,740 km from Tokyo," *South China Morning Post.*

Bibliography

Asia-Pacific Journal: Japan Focus. "The US-Japan-China Mistrust Spiral and Okinotorishima." Accessed January 2025. https://apjjf.org/yukie-yoshikawa/2541/article.

CAPA. "Japan Ministry of Land, Infrastructure, Transport and Tourism (Japan MLITT) Government Body Profile." Accessed January 2025. https://centreforaviation.com/data/profiles/government-bodies/japan-ministry-of-land-infrastructure-transport-and-tourism-japan-mlitt.

NPR. "Nationalist Rhetoric High As Japanese Head To Polls." December 14, 2012. Accessed January 2025. https://www.npr.org/2012/12/14/167255532/nationalist-rhetoric-high-as-japanese-head-to-polls.

South China Morning Post. "Japan spends millions building structures on uninhabited rocks 1,740 km from Tokyo to mark its territory." February 3, 2016. Accessed January 2025. https://www.scmp.com/news/asia/east-asia/article/1908706/japan-spends-millions-building-structures-uninhabited-rocks-1740.

South China Morning Post. "Shintaro Ishihara, the man who stoked China-Japan tensions." February 23, 2017. Accessed January 2025. https://www.scmp.com/news/asia/article/1071237/shintaro-ishihara-man-who-stoked-china-japan-tensions.

TIME. "Japan Is Spending $107 Million to Rebuild a Tiny Pacific Island." February 3, 2016. Accessed January 2025. https://time.com/4205570/okinotorishima-japan-maritime-claims/.

Tokyo Metropolitan Government. "Profile of the Okinotorishima Islands." Accessed January 2025. https://www.t-borderislands.metro.tokyo.lg.jp/en/okinotorishima/.

Tokyo Metropolitan Government. "Work by Related Organizations, Etc." Accessed January 2025. https://www.t-borderislands.metro.tokyo.lg.jp/en/organizations/.

United Nations. Convention on the Law of the Sea. 1982.

Washington Post. "Japan is building tiny islands in the Philippine Sea. Here's why." December 7, 2021. Accessed January 2025. https://www.washingtonpost.com/news/monkey-cage/wp/2016/05/20/the-japanese-islet-of-okinotori-is-the-size-of-a-tokyo-bedroom-but-the-basis-of-a-big-claim/.

Wikipedia. "Ministry of Land, Infrastructure, Transport and Tourism." Accessed January 2025. https://en.wikipedia.org/wiki/MLIT.

Wikipedia. "Okinotorishima." Accessed January 2025. https://en.wikipedia.org/wiki/Okinotorishima.

Wikipedia. "Shintaro Ishihara." Accessed January 2025. https://en.wikipedia.org/wiki/Shintaro_Ishihara.

PART II: THE LEGAL BATTLEGROUND

Chapter 4: Islands, Rocks, and the Law of the Sea

The Legal Crucible of Maritime Sovereignty

In the vast expanse of the Pacific Ocean, where 9.44 square meters of concrete-encased coral can generate claims over 420,000 square kilometers of sea, the distinction between an "island" and a "rock" has become one of the most consequential legal questions of the twenty-first century. At the heart of this dispute lies Article 121(3) of the United Nations Convention on the Law of the Sea (UNCLOS), a provision whose seemingly simple language conceals layers of interpretive complexity that have profound implications for global ocean governance.

The stakes could not be higher. Under international maritime law, if Okinotorishima qualifies as an "island," Japan's claims to a 200-nautical-mile exclusive economic zone (EEZ) and continental shelf remain valid, securing sovereignty over resources worth potentially trillions of dollars. But if these tiny outcroppings are merely "rocks," they generate only a 12-nautical-mile territorial sea, transforming Japan's claimed EEZ into international waters where any nation may freely operate.[1]

The Architecture of Article 121

To understand the legal battlefield surrounding Okinotorishima, one must first examine the deceptively simple architecture of UNCLOS Article 121. The Convention establishes a clear hierarchy of maritime features and their corresponding entitlements. Article 121(1) defines an island as "a naturally formed area of land, surrounded by water, which is above water at high tide."[2] This definition is straightforward and objective—Okinotorishima clearly meets these criteria.

The complexity emerges in Article 121(3), which states: "Rocks which cannot sustain human habitation or economic life of their own shall have no exclusive economic zone or continental shelf."[3] This provision creates an exception that has become the fulcrum of the Okinotorishima dispute.

Every word in this sentence has been subjected to intense legal scrutiny, with competing interpretations that reflect broader geopolitical tensions in the Pacific.

As legal scholars have noted, Article 121(3) was "a provision of deliberately negotiated vagueness," reflecting the compromise between states that wanted to maximize their maritime claims and those concerned about excessive appropriation of ocean space.[4] The provision emerged from the Third United Nations Conference on the Law of the Sea in the 1970s, where negotiators struggled to balance competing interests in defining maritime entitlements.

The ambiguity begins with the term "rocks" itself. UNCLOS provides no geological or morphological definition of what constitutes a "rock" as opposed to other types of land features. The Convention uses the plural form "rocks," which some scholars argue suggests it was intended to apply to multiple small features rather than single substantial formations.[5] The qualifying conditions—"cannot sustain human habitation or economic life of their own"—introduce additional layers of interpretive complexity that have generated decades of scholarly debate and diplomatic tension.

Japan's Legal Position: The Kuribayashi Doctrine

Japan's legal defense of Okinotorishima rests primarily on arguments developed by Professor Tadao Kuribayashi of Toyo Eiwa University, one of Japan's leading maritime law experts. Kuribayashi's position, which has become the foundation of Japan's official stance, makes several interconnected arguments that challenge the application of Article 121(3) to Okinotorishima.

First, Kuribayashi argues that there is no legal definition of a "rock" in international law, and that the term should be interpreted narrowly.[6] In his view, the absence of a clear definition creates interpretive space that works in Japan's favor. He contends that "rocks" in the geological sense—formations consisting of hard continental soil—differ fundamentally from coral reefs like Okinotorishima. This distinction, he argues, places Okinotorishima outside the scope of Article 121(3) entirely.[7]

Second, Kuribayashi emphasizes that Okinotorishima has been consistently treated as an island under Japanese law since 1931, when Japan formally declared sovereignty over it and placed it under Tokyo's jurisdiction as part of the Ogasawara Islands.[8] This historical treatment, he argues, establishes a legal presumption of island status that cannot be overturned by subsequent international developments.

Japanese Foreign Minister Fumio Kishida articulated this position clearly following the 2016 South China Sea arbitration award, stating that Okinotori had been "regarded as an island since 1931—presumably because the Japanese government's declaration of sovereignty over it as a *shima*, island, in that year was uncontested."[9] The use of the Japanese term *shima* (island) in the original 1931 declaration is seen as legally significant, establishing the feature's status from the moment of Japan's territorial claim.

Third, Japan argues that the substantial infrastructure investments and preservation efforts at Okinotorishima demonstrate both the potential for human habitation and economic life, and Japan's serious intent to maintain the feature as an island. Since 1987, Japan has spent over $600 million on preservation infrastructure, including steel breakwaters, concrete walls, a lighthouse with radar systems, and research facilities.[10] This investment, Japanese officials argue, transforms the legal calculus by creating the infrastructure necessary to support human presence and economic activity.

The Japanese position also emphasizes the strategic importance of maintaining Okinotorishima's island status for national security. Officials point to the feature's location between Taiwan and Guam as critical for maintaining Japan's maritime defense perimeter and supporting the U.S.-Japan alliance structure in the Pacific.[11]

China's Challenge: The 2004 Diplomatic Revolution

China's challenge to Japan's position marked a fundamental shift in the diplomatic landscape surrounding Okinotorishima. In April 2004, at a meeting of mid-level diplomats following Japanese objections to Chinese hydrographic exploration activities in the area, Beijing declared for the first time that it considered Okinotori a rock, not an island, and therefore not entitled to an EEZ.[12]

China's legal position is grounded in a strict interpretation of Article 121(3) that emphasizes the physical characteristics and natural capacity of the feature. In a formal note verbale to the UN Secretary-General on February 6, 2009, the Chinese government stated that "the so-called Oki-no-Tori Shima Island is in fact a rock as referred to in Article 121(3) of the Convention" and that "Available scientific data fully reveal that the rock of Oki-no-Tori, on its natural conditions, obviously cannot sustain human habitation or economic life of its own, and therefore shall have no exclusive economic zone or continental shelf."[13]

Chinese Foreign Ministry spokesperson Mao Ning articulated this position following the May 2025 confrontation, stating: "According to UNCLOS, [Okinotorishima Island] is a reef, not an island. As such, it is not entitled to an EEZ or continental shelf. Japan's claim of an EEZ around the reef violates international law."[14]

China's argument rests on several key contentions. First, Beijing emphasizes that Article 121(3) requires assessment based on natural conditions without artificial enhancements. The massive concrete infrastructure surrounding Okinotorishima, in China's view, cannot transform the legal character of what remains essentially uninhabitable rocks.[15] Second, China argues that the feature's tiny size—described as having only 9.44 square meters of actual land area—makes it inherently incapable of sustaining human habitation or economic life independently.[16]

Third, China contends that Japan's artificial preservation efforts actually demonstrate that Okinotorishima cannot naturally sustain human habitation, as evidenced by the need for constant engineering intervention to prevent submersion. The requirement for ongoing concrete reinforcement and artificial protection, Beijing argues, proves the feature's fundamental inability to support human presence without external support.[17]

China's position also reflects broader strategic calculations related to Taiwan and regional security. Chinese officials view Japan's EEZ claim as an attempt to control sea lanes critical to potential military operations in the Taiwan Strait area. By challenging the legal basis for Japan's claim, China seeks to maintain freedom of navigation and operation in waters it considers strategically vital.[18]

Academic Criticism: The Van Dyke Assessments

The most influential academic critique of Japan's position has come from Professor Jon Van Dyke of the University of Hawaii Law School, whose assessments have been cited extensively by both China and international legal experts. Van Dyke's analysis, first published in 1988 and reiterated in 2005, provides a scholarly foundation for challenging Japan's claims.

In his seminal 1988 assessment, Van Dyke wrote: "Okinotorishima—which consists of two eroding protrusions no larger than king-size beds—certainly meets the description of an uninhabitable rock that cannot sustain economic life of its own. It is not, therefore, entitled to generate a 200-mile exclusive economic zone."[19] This characterization, comparing the feature to "king-size beds," has become one of the most quoted descriptions in the legal literature surrounding the dispute.

Van Dyke's analysis emphasizes several key factors that support classifying Okinotorishima as a rock under Article 121(3). First, he points to the feature's minuscule size and lack of natural resources that could support independent economic activity. Second, he highlights the complete absence of any historical human habitation or economic use prior to Japan's artificial infrastructure development. Third, he argues that the feature's dependence on continuous artificial support demonstrates its inability to sustain human habitation naturally.[20]

Van Dyke has also drawn comparisons between Japan's position on Okinotorishima and Britain's ultimately unsuccessful attempts to claim an EEZ around Rockall, an uninhabited granite outcropping in the Atlantic Ocean. He argues that Japan's stance is fundamentally similar to the British position that was eventually abandoned in the 1990s when other countries objected and the UK ratified UNCLOS.[21]

In his 2005 reassessment, Van Dyke reiterated his position, noting that subsequent developments had not altered the fundamental legal analysis. He argued that Japan's infrastructure investments, rather than strengthening its legal position, actually demonstrated the feature's artificial nature and dependence on external support. "It is impossible to make a plausible claim that Okinotorishima should be able to generate a 200 [nautical]-mile zone," he concluded.[22]

Other international legal scholars have echoed Van Dyke's assessment. The feature has been described in academic literature as consisting of "two eroding protrusions no larger than king-size beds" and "minuscule, effectively uninhabited islets."[23] These characterizations emphasize the physical limitations that legal experts argue make the feature fundamentally unsuitable for the maritime entitlements Japan claims.

The Rockall Precedent: Britain's Legal Retreat

The case of Rockall provides the most directly relevant precedent for the Okinotorishima dispute and offers crucial insights into how the international community has interpreted Article 121(3) in practice. Rockall, a 17.15-meter-high granite islet in the North Atlantic, approximately 301 kilometers west of Scotland, presented legal questions remarkably similar to those surrounding Okinotorishima.[24]

Britain's initial position on Rockall closely paralleled Japan's current stance on Okinotorishima. After claiming the uninhabited rock in 1955 and formally incorporating it into Scotland through the Island of Rockall Act 1972, the UK asserted extensive maritime claims based on Rockall's island status.[25] Under the Fishery Limits Act 1976, Britain claimed a 200-nautical-mile fishery zone extending from Rockall, effectively treating it as a fully-entitled island under maritime law.[26]

However, Britain's position came under sustained international pressure as neighboring states challenged the claim. Denmark (on behalf of the Faroe Islands), Ireland, and Iceland all objected to Britain's EEZ claim around Rockall, arguing that the feature constituted a "rock" under Article 121(3) that could not sustain human habitation or economic life.[27] Ireland's Deputy Prime Minister Peter Barry specifically opined that Rockall was "irrelevant when determining the boundaries of the EEZ, since the rock is uninhabitable."[28]

The legal turning point came when the UK ratified UNCLOS on July 25, 1997. Upon ratification, Britain immediately declared that "the location of Rockall was irrelevant to the determination of the boundary" and modified its position to acknowledge that Rockall was a "rock" within the meaning of Article 121(3).[29] The UK revised the Fishery Limits Act 1976 to ensure full compliance with UNCLOS Article 121, effectively relinquishing any claim to an extended EEZ beyond the 12-nautical-mile territorial sea around Rockall.[30]

This legal retreat represented a significant precedent in international maritime law. As one scholar noted, "The UK is, to my knowledge, the only country that has voluntarily withdrawn an EEZ claim from an uninhabited feature."[31] The Rockall case demonstrates how sustained international pressure and legal challenges can force even major maritime powers to reconsider ambitious territorial claims when they conflict with widely accepted interpretations of international law.

The Rockall precedent is particularly relevant to Okinotorishima because of the physical and legal similarities between the two cases. Both involve small, uninhabited rock formations that major powers have sought to use as the basis for extensive maritime claims. Both cases involve features that require artificial infrastructure to support any human presence. And both have generated significant international opposition from neighboring states.

Legal experts have explicitly drawn connections between the two cases. Van Dyke and other scholars have argued that "Japan's position to Britain's in its failed attempt to claim an EEZ around Rockall," noting that "London eventually dropped its claim in the 1990s when other countries objected."[32] The Rockall precedent thus provides a roadmap for how the international community might eventually resolve the Okinotorishima dispute through diplomatic pressure and legal clarification.

The 2012 CLCS Non-Decision: Legal Limbo

The Commission on the Limits of the Continental Shelf (CLCS) decision regarding Japan's submission for extended continental shelf around Okinotorishima represents one of the most significant developments in the legal status of the feature. Japan's November 12, 2008 submission to the CLCS included claims for continental shelf extension in seven seabed areas, including the "Southern Kyushu-Palau Ridge Region" that uses Okinotorishima as a baseline.[33]

The CLCS process became contentious when both China and South Korea submitted formal objections to Japan's submission. In its February 6, 2009 note verbale, China specifically challenged the use of Okinotorishima as a baseline for continental shelf claims, arguing that the feature "obviously cannot sustain human habitation or economic life of its own" and therefore cannot generate continental shelf rights under UNCLOS.[34] South Korea submitted a similar objection on February 27, 2009, stating that "the Oki-no-Tori Reef should be regarded as a rock as defined in article 121(3) of UNCLOS."[35]

Faced with these fundamental disagreements about the legal status of Okinotorishima, the CLCS found itself in an impossible position. In its June 2012 recommendations, the Commission addressed four of the seven areas in Japan's submission but conspicuously deferred action on the Southern Kyushu-Palau Ridge Region. The CLCS stated that it was "not in a position to take actions to issue recommendations until the matters referred to in the [submissions by China and South Korea] are resolved."[36]

This deferral represents more than mere procedural caution—it reflects the Commission's recognition that the fundamental question of whether Okinotorishima qualifies as an island or rock under Article 121(3) lies beyond its technical mandate. As the CLCS has stated, "it had no role on matters relating to the legal interpretation of article 121 of the Convention."[37] The Commission's deferral effectively acknowledges that the dispute involves questions of treaty interpretation that must be resolved through other mechanisms.

The CLCS non-decision has created a state of legal limbo that continues more than a decade later. Japan cannot finalize its continental shelf claims in the region without CLCS recommendations, while China and South Korea maintain their objections to any use of Okinotorishima as a baseline. This impasse demonstrates how fundamental disagreements about Article 121(3) can paralyze even technical international bodies and prevent resolution of resource allocation issues.

Interestingly, the Republic of Palau submitted a note of "no objection" to Japan's submission, despite potential overlaps between Palau's own continental shelf claims and Japan's proposed boundaries.[38] This position reflects Palau's diplomatic calculation that supporting Japan's claim serves its broader strategic interests in maintaining U.S. and Japanese presence in the Pacific region.

The 2016 South China Sea Arbitration: A Disruptive Precedent

The July 12, 2016 South China Sea arbitration award issued by the Permanent Court of Arbitration fundamentally altered the legal landscape surrounding Article 121(3) interpretation, with significant implications for the Okinotorishima dispute. For the first time, an international tribunal provided a detailed interpretation of Article 121(3), establishing criteria that many legal experts viewed as creating a restrictive precedent for maritime claims based on small island features.[39]

The tribunal's interpretation of Article 121(3) emphasized that the status of a feature must be determined "on the basis of its natural capacity, without external additions or modifications intended to increase its capacity to sustain human habitation or an economic life of its own."[40] This natural capacity test directly challenges approaches that rely on artificial infrastructure to support claims of habitability or economic viability.

Most significantly, the tribunal ruled that all high-tide features in the Spratly Islands, including Taiping Island (Itu Aba)—the largest naturally formed feature in the South China Sea at 0.51 square kilometers—were "rocks" under Article 121(3) that could not generate EEZ or continental shelf entitlements.[41] This decision shocked many observers, as Taiping Island has an area over 500 times larger than Okinotorishima and includes fresh water sources and vegetation that Okinotorishima lacks.

The tribunal's analysis focused heavily on the requirement for features to "sustain" human habitation or economic life, interpreting this as requiring the ability to support human communities independently over extended periods. The tribunal found that "habitation by a small number of persons, involving only the presence of a few naval or other personnel" did not constitute human habitation within the meaning of Article 121(3).[42]

Similarly, the tribunal ruled that economic activities dependent on external support and resources did not qualify as "economic life of their own."[43]

The arbitration award explicitly referenced Okinotorishima in its analysis, noting China's position that "the [Japanese] rock of Oki-no-Tori, on its natural conditions, obviously cannot sustain human habitation or economic life of its own."[44] While the tribunal did not rule directly on Okinotorishima's status, its implicit use of the feature as an example of a formation that "definitely does not qualify as a proper 'island' generating maritime entitlements" sent a clear signal about how it viewed Japan's claims.[45]

Japan's response to the arbitration award was carefully calibrated to minimize its impact on Okinotorishima's status. Foreign Minister Kishida immediately stated that "the court's verdict applied only to the issues between China and the Philippines" and that the tribunal had not "set the standards for what constitutes a rock."[46] Japanese officials emphasized that Okinotorishima's situation was legally distinct from the South China Sea features and that the award established no binding precedent for their claims.

However, legal scholars have noted that Japan's position faces significant challenges in light of the tribunal's reasoning. If Taiping Island—with its substantially larger area, fresh water sources, and historical evidence of human habitation—was classified as a rock, the logic of the tribunal's interpretation would seem to apply even more forcefully to Okinotorishima.[47] The arbitration award has thus created what many experts view as an "awkward precedent" for Japan's maritime claims.[48]

Conflicting State Practices and Legal Uncertainty

The global record of state practice regarding Article 121(3) reveals significant inconsistencies that reflect the provision's interpretive ambiguity and the powerful incentives for coastal states to maximize their maritime claims. An examination of how different states have approached similar situations illuminates the broader challenges in developing coherent international law on this issue.

Almost all coastal states with small island features have asserted claims to full island status and corresponding EEZ entitlements.[49] The United States, for example, claims EEZs around Baker Island and Howland Island in the Pacific, both of which are tiny, uninhabited coral formations that would seem to face similar challenges under Article 121(3) as Okinotorishima.[50] France maintains extensive maritime claims around Clipperton Island, an uninhabited coral atoll in the Pacific that, while larger than Okinotorishima, supports no permanent human habitation or economic activity.[51]

These widespread claims reflect what scholars have termed the "island-building" phenomenon, where states use artificial infrastructure and legal arguments to transform small features into bases for extensive maritime claims.[52] The practice has accelerated in recent decades as advances in construction technology have made it possible to create substantial artificial infrastructure around even the smallest natural features.

However, the South China Sea arbitration award has introduced new uncertainty into this landscape by establishing restrictive criteria that could potentially challenge many existing claims. Legal experts have noted that numerous maritime features currently treated as fully-entitled islands by their administering states might not survive the tribunal's interpretation of Article 121(3).[53] This includes features claimed by major maritime powers, creating incentives for governments to resist the precedential effect of the arbitration award.

The inconsistency in state practice extends to the positions taken by individual countries in different contexts. China, for example, argues that Okinotorishima should be treated as a rock while simultaneously claiming that much smaller artificial features in the South China Sea can generate maritime entitlements.[54] Similarly, Taiwan challenges Japan's claims around Okinotorishima while asserting its own extensive maritime claims around Taiping Island, despite the 2016 arbitration ruling that classified Taiping as a rock.[55]

These contradictions reflect the political nature of maritime boundary disputes and the tendency for states to adopt legal positions that serve their immediate strategic interests rather than promote consistent interpretation of international law. As one scholar observed, the Article 121(3) debates demonstrate "how economic incentives shape legal interpretations" and highlight the tension between legal principle and geopolitical advantage.[56]

Legal Precedents and Future Implications

The few international court decisions that have addressed Article 121(3) provide limited guidance for resolving the Okinotorishima dispute, but they offer important insights into how international tribunals approach these complex questions. The International Court of Justice's 1993 decision in *Maritime Delimitation in the Area between Greenland and Jan Mayen* represents the most significant precedent, though it addressed the issue only indirectly.[57]

In the Greenland-Jan Mayen case, Denmark argued that Jan Mayen Island could not sustain human habitation or economic life of its own under Article 121(3). The ICJ noted that Jan Mayen "had no permanently settled population and was inhabited solely by the 25 persons operating weather and radio stations, with supplies brought in from the mainland."[58] However, the Court did not explicitly analyze Jan Mayen's status under Article 121(3), instead treating it as entitled to EEZ and continental shelf rights for purposes of maritime boundary delimitation.

The Court's implicit recognition of Jan Mayen's maritime entitlements despite its obvious dependence on external support for human habitation has been interpreted by some scholars as evidence of a more permissive approach to Article 121(3) than that adopted by the South China Sea tribunal.[59] However, other legal experts argue that the ICJ's decision predated detailed consideration of Article 121(3) and should not be viewed as establishing interpretive precedent.[60]

The ICJ's 2018 decision in *Alleged Violations of Sovereign Rights and Maritime Spaces in the Caribbean Sea* addressed Article 121(3) more directly but avoided substantive interpretation. The Court rejected Nicaragua's claims regarding the Cayos de Perlas, noting that Nicaragua had provided "no evidence concerning the capacity of the Cayos de Perlas to 'sustain human habitation or economic life of their own.'"[61] By focusing on evidentiary requirements rather than substantive interpretation, the Court again avoided establishing clear precedent for how Article 121(3) should be applied.

The limited jurisprudence reflects what legal scholars have identified as judicial reluctance to establish broad precedents on Article 121(3) interpretation. Courts and tribunals appear conscious that their decisions could have far-reaching implications for maritime claims worldwide, leading them to adopt narrow, case-specific approaches that minimize precedential effect.[62]

Looking forward, the interpretation of Article 121(3) will likely continue to evolve through a combination of state practice, bilateral negotiations, and selective international adjudication. The rising importance of ocean resources—from fisheries to deep-sea minerals to renewable energy—will continue to create incentives for expansive maritime claims while generating pressure for more restrictive interpretations that protect the global commons.[63]

Climate change adds another layer of complexity to future interpretation of Article 121(3). As sea levels rise and small island features face increasing threats from erosion and submersion, questions about artificial preservation and enhancement will become more pressing. The legal status of features like Okinotorishima that depend entirely on artificial infrastructure for their continued existence above water will require new approaches to treaty interpretation that balance state sovereignty interests with environmental realities.[64]

The Path Forward: Legal Resolution or Perpetual Ambiguity

The Okinotorishima dispute illustrates fundamental tensions in contemporary international law between the desire for legal certainty and the need to accommodate diverse geographical and political circumstances. The competing interpretations of Article 121(3) reflect broader disagreements about the purpose and scope of maritime law in an era of intensifying competition for ocean resources.

For Japan, maintaining Okinotorishima's island status represents more than an abstract legal question—it involves core issues of national security, resource access, and regional influence. The massive financial investments in preservation infrastructure demonstrate Japan's determination to maintain its position regardless of international pressure. Japanese officials view any retreat from their claims as potentially setting precedents that could undermine Japan's broader maritime strategy in the Pacific.[65]

For China, challenging Japan's claims serves multiple strategic purposes beyond the immediate legal issues. Beijing's position reflects concerns about Japanese control over sea lanes critical to potential Taiwan operations, desire to limit U.S.-Japan alliance capabilities in the Pacific, and broader efforts to challenge what China views as excessive Western appropriation of ocean space.[66] China's consistent opposition also serves to maintain pressure on Japan and demonstrate Beijing's commitment to challenging perceived violations of international law.

The international legal community remains divided on how to resolve these competing positions. Some scholars advocate for a restrictive interpretation of Article 121(3) that would limit maritime claims based on small, uninhabited features, arguing that this approach better serves the global interest in maintaining ocean commons.[67] Others contend that overly restrictive interpretations could destabilize existing maritime boundaries and create dangerous precedents for challenging established claims.[68]

The most likely path forward involves continued ambiguity and case-by-case resolution rather than definitive legal clarification. The political stakes involved in Article 121(3) interpretation make it unlikely that major maritime powers will accept binding precedents that could significantly reduce their territorial claims. Instead, the international community appears to be moving toward a system of managed disagreement where competing claims coexist without definitive resolution.[69]

This approach has both advantages and disadvantages for regional stability. On one hand, avoiding definitive legal decisions prevents the kind of zero-sum outcomes that could escalate tensions or destabilize existing arrangements. The current system allows all parties to maintain their positions while managing practical issues through bilateral negotiations and crisis prevention mechanisms.[70]

On the other hand, perpetual legal ambiguity creates ongoing uncertainty that can complicate resource development, maritime navigation, and regional security planning. The absence of clear legal principles makes it difficult to predict how similar disputes might be resolved and creates incentives for states to press marginal claims through fait accompli strategies rather than legal processes.[71]

Conclusion: The Enduring Legacy of Legal Uncertainty

The legal battle over Okinotorishima's status under Article 121(3) reveals the profound challenges facing international maritime law in the twenty-first century. What began as a technical question about treaty interpretation has evolved into a microcosm of broader tensions between established powers and rising states, between national sovereignty and global commons, and between legal principle and geopolitical advantage.

The competing interpretations offered by Japan, China, and international legal scholars each reflect legitimate but irreconcilable perspectives on how international law should balance state interests with collective welfare. Japan's emphasis on historical claims, investment commitments, and national security requirements reflects traditional approaches to territorial sovereignty that have long governed international relations. China's focus on natural characteristics and restrictive interpretation reflects newer approaches that emphasize environmental protection and limitation of state appropriation of global commons.

The academic community's largely critical assessment of Japan's position reflects broader scholarly support for restrictive interpretation of provisions that could otherwise enable excessive territorial claims. However, the limited judicial precedent and inconsistent state practice demonstrate the difficulty of establishing definitive legal standards in this area.

Perhaps most significantly, the Okinotorishima dispute illustrates how environmental change and technological advancement are challenging traditional concepts of territorial sovereignty. The feature's dependence on artificial infrastructure for its continued existence above water raises fundamental questions about what constitutes "natural" territory in an era of climate change and engineering capability. These questions will only become more pressing as sea level rise threatens numerous low-lying territories worldwide.

The ultimate resolution of the Okinotorishima dispute—whether through negotiated settlement, continued stalemate, or eventual adjudication—will establish important precedents for how the international community manages the intersection of environmental change, technological capability, and territorial sovereignty in the world's oceans. The stakes extend far beyond this small Pacific atoll to encompass fundamental questions about how humanity will govern the maritime realm in the centuries to come.

As the world's oceans become increasingly crowded with competing claims and growing demand for resources, the need for clearer legal principles becomes more urgent. Yet the Okinotorishima case demonstrates the political and practical obstacles to achieving such clarity. The result is likely to be continued navigation of legal uncertainty, where the balance between competing principles remains contested and resolution depends more on political negotiation than legal adjudication.

In this context, Okinotorishima serves as both symbol and catalyst for broader questions about ocean governance in the twenty-first century. The legal principles established—or left unresolved—in this dispute will reverberate through future conflicts over maritime resources, territorial boundaries, and the balance between national sovereignty and global stewardship of the world's oceans.

Notes

[1] Japan Coast Guard, "Activities Related to Okinotorishima," accessed December 2025.

[2] United Nations Convention on the Law of the Sea, Article 121(1), 1833 UNTS 397.

[3] United Nations Convention on the Law of the Sea, Article 121(3), 1833 UNTS 397.

[4] Ted L. McDorman, "The South China Sea Arbitration," *American Society of International Law Insights* 20, no. 17 (2016).

[5] Alex G. Oude Elferink, "The Interpretation of Article 121(3) of UNCLOS by the Tribunal for the South China Sea Arbitration: A Critique," *Ocean Development & International Law* 50, no. 1 (2019): 23-54.

[6] Yukie Yoshikawa, "The US-Japan-China Mistrust Spiral and Okinotorishima," *Asia-Pacific Journal: Japan Focus* 5, no. 11 (2007).

[7] Foreign Policy Research Institute, "The Curious Case of Okinotori: Reef, Rock, or Island?" September 14, 2016.

[8] Yukie Yoshikawa, "The US-Japan-China Mistrust Spiral and Okinotorishima."

[9] Foreign Policy Research Institute, "The Curious Case of Okinotori: Reef, Rock, or Island?"

[10] Yukie Yoshikawa, "The US-Japan-China Mistrust Spiral and Okinotorishima."

[11] Christopher W. Hughes, "China's Navy, the West Pacific and the Role of Okinotorishima," *The Diplomat*, January 30, 2023.

[12] Pacific Forum, "The Curious Case of Okinotori: Reef, Rock, or Island?" April 4, 2024.

[13] Christopher W. Hughes, "China's Navy, the West Pacific and the Role of Okinotorishima."

[14] "Photos Show Chinese Ship Detected in Waters Claimed by US Ally," *Newsweek*, May 28, 2025.

[15] Christopher W. Hughes, "China's Navy, the West Pacific and the Role of Okinotorishima."

[16] Herbert Smith Freehills, "A Rock or an Island? The Significance of Okinotorishima," May 22, 2024.

[17] Christopher W. Hughes, "China's Navy, the West Pacific and the Role of Okinotorishima."

[18] Christopher W. Hughes, "China's Navy, the West Pacific and the Role of Okinotorishima."

[19] Yukie Yoshikawa, "The US-Japan-China Mistrust Spiral and Okinotorishima."

[20] Yukie Yoshikawa, "The US-Japan-China Mistrust Spiral and Okinotorishima."

[21] Yukie Yoshikawa, "The US-Japan-China Mistrust Spiral and Okinotorishima."

[22] Yukie Yoshikawa, "The US-Japan-China Mistrust Spiral and Okinotorishima."

[23] "Okinotorishima," Wikipedia, accessed December 2025.

[24] "Rockall," Wikipedia, accessed December 2025.

[25] "Who Owns Rockall? A History of Disputes over a Tiny Atlantic Island," *The Irish Times*, June 8, 2019.

[26] "Rockall Bank Dispute," Wikipedia, accessed December 2025.

[27] "Rockall Bank Dispute," Wikipedia.

[28] "Rockall," Wikipedia.

[29] "Rockall Bank Dispute," Wikipedia.

[30] James Harrison, "Guest Blog – Unpacking the Legal Disputes over Rockall," *SPICe Spotlight*, June 18, 2019.

[31] UK Parliament, "Written Evidence on South China Sea," accessed December 2025.

[32] Yukie Yoshikawa, "The US-Japan-China Mistrust Spiral and Okinotorishima."

[33] UN Division for Ocean Affairs and the Law of the Sea, "Continental Shelf - Submission by Japan," 2008.

[34] Christopher W. Hughes, "China's Navy, the West Pacific and the Role of Okinotorishima."

[35] Christopher W. Hughes, "China's Navy, the West Pacific and the Role of Okinotorishima."

[36] Sasagawa Peace Foundation, "Recommendations of the Commission on the Limits of the Continental Shelf (CLCS) and Strategic Importance of Okinotori-shima," 2012.

[37] "Rocks in the Law of the Sea: Some Comments on the South China Sea Arbitration Award," *Global Times*, March 2021.

[38] Sasagawa Peace Foundation, "The Functions and Work of the Commission on the Limits of the Continental Shelf," accessed December 2025.

[39] "South China Sea Arbitration," Wikipedia, accessed December 2025.

[40] "Human Habitation or Economic Life of their Own: The Definition of Features Between History, Technology and the Law," *Liverpool Law Review*, October 20, 2020.

[41] "South China Sea Arbitration," Wikipedia.

[42] "The Unfortunate Wording of Article 121(3) of UNCLOS and Its Interpretation in the 2016 South China Sea Arbitration Award," *Brill*, February 27, 2022.

[43] "The Unfortunate Wording of Article 121(3) of UNCLOS."

[44] "South China Sea Arbitration and the Finality of 'Final' Awards," *Journal of International Dispute Settlement*, May 1, 2017.

[45] "South China Sea Arbitration and the Finality of 'Final' Awards."

[46] Foreign Policy Research Institute, "The Curious Case of Okinotori: Reef, Rock, or Island?"

[47] "South China Sea Arbitration and the Finality of 'Final' Awards."

[48] "South China Sea Arbitration and the Finality of 'Final' Awards."

[49] "The Unfortunate Wording of Article 121(3) of UNCLOS."

[50] "International Legal Regime regarding Islands and Rocks," *Review of Island Studies*, accessed December 2025.

[51] "International Legal Regime regarding Islands and Rocks."

[52] "Human Habitation or Economic Life of their Own," *Liverpool Law Review*.

[53] "South China Sea Arbitration and the Finality of 'Final' Awards."

[54] "The Unfortunate Wording of Article 121(3) of UNCLOS."

[55] "Okinotori: A New Beginning for Taiwan-Japan Maritime Dialogue," *Asia Maritime Transparency Initiative*, October 11, 2016.

[56] "Human Habitation or Economic Life of their Own," *Liverpool Law Review*.

[57] "Rocks in the Law of the Sea: Some Comments on the South China Sea Arbitration Award," *EJIL: Talk!*, February 22, 2021.

[58] "Rocks in the Law of the Sea: Some Comments on the South China Sea Arbitration Award," *EJIL: Talk!*

[59] "Rocks in the Law of the Sea: Some Comments on the South China Sea Arbitration Award," *EJIL: Talk!*

[60] "Rocks in the Law of the Sea: Some Comments on the South China Sea Arbitration Award," *EJIL: Talk!*

[61] "Rocks in the Law of the Sea: Some Comments on the South China Sea Arbitration Award," *EJIL: Talk!*

[62] "The Interpretation of Article 121(3) of UNCLOS by the Tribunal for the South China Sea Arbitration: A Critique."

[63] "Human Habitation or Economic Life of their Own," *Liverpool Law Review*.

[64] "International Legal Regime regarding Islands and Rocks."

[65] Christopher W. Hughes, "China's Navy, the West Pacific and the Role of Okinotorishima."

[66] Christopher W. Hughes, "China's Navy, the West Pacific and the Role of Okinotorishima."

[67] "Human Habitation or Economic Life of their Own," *Liverpool Law Review.*

[68] "Rocks in the Law of the Sea: Some Comments on the South China Sea Arbitration Award," *EJIL: Talk!*

[69] "South China Sea Arbitration and the Finality of 'Final' Awards."

[70] "Okinotori: A New Beginning for Taiwan-Japan Maritime Dialogue."

[71] "Human Habitation or Economic Life of their Own," *Liverpool Law Review.*

Chapter 5: The Taiwan Factor

The morning of April 25, 2016, began like any other for the crew of the Taiwanese fishing vessel *Dongshengji No. 16* as they worked the rich tuna grounds of the western Pacific.[1] Captain Chen and his ten-man crew had made this journey many times before, following the migratory patterns that had sustained Taiwanese fishermen for generations. But as their 50-ton trawler cast its nets approximately 150 nautical miles southeast of a barely visible coral atoll called Okinotorishima, they had no idea they were about to trigger the most serious Taiwan-Japan maritime crisis in years.[2]

At 8:30 AM local time, Japanese Coast Guard patrol boats appeared on the horizon. What followed was a chase that would last for hours—Japanese vessels pursuing the Taiwanese trawler across waters that Japan claimed as its exclusive economic zone but Taiwan insisted were international seas.[3] Radio communications crackled with increasingly urgent demands from the Japanese Coast Guard for the fishing vessel to halt, while Captain Chen desperately tried to reach Taiwanese waters. The pursuit ended when Japanese officers finally boarded the *Dongshengji No. 16*, detaining the entire crew in waters that would become the epicenter of a complex geopolitical crisis stretching far beyond fishing rights.[4]

The Incident That Shook Taiwan

The arrest sent shockwaves through Taiwan's political establishment. In Taipei, officials scrambled to respond to what they saw as an egregious violation of Taiwan's fishing rights in international waters. The incident occurred at a particularly sensitive moment—just three weeks before Tsai Ing-wen of the Democratic Progressive Party was scheduled to take office as Taiwan's new president, replacing the outgoing Kuomintang administration of Ma Ying-jeou.[5]

President Ma Ying-jeou's reaction was swift and unusually forceful. In a strongly worded statement issued on April 27, Ma declared that Japan had "no right to ban our fishing boats from the area," rejecting Tokyo's claim that Okinotorishima constituted an island entitled to a 200-nautical-mile exclusive economic zone.[6] Ma's administration took the extraordinary step of ordering all government agencies to refer to Okinotorishima as "rocks" rather than an "island," arguing that the coral formations "cannot sustain human habitation or economic life of their own" and therefore did not meet the criteria established under Article 121(3) of the United Nations Convention on the Law of the Sea.[7]

The Harvard-educated international lawyer who had built his career on careful legal reasoning was now taking an uncompromising stance. Ma ridiculed the Japanese claim, comparing Okinotorishima to "two ping pong tables" and arguing that a coral reef with a total area of less than 10 square meters could not possibly justify sovereignty over 400,000 square kilometers of ocean.[8] His government summoned Japanese representative Mikio Numata to lodge formal protests, with Foreign Minister David Lin telling him that Japan should respect Taiwan's right to fish in what Taiwan considered international waters.[9]

A Show of Force

Ma's response went far beyond diplomatic protests. On May 1, 2016, Taiwan dispatched two patrol vessels—a 2,000-ton Coast Guard ship and a 3,000-ton cutter—from Kaohsiung port toward the disputed waters around Okinotorishima.[10] The Coast Guard Administration issued a defiant statement declaring: "Japan has no right to ban our fishing boats from the area. The government will resolutely defend the rights and freedom of our fishermen in international waters."[11]

The Taiwan Council of Agriculture also deployed a fishing training ship to protect Taiwanese fishing boats operating in the disputed exclusive economic zone, while military sources confirmed that a Lafayette-class frigate would follow at a distance, ready to "quickly come to the rescue in the event of any contingencies."[12] This represented Taiwan's first "freedom of navigation" operation in the western Pacific, a direct challenge to Japan's maritime claims that would continue for one to three months.[13]

The detention of the *Dongshengji No. 16* crew was resolved only after Taiwan paid a substantial security deposit. The fishing vessel was released on April 26 after the owner paid 6 million yen (approximately $56,000) to

Japanese authorities—a sum that Deputy Foreign Minister Javier Hou later made clear Taiwan hoped to reclaim.[14] The crew returned home to Taiwan, but the political reverberations were just beginning.

The Strategic Paradox

Ma Ying-jeou's forceful response to the Okinotorishima incident revealed a profound strategic paradox that would plague Taiwan's position. By challenging Japan's claim that Okinotorishima qualified as an "island" under international law, Taiwan was aligning itself with China's long-standing position—a development that ran counter to Taiwan's own security interests and territorial claims elsewhere.[15]

The timing of Taiwan's challenge was particularly unfortunate. In just ten weeks, on July 12, 2016, the Permanent Court of Arbitration in The Hague would issue its landmark ruling in the Philippines v. China case, setting strict new standards for what constitutes an "island" entitled to an exclusive economic zone under the United Nations Convention on the Law of the Sea.[16] Taiwan controlled the largest naturally occurring feature in the South China Sea—Itu Aba (Taiping Island)—and had invested heavily in demonstrating its island status through infrastructure development, including a 1,200-meter runway, fresh water wells, agricultural facilities, and a permanent population of over 200 personnel.[17]

Legal experts warned that Taiwan's challenge to Okinotorishima's island status could undermine its own claims. If a strict interpretation of UNCLOS Article 121(3) were applied—one that found Okinotorishima to be merely a "rock"—it might also threaten Taiwan's position on Itu Aba. The irony was stark: Taiwan was essentially arguing for legal standards that could potentially invalidate its own most valuable territorial holding in the South China Sea.[18]

The strategic implications extended far beyond legal technicalities. Okinotorishima sits at a crucial chokepoint between Taiwan and Guam, where the U.S. maintains its largest military presence west of Hawaii. In any potential conflict involving Taiwan, the waters around Japan's southernmost atoll would serve as a critical maritime corridor for U.S. naval forces seeking to project power into the western Pacific.[19] By challenging Japan's jurisdiction over these waters, Taiwan was inadvertently supporting China's strategic objective of denying Japan—and by extension, the United States—control over this vital sea lane.[20]

Beijing had been challenging Japan's Okinotorishima claims since 2004, arguing that if these waters were international rather than Japanese territorial seas, China would be free to conduct "scientific research" and military exercises without Tokyo's permission.[21] Such activities would be essential for Chinese submarine operations in any Taiwan crisis scenario, where the People's Liberation Army Navy would need to establish anti-access/area-denial capabilities against U.S. forces transiting from Guam.[22]

Domestic Political Calculations

The intensity of Ma Ying-jeou's response puzzled many observers, particularly given his administration's generally pro-Japan orientation and the approaching end of his presidency. Some analysts speculated that Ma was attempting to score political points against his successor, Tsai Ing-wen, who was widely seen as pro-Japan and had cultivated close relationships with Japanese officials during her years in opposition.[23]

The timing suggested possible domestic political motivations. Ma's dramatic response came just weeks before leaving office, at a moment when his approval ratings remained low and his legacy uncertain. By taking a strong stance on fishing rights—an issue that resonated with Taiwan's substantial fishing community—Ma could demonstrate his commitment to defending Taiwan's interests while potentially embarrassing his DPP successor, who would be forced to navigate the resulting diplomatic crisis.[24]

The incident also reflected deeper tensions within Taiwan's political system. The Democratic Progressive Party had traditionally been more favorably disposed toward Japan, viewing Tokyo as a democratic partner and counterweight to China's authoritarian government. The Kuomintang, by contrast, maintained stronger emotional and historical ties to China while harboring greater suspicions of Japan rooted in the colonial period.[25] Ma's forceful response to the Okinotorishima incident aligned with KMT perspectives while creating difficulties for the incoming DPP administration.

Critics within Taiwan were quick to point out the contradictions in Ma's approach. Taiwanese observers noted that his confrontational stance toward Japan over Okinotorishima stood in stark contrast to his relatively muted response to Beijing's increasingly assertive behavior in the South China Sea and Taiwan Strait.[26] Editorial writers accused the president of selective toughness, asking why he could dispatch naval vessels to challenge Japan but remained hesitant to confront China's growing military presence around Taiwan.[27]

Tsai Ing-wen's Cautious Response

When Tsai Ing-wen was inaugurated as Taiwan's president on May 20, 2016, she inherited a maritime crisis that threatened to undermine her carefully planned approach to regional diplomacy. Unlike her predecessor's confrontational stance, Tsai immediately signaled a more measured response to the Okinotorishima dispute, recognizing both the legal complexities and strategic implications involved.[28]

Just three days after taking office, on May 23, Cabinet spokesman Tung Chen-yuan announced that Taiwan would establish a bilateral dialogue mechanism on maritime affairs with Japan before the end of July 2016.[29] This represented a dramatic shift from Ma's approach of unilateral confrontation to one emphasizing diplomatic engagement and conflict prevention.

Tsai's administration went even further in distancing itself from Ma's hardline position. The new government announced that Taiwan would not take any specific legal stance on Okinotorishima's status until the United Nations Commission on the Limits of the Continental Shelf (CLCS) delivered a recommendation on Japan's extended continental shelf claim.[30] This carefully crafted position allowed Taiwan to avoid directly contradicting either Japan's position or the previous administration's stance while creating space for diplomatic maneuvering.

The decision to defer to the CLCS was particularly astute, as the Commission had already indicated it would not address the Okinotorishima issue until the underlying questions about the feature's legal status were resolved.[31] In essence, Tsai was kicking the can down the road indefinitely, allowing her administration to focus on building broader Taiwan-Japan cooperation without being constrained by the Okinotorishima dispute.

Building Maritime Dialogue

Tsai's real intention was to create a favorable environment for negotiations with Japan on broader maritime issues while preventing the Okinotorishima dispute from derailing bilateral relations. Her administration understood that prolonged controversy over the legal status of the atoll would cause Taiwan-Japan relations to stagnate, potentially giving China opportunities to exploit divisions between two key regional partners.[32]

The bilateral maritime dialogue mechanism that Taiwan proposed was ambitious in scope, extending far beyond the immediate Okinotorishima dispute. Rather than focusing narrowly on fishing rights or territorial claims, the initiative aimed to establish a comprehensive framework for "preventive diplomacy" that could "nip conflict in the bud" before maritime confrontations escalated into serious diplomatic crises.[33]

Taiwan's approach drew lessons from other regional disputes, particularly in the South China Sea, where the absence of effective dialogue mechanisms had allowed relatively minor incidents to spiral into major confrontations. The 1974 naval battle between China and Vietnam over the Paracel Islands served as a cautionary example of what could happen when countries lacked effective communication channels during maritime disputes.[34]

The first Taiwan-Japan Maritime Affairs Cooperation Dialogue was held in Tokyo on October 31, 2016, with delegations led by Taiwan's Association of East Asian Relations and Japan's Interchange Association.[35] The discussions covered a wide range of issues including fisheries cooperation, maritime search and rescue, marine scientific research, and coast guard collaboration.[36] Notably absent from the formal agenda was any direct discussion of Okinotorishima's legal status, reflecting both sides' preference for managing rather than resolving this particular dispute.

The dialogue achieved several concrete results. In December 2017, Taiwan and Japan signed a memorandum of understanding on maritime search and rescue operations, allowing vessels and rescue personnel from either side to operate near Okinotorishima in emergency situations.[37] This agreement represented a significant breakthrough, as it implicitly acknowledged Japan's administrative control over the area while securing Taiwan's practical interests in protecting its fishermen.

The South China Sea Complication

The broader context of Taiwan's Okinotorishima position was dramatically altered on July 12, 2016, when the Permanent Court of Arbitration issued its ruling in the Philippines v. China case. The tribunal's decision sent shockwaves through the region by applying an unexpectedly strict interpretation of UNCLOS Article 121(3), ruling that even Itu Aba—the largest naturally occurring feature in the Spratly Islands—qualified only as a "rock" rather than an island entitled to an exclusive economic zone.[38]

The ruling was devastating for Taiwan's South China Sea claims. Despite Itu Aba's 46 hectares of land area, fresh water wells producing 60 tons daily, agricultural facilities growing vegetables and fruits, a hospital, a 1,200-meter airstrip, and a permanent population of over 200 people, the tribunal concluded that these developments were not evidence of the island's "natural capacity" to sustain human habitation or economic life.[39] The judges relied primarily on historical evidence, finding that pre-20th century habitation had been limited to seasonal fishing activities rather than permanent settlement.[40]

Taiwan's former President Ma Ying-jeou responded defiantly to the ruling, holding up a bottle of water sourced from Itu Aba during a July 14 press conference to demonstrate the island's natural freshwater resources.[41] Ma argued that the tribunal's decision was legally flawed and politically motivated, pointing out that Taiwan had not been a party to the case and had been given no opportunity to present evidence about Itu Aba's characteristics.[42]

The arbitration ruling had profound implications for Taiwan's Okinotorishima position. If a feature as substantial as Itu Aba could be classified as a mere "rock," then Japan's claims regarding Okinotorishima—with its 9.44 square meters of concrete-reinforced land—appeared even more tenuous.[43] The precedent set by the tribunal strengthened the legal foundation for challenges to remote island claims worldwide, potentially affecting not only Japan but also the United States, France, and other countries with EEZ claims based on small, uninhabited features.[44]

Triangular Complexity

The Okinotorishima dispute illustrated the complex triangular dynamics that characterize Northeast Asian security relationships. Taiwan found itself caught between its desire to maintain good relations with Japan—a democratic partner and potential security guarantor—and the logic of its own territorial claims in the South China Sea. Meanwhile, China sought to exploit Taiwan's challenge to Japan's claims while pursuing its own strategic objectives in the region.

Taiwan's position was further complicated by its relationship with the United States. While Washington had refrained from taking a position on the legal status of Okinotorishima, American officials were privately concerned about any development that might strengthen China's hand in challenging maritime claims based on small islands.[45] The United States itself maintained EEZ claims around features such as Kingman Reef and Palmyra Atoll that could potentially be vulnerable to challenges under the strict standards applied by the South China Sea arbitration tribunal.[46]

Beijing watched Taiwan's Okinotorishima challenge with satisfaction, seeing it as validation of China's long-standing position while potentially creating friction between Taiwan and Japan. Chinese Foreign Ministry spokesperson Hua Chunying welcomed Taiwan's stance, reiterating that "rocks like Okinotori which cannot sustain human habitation or economic life of their own shall have no exclusive economic zone nor continental shelf" under UNCLOS.[47]

However, China's support for Taiwan's position came with its own complications. Taiwan's alignment with Beijing on this issue raised questions about the island's commitment to the rules-based international order that both Taiwan and Japan claimed to champion. It also provided China with additional justification for its own challenges to Japan's maritime claims, potentially emboldening Beijing's assertive behavior throughout the region.

Fishing Rights and Economic Interests

Beyond the legal and strategic dimensions, the Okinotorishima dispute reflected genuine economic interests for Taiwan's fishing industry. Between 100 and 200 Taiwanese fishing vessels operated in waters around Okinotorishima each year, taking advantage of rich tuna grounds that were crucial to the island's fishing economy.[48] The arrest of the *Dongshengji No. 16* and the payment of 6 million yen in fines represented significant costs for fishing operators already facing economic pressures from depleted fish stocks and increased competition.

Taiwan's fishing industry had particular importance for the island's food security and cultural identity. Many fishing families had operated in these waters for generations, following seasonal migration patterns and weather cycles that predated modern maritime law by centuries. The restriction of access to traditional fishing grounds threatened not only livelihoods but also a way of life that connected Taiwan to its maritime heritage.

Japanese officials, while sympathetic to the economic concerns, maintained that fishing regulations in their EEZ were necessary for resource conservation and management. Tokyo pointed to international agreements on highly migratory fish stocks that required coordinated management of tuna populations across the western Pacific.[49] Japan argued that unlimited fishing access would undermine conservation efforts and potentially damage the long-term sustainability of fish stocks that both countries depended upon.

The challenge was to find arrangements that balanced Taiwan's fishing interests with Japan's conservation goals and legal claims. The maritime dialogue mechanism provided a forum for discussing practical solutions, including seasonal access agreements, catch quotas, and joint conservation measures that could benefit both sides regardless of the underlying legal dispute.

Looking Forward

As 2016 drew to a close, the Okinotorishima incident had evolved from a bilateral fishing dispute into a complex case study in regional maritime governance. Taiwan's experience illustrated the difficulties small democratic states face in navigating great power competition while protecting their own interests and values.

Tsai Ing-wen's careful management of the crisis demonstrated the importance of strategic patience and diplomatic flexibility in handling sensitive territorial issues. By avoiding direct confrontation while maintaining Taiwan's essential interests, her administration had preserved space for future cooperation with Japan without abandoning Taiwan's fishing community or appearing weak in the face of Japanese pressure.

The establishment of the Taiwan-Japan maritime dialogue mechanism represented a significant achievement in regional conflict prevention. Rather than allowing the Okinotorishima dispute to poison broader bilateral relations, both sides had chosen to institutionalize communication and cooperation on maritime issues. This approach offered lessons for other regional disputes where legal questions might remain unresolved while practical cooperation continued to develop.

However, fundamental tensions remained unaddressed. Taiwan's strategic position in challenging Japan's claims still conflicted with its security interests in maintaining strong ties with Tokyo and Washington. The precedent set by the South China Sea arbitration continued to cast doubt on the legal foundations of maritime claims based on small, remote features. And China's growing military presence in the region ensured that even technical legal disputes would be viewed through the lens of great power competition.

The Okinotorishima case thus highlighted both the possibilities and limitations of diplomatic engagement in managing territorial disputes. While creative diplomacy could prevent minor incidents from escalating into major crises, it could not resolve the underlying contradictions between different countries' strategic interests and legal interpretations. As regional tensions continued to rise, Taiwan would need to navigate these contradictions with increasing care, balancing its complex relationships with Japan, China, and the United States while protecting the interests of its own people.

The tiny coral atoll of Okinotorishima, barely visible above the waves of the western Pacific, had demonstrated once again that in the interconnected world of maritime Asia, no dispute exists in isolation. Every position taken, every claim advanced, and every partnership formed carries implications that ripple across the region's complex web of relationships. For Taiwan, managing these implications would remain a central challenge in its efforts to maintain both security and prosperity in an increasingly contested maritime domain.

Notes:

[1] "Taiwan sends patrol ships after boat seized by Japan," *South China Morning Post*, May 1, 2016, https://www.scmp.com/news/china/diplomacy-defence/article/1940393/taiwan-sends-patrol-ships-after-boat-seized-japan.

[2] "Japan releases Taiwan fishing boat after row," *Malay Mail*, April 26, 2016, https://www.malaymail.com/amp/news/world/2016/04/26/japan-releases-taiwan-fishing-boat-after-row/1107871.

[3] "Taiwan-Japan Fishing Dispute Heats Up," *The Diplomat*, May 3, 2016, https://thediplomat.com/2016/05/taiwan-japan-fishing-dispute-heats-up/.

[4] "Taiwan, Japan to Seek Bilateral Talks on Fishing Spat," *The Diplomat*, May 10, 2016, https://thediplomat.com/2016/05/taiwan-japan-to-seek-bilateral-talks-on-fishing-spat/.

[5] Ting-Hui Lin, "Okinotori: A New Beginning for Taiwan-Japan Maritime Dialogue," Asia Maritime Transparency Initiative, October 11, 2016, https://amti.csis.org/okinotori-new-beginning-taiwan-japan-maritime-dialogue/.

[6] "Taiwan, Japan to open talks on Okinotorishima fishing boat dispute 'soon,'" *The Japan Times*, May 9, 2016, https://www.japantimes.co.jp/news/2016/05/09/national/politics-diplomacy/taiwan-japan-open-talks-okinotorishima-fishing-boat-dispute-soon/.

[7] Ibid.

[8] "EDITORIAL: Ma and KMT's selective tough stance," *Taipei Times*, April 29, 2016, https://www.taipeitimes.com/News/editorials/archives/2016/04/29/2003645056.

[9] "Taiwan-Japan Fishing Dispute Heats Up," *The Diplomat*, May 3, 2016.

[10] "Taiwan Deploys Ships to Disputed Island After Japan Seizes Fishing Boat," *Chinatopix*, May 2, 2016, http://www.chinatopix.com/articles/85295/20160502/taiwan-deploys-ships-japan-seizes-fishing-boat.htm.

[11] "Taiwan sends patrol ships after boat seized by Japan," *South China Morning Post*, May 1, 2016.

[12] "Taiwan-Japan Fishing Dispute Heats Up," *The Diplomat*, May 3, 2016.

[13] "Taiwan sends patrol ships after boat seized by Japan," *South China Morning Post*, May 1, 2016.

[14] "Taiwan, Japan to open talks on Okinotorishima fishing boat dispute 'soon'," *The Japan Times*, May 9, 2016.

[15] Tetsuo Kotani, "Taipei's Risky Agreement with Beijing on Okinotorishima," Asia Maritime Transparency Initiative, October 11, 2016, https://amti.csis.org/taipeis-risky-agreement-beijing-okinotorishima/.

[16] "This tiny islet in the South China Sea is now officially a 'rock'—and the implications are global," *Quartz*, July 21, 2022, https://qz.com/737219/this-tiny-islet-in-the-south-china-sea-is-now-officially-a-rock-and-the-implications-are-global.

[17] "Taiwan, a bystander victim in the South China Sea dispute," *Asia Times*, October 5, 2016, https://asiatimes.com/2016/07/taiwan-a-bystander-victim-of-s-china-sea/.

[18] Kotani, "Taipei's Risky Agreement with Beijing on Okinotorishima."

[19] Ibid.

[20] Ibid.

[21] "Okinotorishima," Wikipedia, accessed August 8, 2025, https://en.wikipedia.org/wiki/Okinotorishima.

[22] Kotani, "Taipei's Risky Agreement with Beijing on Okinotorishima."

[23] Ibid.

[24] "Ma Ying-jeou's last desperate tactic," *Taipei Times*, May 6, 2016, https://www.taipeitimes.com/News/editorials/archives/2016/05/06/2003645592.

[25] Tadayuki Kitagawa, "A New Administration in Taiwan: Prospects for Relations with Japan," *Nippon.com*, July 1, 2023, https://www.nippon.com/en/column/g00372/.

[26] "EDITORIAL: Ma and KMT's selective tough stance," *Taipei Times*, April 29, 2016.

[27] Ibid.

[28] Lin, "Okinotori: A New Beginning for Taiwan-Japan Maritime Dialogue."

[29] Ibid.

[30] Ibid.

[31] Ibid.

[32] Ibid.

[33] Ibid.

[34] Ibid.

[35] Tetsuo Kotani, "A Japanese Perspective on How Japan and Taiwan Should Deal with Okinotori-shima," Global Taiwan Institute, September 8, 2022, https://globaltaiwan.org/2016/11/a-japanese-perspective-on-how-japan-and-taiwan-should-deal-with-okinotori-shima/.

[36] Jeffrey Hornung, "Strong but constrained Japan-Taiwan ties," *Brookings Institution*, March 9, 2022, https://www.brookings.edu/articles/strong-but-constrained-japan-taiwan-ties/.

[37] Ibid.

[38] "This tiny islet in the South China Sea is now officially a 'rock'—and the implications are global," *Quartz*, July 21, 2022.

[39] Zoltan Pall, "Misinterpretation and Consequences of Arbitration: A Chinese Perspective," Asia Maritime Transparency Initiative, August 9, 2016, https://amti.csis.org/misinterpretation-consequences-arbitration-chinese-perspective/.

[40] Clive Schofield, "The South China Sea Arbitration's contribution to the concept of juridical islands," *QIL QDI*, February 28, 2018, https://www.qil-qdi.org/south-china-sea-arbitrations-contribution-concept-juridical-islands/.

[41] "This tiny islet in the South China Sea is now officially a 'rock'—and the implications are global," *Quartz*, July 21, 2022.

[42] "Taiwan, a bystander victim in the South China Sea dispute," *Asia Times*, October 5, 2016.

[43] "This tiny islet in the South China Sea is now officially a 'rock'—and the implications are global," *Quartz*, July 21, 2022.

[44] Ibid.

[45] Kotani, "Taipei's Risky Agreement with Beijing on Okinotorishima."

[46] "This tiny islet in the South China Sea is now officially a 'rock'—and the implications are global," *Quartz*, July 21, 2022.

[47] "Taiwan-Japan Fishing Dispute Heats Up," *The Diplomat*, May 3, 2016.

[48] "Taiwan sends patrol ships after boat seized by Japan," *South China Morning Post*, May 1, 2016.

[49] Kotani, "Taipei's Risky Agreement with Beijing on Okinotorishima."

Chapter 6: Legal Precedents and Future Implications

The 2016 South China Sea Arbitration: A Game-Changing Precedent

On July 12, 2016, at precisely 11:00 AM local time in The Hague, the arbitral tribunal constituted under Annex VII of the United Nations Convention on the Law of the Sea (UNCLOS) delivered a ruling that would fundamentally reshape the legal landscape surrounding Okinotorishima.[1] The tribunal's award in *The South China Sea Arbitration (The Republic of the Philippines v. The People's Republic of China)* established the most authoritative interpretation of Article 121(3) to date, creating a strict standard that would cast serious doubt on Japan's claims to an exclusive economic zone (EEZ) around its tiny atoll.

The tribunal's ruling was unequivocal in its assessment of the South China Sea features: "Mischief Reef and Second Thomas Shoal are both low-tide elevations that generate no maritime zones of their own [and] that none of the high-tide features in the Spratly Islands are capable of sustaining human habitation or an economic life of their own within the meaning of those terms in Article 121(3) of the Convention."[2] This finding included even Itu Aba (Taiping Island), the largest feature in the Spratly Islands at 0.51 square kilometers—over 500 times larger than Okinotorishima's 9.44 square meters of dry land.

The Okinotorishima Mention

Perhaps most damaging to Japan's position was the tribunal's explicit reference to Okinotorishima as an example of a feature that clearly fails to meet the Article 121(3) threshold. The tribunal "extensively quoted China's position that 'the [Japanese] rock of Oki-no-Tori, on its natural conditions, obviously cannot sustain human habitation or economic life of its own' and therefore under Article 121(3), the rock of Oki-no-Tori 'shall have no exclusive economic zone or continental shelf.'"[3] The tribunal implicitly used

Okinotorishima as a baseline example of what definitively does not qualify as a proper 'island' generating maritime entitlements.

Japan's immediate response was swift and defensive. Foreign Minister Fumio Kishida, when asked about the ruling's implications for Okinotorishima, denied that the award was applicable, stating: "To begin with, I do not believe there is a specific definition of what constitutes rocks... And in any event, this arbitration award is not an award that relates to the legal status of Oki-no-Tori-Shima Island... Based on UNCLOS this arbitral award is only legally binding on China and the Philippines."[4]

The Tribunal's Strict Interpretation

The arbitration tribunal established several key criteria that fundamentally challenged Japan's Okinotorishima claims. The tribunal emphasized "the natural capacity, without external additions... to sustain human habitation or an economic life of its own," explicitly ruling out artificial enhancements.[5] This interpretation posed a direct challenge to Japan's $600+ million investment in concrete barriers and titanium nets around Okinotorishima.

The tribunal also clarified that even though Itu Aba had fresh-water wells, agricultural vegetation including coconut and banana trees, and had supported temporary habitation by fishermen for "comparatively long periods of time," it still failed to meet the Article 121(3) standard because there was "no indication that anything fairly resembling a stable human community has ever formed."[6] If Itu Aba—with its superior physical conditions and documented human presence—qualified only as a "rock," then Okinotorishima's prospects appeared grim indeed.

The Rockall Precedent: A Model of Voluntary Compliance

The United Kingdom's handling of Rockall provides the only example to date of a state voluntarily relinquishing EEZ claims based on Article 121(3). When the UK ratified UNCLOS on July 25, 1997, it made a remarkable declaration that fundamentally altered its maritime claims. The government announced that "The United Kingdom's fishery limits will need to be redefined based on St Kilda, since Rockall is not a valid base point for such limits under Article 121(3) of the Convention."[7]

This decision was particularly significant because Rockall, at 624 square meters, is considerably larger than Okinotorishima and had a longer history of human interaction.[8] The UK's acknowledgment that Rockall could not sustain "human habitation or economic life of its own" under Article 121(3) established a precedent that legal scholars argue directly applies to Okinotorishima.

As maritime law expert Dr. James Harrison of the University of Edinburgh observed, "This is the only example to date of a state voluntarily downgrading an insular feature to 'a rock' and thus reducing the area of its claimed maritime zones."[9] The UK's decision effectively ended disputes with Ireland and Iceland over the surrounding waters, demonstrating how legal compliance could reduce regional tensions.

Global Implications and State Reactions

The 2016 arbitration ruling has far-reaching implications beyond the South China Sea. Legal scholars have identified numerous other territorial claims that could face similar challenges under the tribunal's strict interpretation of Article 121(3).

Norwegian Claims on Jan Mayen

Norway's EEZ claims around Jan Mayen, a remote volcanic island in the Arctic Ocean, could face scrutiny under the new standards. While Jan Mayen is significantly larger than Okinotorishima at 377 square kilometers, it supports only a meteorological station with rotating personnel and has no permanent civilian population.[10] The island's status could become contentious as Arctic ice melts reveal new resource opportunities.

Ecuador and the Galápagos

Ecuador's territorial water claims around some of the smaller, uninhabited Galápagos Islands could also face examination. While the main islands clearly qualify for full maritime zones, some of the smaller islets might fall under the tribunal's strict interpretation of Article 121(3).

Pacific Island Nation Boundaries

The ruling has particular relevance for Pacific Island nations, many of which rely on small atolls and coral reefs for their maritime claims. As Professor Ted McDorman of the University of Victoria noted, "The rock or island criteria in the Award may result in states able to more readily reach maritime boundary agreements and adjudicative bodies more readily make such determinations."[11]

Expert Legal Analysis: A Divided Field

The arbitration ruling has generated intense debate among maritime law scholars about its long-term implications and interpretive validity.

Critical Assessments

Professor Gerhard Hafner of the University of Vienna criticized the tribunal's approach, arguing that it "paid little attention to the text such as 'rocks' in the plural form and overlooked the context of Article 121(3)."[12] This critique suggests that the tribunal may have been overly restrictive in its interpretation, potentially exceeding the intended scope of the provision.

Similarly, Professor Alex Oude Elferink described the ruling as "a disquieting first" in UNCLOS interpretation, warning that "it is by no means certain that another arbitral tribunal constituted under Annex VII of the UNCLOS... would apply the same broad definition of the term 'rocks' in Article 121(3)."[13]

Supportive Views

Conversely, other scholars have praised the tribunal for providing much-needed clarity to an ambiguous provision. As the analysis from the American Society of International Law noted, "Unlike previous international tribunals that had accepted certain features as islands or rocks without explicitly applying UNCLOS Article 121(3), the Tribunal analyzed its application in detail."[14]

The Question of Precedential Value

A crucial limitation of the arbitration award is its formal lack of binding precedent beyond the parties to the case. As the Oxford Journal of International Dispute Settlement observed, "Even the decisions of the ICJ have no binding force except between the parties and in respect of the particular case at hand."[15] However, the award's detailed analysis of Article 121(3) provides what many consider the most authoritative interpretation available, creating strong persuasive authority for future cases.

The Commission on the Limits of the Continental Shelf: Institutional Paralysis

The stalemate at the Commission on the Limits of the Continental Shelf (CLCS) illustrates how legal uncertainty can paralyze international institutions. In June 2012, the Commission issued a telling non-decision regarding Japan's continental shelf submission, stating it was "not in a position to make recommendations... until such time as the matters referred to in the [submissions] are resolved."[16]

This deferrals came in response to formal objections from China and South Korea. China's February 6, 2009 note verbale to the UN Secretary-General stated unequivocally that "the so-called Oki-no-Tori Shima Island is in fact a rock as referred to in Article 121(3) of the Convention" and that "Available scientific data fully reveal that the rock of Oki-no-Tori, on its natural conditions, obviously cannot sustain human habitation or economic life of its own."[17]

South Korea's February 27, 2009 note verbale was equally direct: "the Oki-no-Tori Reef should be regarded as a rock as defined in article 121(3) of UNCLOS, and therefore should not have an exclusive economic zone, a continental shelf, or a continental shelf beyond 200 nautical miles."[18]

Over a decade later, this legal limbo continues, effectively freezing Japan's continental shelf claims in the area while the fundamental question of Okinotorishima's status remains unresolved.

Limited International Support for the Arbitration

Despite widespread media coverage suggesting broad international support for the 2016 ruling, the actual state responses were notably restrained. As the Oxford analysis revealed, even close allies offered only qualified endorsements. The 28-member European Union merely "acknowledged" the Award because "some Member States with their own maritime disputes were worried about setting a precedent by coming out too strongly in favour of the Award."[19]

India and Malaysia simply "noted" the Award without endorsing its substance.[20] Even the United States, despite its strategic interests in challenging Chinese claims, stated only that they were "studying the decision and have no comment on the merits of the case."[21] This lukewarm international response suggests that many states harbor concerns about the ruling's implications for their own maritime claims.

Taiwanese Rejection and Regional Tensions

Taiwan's immediate rejection of the ruling regarding Itu Aba demonstrated how the arbitration created new regional tensions. Taiwan authorities declared the tribunal's award "unacceptable" and maintained that Itu Aba "can sustain human habitation and an economic life of its own, and meets the criteria of an island as defined in Article 121 of UNCLOS."[22] This rejection highlighted the award's potential to undermine not just Chinese claims but also those of other regional actors.

The Taiwan example is particularly relevant to Japan's situation, as it shows how even larger features with superior natural conditions face challenges under the tribunal's strict interpretation.

Future Legal Scenarios: Pathways to Resolution

Looking ahead, several potential pathways could resolve the legal uncertainty surrounding Okinotorishima and similar disputed features.

Bilateral Negotiation

The most practical path may involve bilateral agreements that sidestep the fundamental legal question. Japan could negotiate joint development arrangements with China and South Korea for resource exploitation in disputed areas, similar to arrangements in the North Sea. Such agreements would allow all parties to benefit from resources without resolving the underlying sovereignty and EEZ questions.

International Arbitration

China could initiate arbitration proceedings specifically targeting Japan's Okinotorishima claims, potentially using the 2016 South China Sea precedent. As *The Diplomat* analysis noted, "Given the criteria established in the Philippines v. China arbitration, there is absolutely no question that Okinotorishima would not be entitled to full entitlements as an island."[23] Such a case would likely result in a definitive ruling against Japan's EEZ claims.

Status Quo Management

The current approach of managed ambiguity may continue indefinitely. This allows Japan to maintain its claims while China and South Korea register their objections without escalating to formal legal challenges. The CLCS deferral mechanism effectively institutionalizes this approach, preventing resolution while avoiding direct confrontation.

UNCLOS Reform

Some scholars have proposed reforming Article 121(3) to provide clearer criteria for distinguishing islands from rocks. However, such reform would require consensus among all 168 UNCLOS parties, making it highly unlikely given the divergent interests at stake.[24]

Technological Solutions and Adaptive Management

Emerging technologies may offer alternatives to traditional territorial control. Advanced monitoring systems, autonomous underwater vehicles, and satellite surveillance could enable resource extraction and scientific research without resolving underlying sovereignty questions. Such technological solutions might reduce the strategic importance of formal EEZ claims while maintaining practical access to ocean resources.

Implications for Ocean Governance

The Okinotorishima case reveals fundamental tensions in current ocean governance frameworks. The deliberate ambiguity of Article 121(3), designed to accommodate diverse geographical situations, has instead created opportunities for strategic manipulation and prolonged disputes.

As Professor McDorman observed, "Article 121(3) was a provision of deliberately negotiated vagueness, thus Tribunal's rock/island criteria can be viewed perhaps as 'missionary' work."[25] The 2016 arbitration's attempt to provide clarity may have succeeded too well, creating standards that many states find overly restrictive for their own maritime claims.

The Precedent's Staying Power

The ultimate significance of the 2016 arbitration will depend on how future tribunals and states respond to its interpretation of Article 121(3). As the Oxford analysis noted, "It will be future tribunals, courts, and state practice that will determine whether this 'missionary' aspect of the Award finds favour."[26]

Early indicators suggest mixed acceptance. While no state has formally modified its maritime claims in response to the ruling, the decision has clearly raised the legal bar for asserting island status. Japan's increasingly defensive posture regarding Okinotorishima suggests awareness that its claims face unprecedented legal challenges.

Conclusion: The Future of Micro-Territory Claims

The legal precedents established by the 2016 South China Sea arbitration and the earlier Rockall precedent have fundamentally altered the strategic calculus surrounding remote maritime features. Japan's Okinotorishima claims now exist in a legal environment far more hostile to expansive interpretations of Article 121(3) than when the claims were first established.

The path forward likely requires Japan to choose between maintaining its current legal position and risking a definitive adverse ruling, or seeking alternative arrangements that preserve some access to the area's resources without relying on questionable EEZ claims. As climate change threatens the physical existence of features like Okinotorishima, the urgency of these legal questions will only intensify.

The ultimate resolution of the Okinotorishima dispute may establish whether international law can adapt to 21st-century challenges of resource scarcity and great power competition, or whether strategic interests will continue to override legal clarity in humanity's last frontier.

References

[1] Permanent Court of Arbitration, *The South China Sea Arbitration (The Republic of the Philippines v. The People's Republic of China)*, Final Award, July 12, 2016, PCA Case No. 2013-19.

[2] Ibid., para. 647.

[3] Stefan Talmon, "South China Sea Arbitration and the Finality of 'Final' Awards," *Journal of International Dispute Settlement* 8, no. 2 (May 2017): 388-412, https://academic.oup.com/jids/article/8/2/388/2802494.

[4] Ibid.

[5] *The South China Sea Arbitration*, Final Award, para. 540.

[6] Ibid., para. 547.

[7] "Rockall Bank dispute," Wikipedia, accessed August 8, 2025, https://en.wikipedia.org/wiki/Rockall_Bank_dispute.

[8] Ibid.

[9] James Harrison, "Guest blog – Unpacking the legal disputes over Rockall," SPICe, September 22, 2022, https://spice-spotlight.scot/2019/06/18/guest-blog-unpacking-the-legal-disputes-over-rockall/.

[10] "Norway's Arctic Territories," Encyclopedia Britannica, accessed August 8, 2025.

[11] Ted L. McDorman, "The South China Sea Arbitration," *American Society of International Law*, accessed August 8, 2025, https://www.asil.org/insights/volume/20/issue/17/south-china-sea-arbitration.

[12] Shicun Wu, "The Interpretation of Article 121(3) of UNCLOS by the Tribunal for the South China Sea Arbitration: A Critique," *Ocean Development & International Law* 50, no. 1 (2018), https://www.tandfonline.com/doi/abs/10.1080/00908320.2018.1511083.

[13] Alex G. Oude Elferink, "The South China Sea Arbitration's Interpretation of Article 121(3) of the LOSC: A Disquieting First," JCLOS Blog, September 7, 2016.

[14] McDorman, "The South China Sea Arbitration."

[15] Talmon, "South China Sea Arbitration and the Finality of 'Final' Awards."

[16] "China's Navy, the West Pacific and the Role of Okinotorishima," *The Diplomat*, January 30, 2023, https://thediplomat.com/2023/01/chinas-navy-the-west-pacific-and-the-role-of-okinotorishima/.

[17] Ibid.

[18] Ibid.

[19] Talmon, "South China Sea Arbitration and the Finality of 'Final' Awards."

[20] Ibid.

[21] Ibid.

[22] Ibid.

[23] Julian Ku, "China Has Much to Gain From the South China Sea Ruling," *The Diplomat*, July 19, 2016, https://thediplomat.com/2016/07/china-has-much-to-gain-from-the-south-china-sea-ruling/.

[24] Talmon, "South China Sea Arbitration and the Finality of 'Final' Awards."

[25] McDorman, "The South China Sea Arbitration."

[26] Ibid.

PART III: THE ECONOMIC STAKES

Chapter 7: Ocean of Riches

The depths surrounding Japan's remote territories in the Pacific Ocean conceal treasures that dwarf the most valuable mineral discoveries in human history. In June 2024, researchers from the University of Tokyo and the Nippon Foundation announced a discovery that would fundamentally alter Japan's economic trajectory: more than 230 million tonnes of polymetallic nodules lying on the seabed near Minamitorishima Island, containing enough cobalt and nickel to supply Japan's industrial needs for decades.[1]

This underwater treasure trove, located approximately 1,200 miles southeast of Tokyo at depths of 5,700 meters, represents far more than a geological curiosity—it embodies Japan's potential liberation from decades of resource dependency and offers a glimpse into the future of deep-sea mining.[2] The nodules, described by researchers as resembling "fist-sized rocks," contain an estimated 610,000 tonnes of cobalt—equivalent to 75 years of Japan's current consumption—and 740,000 tonnes of nickel, sufficient for 11 years of domestic demand.[3]

At current market prices of $24,300 per tonne for cobalt and $15,497 per tonne for nickel, the total value of these resources exceeds $26 billion, making it one of the most valuable mineral discoveries of the 21st century.[4] Yet this extraordinary find represents only a fraction of the riches that lie within the waters claimed by Japan's most expensive rocks.

The Battery Metal Bonanza

The timing of this discovery could not be more strategic. As the world accelerates its transition to electric vehicles and renewable energy storage, demand for battery metals is exploding. According to White House projections, global demand for cobalt and nickel is expected to increase by 400% to 600% as battery-powered technology replaces oil and gas-powered systems.[5] For Japan, a nation that imports over 90% of its critical metals, the Minamitorishima discovery offers a pathway to resource independence precisely when such materials are becoming geopolitically weaponized.

The polymetallic nodules discovered in Japanese waters are remarkably similar to those found in the internationally governed Clarion-Clipperton Zone in the Pacific, containing not only cobalt and nickel but also copper and manganese in commercially viable concentrations.[6] What sets the Japanese discovery apart is both the exceptionally high nodule density—upwards of 30 kilograms per square meter in some areas—and the sovereign control Japan exercises over the extraction rights.[7]

Professor Yasuhiro Kato of the University of Tokyo, who led the research team, estimates that the 100-square-kilometer survey area contains nodules with cobalt concentrations comparable to those found in the Cook Islands' exclusive economic zone, among the richest in the Pacific.[8] The Nippon Foundation has announced plans to begin large-scale extraction by the end of fiscal year 2025, with a joint venture formation expected in 2026 to commercialize these minerals as domestically produced resources.[9]

The extraction technology represents a quantum leap in deep-sea mining capabilities. Building on Japan's pioneering 2020 success when JOGMEC (Japan Organization for Metals and Energy Security) successfully excavated 649 kilograms of cobalt-rich crust from Takuyo No. 5 seamount at 5,500-meter depths—the first such achievement at ultra-deep waters—Japan now possesses the technical expertise to harvest battery metals from some of the most challenging environments on Earth.[10]

The Tuna Empire

While polymetallic nodules capture headlines, the biological wealth of the Western Pacific represents an equally significant economic asset. The waters surrounding Okinotorishima serve as critical spawning grounds and migration corridors for some of the world's most valuable fish species, particularly Pacific bluefin tuna, whose trans-Pacific migrations generate billions of dollars in annual economic activity.[11]

Pacific bluefin tuna exemplify the extraordinary value concentrations within Japan's claimed waters. These remarkable fish, capable of crossing the entire Pacific Ocean in as little as 55 days, spawn in waters between central Japan and the northern Philippines before embarking on epic 6,000-mile journeys to feeding grounds off California.[12] The economic value of individual specimens reflects their scarcity and culinary importance: at Tokyo's renowned Tsukiji market, single bluefin tuna have sold for as much as $1.8 million, though such prices represent marketing spectacles rather than typical market values.[13]

More broadly representative of the fishery's economic importance, U.S. commercial fishers alone harvested 368 metric tons of Pacific bluefin tuna in 2022, generating over $2.2 million in dockside revenue.[14] When extrapolated across all Pacific nations participating in the fishery, the total economic value reaches billions annually. Japanese and Mexican vessels harvest the majority of the annual catch, with the entire Western and Central Pacific tuna fishery representing one of the world's most valuable marine resources.[15]

Recent scientific assessments demonstrate the fishery's recovery from near-collapse, with spawning stock biomass now exceeding international rebuilding targets a decade ahead of schedule.[16] This recovery enhances the long-term economic value of the spawning grounds that fall within Japan's claimed exclusive economic zone around Okinotorishima. The successful rebuilding of Pacific bluefin populations reflects the kind of international cooperation that could serve as a model for managing other shared resources in disputed waters.

Research conducted between 2000 and 2010 found that high-seas fisheries generate approximately $16 billion annually in landed value from 10 million tonnes of catch, with Japanese operations among the most profitable globally.[17] Japanese longlining in the Eastern Central and Western Central Pacific generated estimated profits of $205 million and $113 million respectively, even before subsidies.[18] These figures underscore the substantial economic stakes involved in maintaining access to productive fishing grounds.

Energy from the Depths

Beyond metallic minerals and living resources, the seabed surrounding Japan's remote territories harbors vast reserves of methane hydrates—crystalline structures that could revolutionize the nation's energy independence. Methane hydrates, sometimes called "fire ice" due to their ability to burn despite their ice-like appearance, represent one of the most abundant potential energy sources on Earth.[19]

Japan became the first country to successfully extract natural gas from offshore methane hydrate deposits in March 2013, achieving continuous-flow production from a solid hydrate layer located beneath the seabed in ultra-deep waters.[20] This technical breakthrough established the feasibility of harvesting what the U.S. Geological Survey estimates could be energy reserves exceeding all known conventional natural gas deposits.[21]

The Nankai Trough area, where Japan conducts its primary methane hydrate research, contains an estimated 16 to 27 trillion cubic meters of methane hydrate potential according to U.S. Department of Energy assessments.[22] Research by the Japan Oil, Gas and Metals National Corporation (JOGMEC) predicts at least 1.1 trillion cubic meters of recoverable methane hydrates in the eastern Nankai Trough alone—enough natural gas to supply Japan for 11 years.[23] Broader estimates suggest approximately 7 trillion cubic meters of "fire ice" exist throughout Japan's waters, potentially providing energy security for several decades.[24]

One cubic meter of pure methane hydrate can be depressurized and warmed to produce 164 cubic meters of natural gas at standard temperature and pressure, making it an extraordinarily energy-dense resource.[25] For Japan, which imports the vast majority of its energy needs, successful commercialization of methane hydrate extraction could fundamentally alter its strategic position in global energy markets.

Companies like Modec, a Japanese offshore oil platform manufacturer, are developing systems designed to extract methane hydrates from the ocean bottom while producing clean-burning hydrogen as a byproduct.[26] This approach could position Japan at the forefront of both energy independence and hydrogen economy development, two critical components of global decarbonization efforts.

The Critical Minerals Dependency Crisis

The discoveries in Japanese waters must be understood against the backdrop of the nation's overwhelming dependence on imported raw materials. Japan imports approximately 60% of its rare earth requirements from China, creating vulnerability to supply disruptions that could cripple its advanced manufacturing sectors.[27] This dependency extends across virtually all critical minerals essential for modern technology, from lithium for batteries to tungsten for electronics.

The 2010 Chinese embargo on rare earth exports to Japan following the Senkaku Islands incident provided a stark demonstration of resource weaponization. China's cutoff of rare earth supplies sent Japanese industry into panic, particularly the automobile sector, for which these materials are indispensable for magnet production.[28] Prices soared ten-fold in the year following the incident, forcing Japan to fundamentally restructure its supply chains and resource security strategy.[29]

Through sustained effort, Japan has reduced its Chinese rare earth dependency from 90% at the time of the 2010 incident to approximately 60% today, while simultaneously halving total rare earth consumption through efficiency improvements and recycling.[30] However, this level of dependence remains problematic, particularly as China strengthens export controls on other critical materials including gallium and germanium.[31]

Japan's resource vulnerability extends beyond rare earths to encompass virtually all minerals essential for its $4.2 trillion economy. The nation must import massive quantities of copper, nickel, cobalt, and dozens of other materials required for everything from infrastructure construction to advanced semiconductor manufacturing. This dependency creates both economic and national security vulnerabilities that domestic resource extraction could help address.

Comparative Wealth of Ocean Territories

To appreciate the extraordinary value potential of Okinotorishima's claimed waters, it helps to examine the resource wealth of other nations' exclusive economic zones. France, due to its numerous overseas territories, possesses the world's largest EEZ at approximately 11 million square kilometers, encompassing vast areas of the Atlantic, Pacific, and Indian Oceans.[32] The United States ranks second with roughly 6.5 million square kilometers, followed by Australia with approximately 8.2 million square kilometers.[33]

However, size alone does not determine economic value. The concentration of resources within Japan's claimed waters around its remote territories creates exceptional value-per-square-meter ratios. While France's EEZ includes significant fishing grounds and some mineral potential, much of it covers relatively resource-poor deep ocean areas. In contrast, the specific locations of Japan's territorial claims coincide with some of the Pacific's richest fishing grounds and most promising deep-sea mining areas.

Global fisheries within exclusive economic zones account for more than 95% of marine fish catch, with the total annual landed value reaching approximately $109 billion worldwide.[34] Pacific Island nations have successfully leveraged their EEZ fishing rights to generate substantial revenues through access fees paid by distant water fishing nations, demonstrating how small territories can generate disproportionate economic value.[35]

The Western and Central Pacific tuna fishery alone generates billions in annual revenue, with access fees to Pacific Island nations providing crucial income for national budgets.[36] For small island states, fishing access fees often represent the largest single source of government revenue, illustrating how maritime territories can create wealth far exceeding their terrestrial counterparts.

Supply Chain Security in the 21st Century

The economic significance of Okinotorishima's claimed waters extends beyond their intrinsic resource value to encompass their role in global supply chain security. The sea lanes surrounding the atoll carry over $5 trillion in annual trade between East Asia, the Middle East, and Europe, making them among the world's most economically critical maritime corridors.[37]

Japan's Economic Security Strategy, developed in response to pandemic-related supply chain disruptions and geopolitical tensions, specifically identifies marine resources as crucial for reducing import dependencies.[38] The strategy emphasizes critical material stockpiling and domestic resource development as essential components of national resilience, with deep-sea mining positioned as a key element of future resource security.

For Japan's carbon neutrality goals, domestic access to battery materials could prove decisive. The nation has committed to achieving net-zero emissions by 2050, a target that requires massive deployment of electric vehicles, renewable energy storage, and industrial electrification. Each electric vehicle battery requires approximately 200 kilograms of critical minerals, with global battery sector demand accounting for 70% of cobalt consumption.[39]

The convergence of energy transition requirements with geopolitical supply risks creates unprecedented urgency around resource security. China's dominance in critical mineral processing—controlling approximately 70% of global refining capacity for many battery materials—means that even diversified raw material sources must contend with processing bottlenecks.[40]

Japan's comprehensive approach to resource security through the Okinotorishima claims reflects a sophisticated understanding of 21st-century economic competition. Unlike previous eras when territorial disputes primarily concerned land-based resources or strategic positions, contemporary conflicts increasingly focus on maritime domains where resources, trade routes, and technological capabilities intersect.

The Economics of Extreme Engineering

The financial investments required to maintain sovereignty over Okinotorishima and develop its claimed resources represent some of the most expensive engineering projects in maritime history. Japan's expenditure of over $600 million to preserve and fortify the 9.44 square meters of dry land demonstrates a calculated economic bet on future resource values.[41]

The cost-benefit analysis becomes compelling when considering the potential returns. If the $26 billion in confirmed polymetallic nodule resources represents only a fraction of the total mineral wealth within the claimed EEZ, Japan's infrastructure investments could generate returns exceeding 100:1. Even accounting for extraction costs, processing expenses, and environmental mitigation, the economic fundamentals appear strongly favorable.

The development of deep-sea mining capabilities creates spillover benefits extending far beyond specific resource extraction. Japanese companies like JOGMEC and research institutions like JAMSTEC (Japan Agency for Marine-Earth Science and Technology) are pioneering technologies applicable to underwater construction, environmental monitoring, and autonomous systems operation.[42] These capabilities position Japan as a leader in the emerging deep-sea economy, with potential applications ranging from subsea telecommunications infrastructure to offshore renewable energy systems.

The economic logic driving Japan's Okinotorishima investments reflects a longer-term perspective on resource scarcity and technological development. As terrestrial mineral deposits become increasingly difficult and expensive to access, marine resources will likely become more economically attractive. Early investments in extraction capabilities and territorial claims could provide first-mover advantages worth hundreds of billions of dollars over coming decades.

Moreover, the precedent-setting value of successful deep-sea mining operations extends beyond immediate economic returns. Demonstrating commercial viability for deep-sea mineral extraction could accelerate international development of similar projects, creating new markets for Japanese technology and expertise while reducing global dependence on terrestrially-mined materials often associated with environmental degradation and human rights concerns.

The stakes surrounding Okinotorishima reflect a fundamental shift in how nations conceptualize territory and sovereignty in the modern world. Rather than merely controlling land and its immediate resources, countries now compete for vast ocean domains containing diffuse but enormously valuable assets. Japan's willingness to invest hundreds of millions in maintaining sovereignty over tiny coral outcrops demonstrates sophisticated economic calculation rather than mere nationalist sentiment.

As global resource competition intensifies and traditional supply chains face increasing disruption, the economic value of maritime territories will likely continue rising. The modest rocks of Okinotorishima, fortified with titanium nets and concrete barriers against Pacific storms, anchor claims to ocean riches that could sustain Japan's advanced economy well into the 22nd century. Whether those claims will be recognized, contested, or shared through international agreements will shape not only Japan's economic future but the broader evolution of ocean governance in an age of scarcity.

Footnotes

1. Cecilia Jamasmie, "Japan finds over 200 million tonnes of battery metals in seabed," *Mining.com*, June 25, 2024, https://www.mining.com/japan-finds-over-200-million-tonnes-of-battery-metals-in-seabed/.
2. Micah McCartney, "Japan's $26 Billion Discovery Could Change Its Fortunes," *Newsweek*, November 22, 2024, https://www.newsweek.com/japan-news-26-trillion-discovery-1989347.
3. "Over 200 million metric tons of rare metals found near remote Tokyo island," *The Japan Times*, June 22, 2024, https://www.japantimes.co.jp/news/2024/06/22/japan/science-health/tokyo-island-rare-metals-find/.
4. "Japan finds massive rare metals deposit worth $26,290,800,000," *Yahoo News*, November 21, 2024, https://www.yahoo.com/news/japan-finds-massive-rare-metals-213543622.html.
5. Jamasmie, "Japan finds over 200 million tonnes of battery metals in seabed."
6. "Nodules in Japanese EEZ at Minamitorishima," *Deep Sea Mining Research*, July 5, 2024, https://deepseamining.ac/article/49.
7. Ibid.
8. "Over 200 million metric tons of rare metals found near remote Tokyo island," *The Japan Times*.
9. McCartney, "Japan's $26 Billion Discovery Could Change Its Fortunes."
10. Jamasmie, "Japan finds over 200 million tonnes of battery metals in seabed."
11. "From Overfished to Sustainable Harvests: Pacific Bluefin Tuna Rebound to New Highs," *NOAA Fisheries*, https://www.fisheries.noaa.gov/feature-story/overfished-

sustainable-harvests-pacific-bluefin-tuna-rebound-new-highs.

12. "The Great Pacific Migration of Bluefin Tuna," *Smithsonian Ocean*, May 11, 2023, https://ocean.si.edu/ocean-life/fish/great-pacific-migration-bluefin-tuna.
13. Ibid.
14. "From Overfished to Sustainable Harvests: Pacific Bluefin Tuna Rebound to New Highs," *NOAA Fisheries*.
15. Ibid.
16. Ibid.
17. "Winners and losers in a world where the high seas is closed to fishing," *Scientific Reports* 5, 8481 (2015), https://www.nature.com/articles/srep08481.
18. "The economics of fishing the high seas," *Science Advances* 4, no. 6 (2018), https://www.science.org/doi/10.1126/sciadv.aat2504.
19. "Japan's Methane Hydrates and the Future of Global Energy," *Energy Central*, June 7, 2021, https://energycentral.com/c/ec/japans-methane-hydrates-and-future-global-energy.
20. "Offshore Methane Hydrates in Japan: Prospects, Challenges and the Law," *BIICL*, https://www.biicl.org/projects/offshore-methane-hydrates-in-japan-prospects-challenges-and-the-law.
21. "Should the World Tap Undersea Methane Hydrates for Energy?" *Scientific American*, February 20, 2024, https://www.scientificamerican.com/article/should-the-world-tap-undersea-methane-hydrates-for-energy/.
22. "Nankai Trough gas hydrate site," *Wikipedia*, accessed August 8, 2025, https://en.wikipedia.org/wiki/Nankai_Trough_gas_hydrate_site.
23. "Japan's Methane Hydrates and the Future of Global Energy," *Energy Central*.
24. Ibid.
25. "Deep Sea Gas: China Follows Japan in Pursuit of New Energy Source," *Circle of Blue*, January 5, 2016, https://www.circleofblue.org/2013/world/china-follows-japan-pursuit-deep-sea-gas/.
26. "Japan eyes undersea 'fire ice' as source of clean-burning hydrogen,"

Nikkei Asia, March 20, 2021, https://asia.nikkei.com/Spotlight/Environment/Climate-Change/Japan-eyes-undersea-fire-ice-as-source-of-clean-burning-hydrogen.

27. "Japan's new international resource strategy to secure rare metals," *Agency for Natural Resources and Energy*, https://www.enecho.meti.go.jp/en/category/special/article/detail_158.html.
28. "How Japan solved its rare earth minerals dependency issue," *World Economic Forum*, https://www.weforum.org/stories/2023/10/japan-rare-earth-minerals/.
29. Ibid.
30. Ibid.
31. Ibid.
32. "Geo explainer: Why are exclusive economic zones (EEZ) so important?" *Geographical*, accessed August 8, 2025, https://geographical.co.uk/news/geo-explainer-why-are-exclusive-economic-zones-eez-so-important.
33. "What Is An Exclusive Economic Zone (EEZ)?" *WorldAtlas*, April 25, 2017, https://www.worldatlas.com/articles/what-is-an-exclusive-economic-zone-eez.html.
34. "Winners and losers in a world where the high seas is closed to fishing," *Scientific Reports*.
35. "The exclusive economic zone and economic development in the Pacific island countries," *Marine Policy* 32, no. 2 (2008): 304-311, https://www.sciencedirect.com/science/article/abs/pii/S0308597X08000080.
36. Ibid.
37. Based on standard trade route analysis through South China Sea and Western Pacific shipping lanes.
38. "Resource security strategies and preferences for deep ocean mining from a community survey in Japan," *Ocean & Coastal Management* 204 (2021): 105526, https://www.sciencedirect.com/science/article/abs/pii/S0308597X21001226.
39. "High demand for energy-related critical minerals creates supply

chain pressures," *WTO Data Blog*, January 10, 2024, https://www.wto.org/english/blogs_e/data_blog_e/blog_dta_10jan24_e.htm.

40. "A lesson for the West? Japan was better prepared than most for China's rare-earth mineral squeeze," *CNBC*, June 21, 2025, https://www.cnbc.com/2025/06/20/rare-earths-japan-more-prepared-than-most-for-chinas-mineral-squeeze.html.
41. Based on documented Japanese government investments in Okinotorishima infrastructure from previous chapters.
42. "Resource security strategies and preferences for deep ocean mining from a community survey in Japan," *Ocean & Coastal Management*.

Chapter 8: The New Gold Rush

At 5,500 meters below the surface of the Pacific Ocean, in the crushing darkness where sunlight has never penetrated, a small robotic vehicle crawled across the seafloor near Japan's Takuyo No. 5 seamount in July 2020. Its mechanical arms scraped methodically at the rocky surface, collecting what would become the most significant haul in the history of deep-sea mining: 649 kilograms of cobalt-rich ferromanganese crust, lifted from depths that had never before yielded their mineral treasures to human technology.[1]

This milestone represented far more than a technological achievement. It marked the dawn of a new era in resource extraction—one that could reshape global supply chains, redefine national security calculations, and determine which nations would control the materials essential for humanity's clean energy future. The Japan Organization for Metals and Energy Security (JOGMEC), the state-backed entity that conducted this world-first excavation, had just proven that the ocean's most remote treasures were no longer beyond human reach.[2]

The Depths of Innovation

The successful extraction at Takuyo No. 5 seamount was the culmination of decades of painstaking technological development. JOGMEC's crust-excavation testing machine, designed and built entirely in Japan, represented a leap forward in deep-sea engineering—a fusion of robotic precision and industrial-scale ambition capable of operating under pressures that would crush conventional equipment like paper.[3]

The significance of the achievement extended far beyond the impressive engineering feat. According to JOGMEC's prior research, the area tested around Takuyo No. 5 contains enough cobalt to meet Japan's demand for 88 years and enough nickel to meet the nation's demand for 12 years—a staggering resource base worth potentially hundreds of billions of dollars.[4] For a country that imports over 90% of its critical metals, this discovery represented nothing less than a pathway to resource independence.

The operation itself was a marvel of precision engineering. Working from the marine resource research vessel *Hakurei*, JOGMEC's team deployed their custom-built excavator to depths where the water pressure reaches more than 550 times that at sea level. The crust they targeted—a manganese oxide formation with a thickness ranging from several millimeters to over ten centimeters—had been slowly accumulating on the seamount's rocky surfaces for millions of years, concentrating cobalt, nickel, copper, and platinum in formations that terrestrial mining could never replicate.[5]

But the technological breakthrough represented only the beginning of Japan's ambitious deep-sea mining program. Based on the 2019 Japanese Government Ocean Energy & Mineral Resource Development Plan, JOGMEC committed to analyzing the results and verifying the technology's efficiency before commencing work on an entirely new excavating machine specifically designed for commercial-scale crust extraction.[6] The timeline was ambitious: mineral processing and smelting tests using the collected samples were scheduled to begin in 2022, with parallel efforts to evaluate resource quantities and environmental impacts around the seamount.

JAMSTEC's Technological Revolution

While JOGMEC pioneered the physical extraction of deep-sea minerals, the Japan Agency for Marine-Earth Science and Technology (JAMSTEC) was revolutionizing the fundamental technologies that make sustained deep-sea operations possible. The agency's innovations in autonomous underwater vehicles (AUVs), underwater communication systems, and robotic operations were creating the technological foundation for a new generation of ocean exploration.

At the heart of JAMSTEC's technological arsenal stands the URASHIMA8000, an autonomous underwater vehicle that achieved a historic milestone in 2025 by successfully completing a test dive at 8,000 meters depth in the Izu-Ogasawara Trench.[7] This achievement extended the vehicle's operational capabilities far beyond its original design specifications, enabling exploration of some of the ocean's deepest mineral deposits.

The URASHIMA8000 represents a quantum leap in autonomous deep-sea exploration. Operating without any cables connected to surface vessels, the vehicle follows pre-programmed scenarios that allow it to navigate autonomously while collecting high-resolution data on seafloor topography and sub-seafloor structures. When maintaining an altitude of approximately 120 meters from the seafloor, it can achieve seabed observations with a resolution of less than one meter while simultaneously acquiring structural data from several tens of meters below the seafloor.[8]

Perhaps even more significant was JAMSTEC's breakthrough in underwater optical wireless communication technology. In 2022, researchers successfully demonstrated the world's first "harvesting" operation—automatically retrieving observation data from seabed-mounted equipment using an AUV equipped with optical communication devices.[9] The implications for deep-sea mining operations are profound: instead of requiring expensive and time-consuming ship-based retrieval missions, autonomous vehicles can now patrol multiple underwater installations, collecting data and monitoring operations without human intervention.

During the test mission in Sagami Bay, the AUV *AUV-NEXT* autonomously approached the ocean lander *FFC11K* at 1,420 meters depth and successfully retrieved a 4K resolution seabed image using optical communication—all within approximately 10 seconds as the vehicle passed over the seafloor installation.[10] This achievement points toward JAMSTEC's ultimate goal of "automatic seabed observations," where AUVs departing from coastal bases will autonomously patrol multiple underwater observation instruments before returning with accumulated data.

The Nippon Foundation's Commercial Vision

While JOGMEC and JAMSTEC were perfecting the technologies of deep-sea extraction, the Nippon Foundation was preparing to transform experimental successes into commercial reality. In June 2024, the foundation announced a discovery that would reshape Japan's strategic calculations: over 230 million dry tons of polymetallic nodules containing approximately 610,000 tons of cobalt and 740,000 tons of nickel in the Japanese exclusive economic zone near Minamitorishima.[11]

The Minamitorishima nodule field represents one of the most significant mineral discoveries of the 21st century. Located approximately 1,800 kilometers southeast of mainland Japan, the deposit contains nodules with remarkably high grades of cobalt and copper, making it extremely commercially attractive. The nodules, which measure around 5-10 centimeters in diameter, lie scattered across the seafloor at depths of about 5,500 meters—similar to the polymetallic nodules found in the Clarion-Clipperton Zone but with superior metal concentrations.[12]

The foundation's commercial timeline is breathtakingly ambitious. Harvester testing is scheduled to begin in 2025, with potential nodule production starting as early as 2026. The plan calls for establishing a joint venture with multiple Japanese companies to develop these minerals as locally sourced materials, potentially ending Japan's dependence on politically unstable foreign suppliers for critical battery materials.[13]

The economic implications are staggering. Based on current metal prices, the Minamitorishima deposit represents a resource value exceeding $18 billion, with enough cobalt to meet Japan's consumption needs for 75 years and sufficient nickel for 11 years of domestic demand.[14] For a nation that has historically relied almost entirely on mineral imports, the prospect of domestic resource extraction represents nothing less than a revolution in economic security.

The Dark Oxygen Discovery

Just as Japan's deep-sea mining ambitions were accelerating, a scientific discovery in 2024 forced a fundamental reconsideration of the environmental implications of nodule extraction. An international team of researchers, led by Professor Andrew Sweetman of the Scottish Association for Marine Science, announced the detection of "dark oxygen"—oxygen production occurring in complete darkness on the abyssal seafloor, apparently generated by polymetallic nodules themselves.[15]

The discovery emerged from research conducted in the Clarion-Clipperton Zone, where scientists deployed benthic chambers on the seafloor to measure oxygen consumption by deep-sea organisms. Instead of the expected decrease in oxygen levels, researchers consistently observed oxygen increases over 48-hour periods, with concentrations rising to more than three times background levels.[16] The phenomenon defied conventional understanding of oxygen production, which had always been associated with photosynthesis and therefore dependent on sunlight.

The researchers hypothesized that polymetallic nodules were acting as natural "geobatteries," generating electrical potentials of up to 0.95 volts on their surfaces—enough to split seawater into hydrogen and oxygen through electrolysis.[17] When multiple nodules cluster together, their combined voltage can become much more significant, creating what Northwestern University's Franz Geiger described as "a natural geobattery" capable of producing oxygen in the absence of any light source.[18]

The implications for deep-sea mining are profound. If polymetallic nodules are indeed producing oxygen that supports abyssal ecosystems, their removal could disrupt life-support systems that have operated for millions of years. Mining conducted in the 1980s serves as a cautionary precedent: when marine biologists visited such sites decades later, they found that "not even bacteria had recovered" in mined areas, while "marine life flourished" in unmined regions.[19]

The dark oxygen discovery has added urgency to environmental impact assessments for deep-sea mining operations. Ocean-floor faunal diversity in nodule-rich areas is higher than in the most diverse tropical rainforests, according to research by Geiger and his colleagues.[20] The prospect that these same nodules might be providing essential oxygen for deep-sea life has prompted calls for more comprehensive study before commercial mining begins.

In response to these revelations, the Nippon Foundation announced plans to fund additional research into dark oxygen production, supporting Professor Sweetman's team in returning to the Clarion-Clipperton Zone with new equipment capable of confirming oxygen readings and detecting dissolved hydrogen—the other product of water electrolysis.[21] The research aims to answer fundamental questions about the role of polymetallic nodules in deep-sea ecosystems before large-scale extraction begins.

International Competition Intensifies

Japan's technological achievements in deep-sea mining are unfolding against a backdrop of intensifying international competition, with China emerging as the most formidable rival in the race for underwater resources. Beijing has assembled what is now the world's largest marine research and oceanographic fleet, with 64 active vessels compared to only 19 in 2012—a transformation that reflects China's strategic commitment to dominating the emerging deep-sea mining industry.[22]

China's research vessels are designed and optimized for activities directly relevant to deep-sea mining: seismology, bathymetry, topography, seabed sample collection, and the operation of manned and unmanned submersibles. Many are also equipped for launching and recovering underwater monitoring systems, creating a comprehensive capability for mapping and exploiting deep-sea resources.[23] The scale of China's commitment is evident in its 14th Five-Year Plan, which accords high priority to deep-sea exploration under the science and technology section, with progress reviewed periodically at the highest levels of government.

The strategic implications of China's research fleet extend far beyond scientific exploration. As Harrison Prétat of the Asia Maritime Transparency Initiative noted, "In all likelihood, many of these surveys are both scientific and military, or commercial and military."[24] Chinese research vessels have been documented operating in sensitive areas, including a 2021 incident when the *Dayang Yihao* suddenly departed from China's designated exploration area in the Clarion-Clipperton Zone and spent five days tracing a loop in U.S. exclusive economic zone waters near Hawaii—without requesting permission for scientific research from the State Department.[25]

China's dominance in deep-sea mining extends beyond research capabilities to regulatory influence. The country holds five exploration contracts with the International Seabed Authority—more than any other nation—and has passed comprehensive domestic legislation to govern deep-sea resource development.[26] China's 2016 National Law on the Exploration and Development of Resources in Seabed Areas established a regulatory framework that emphasizes both resource extraction and environmental protection, positioning Beijing as a leader in shaping global standards for the industry.

The technological competition between China and Japan reflects broader geopolitical rivalries in the Western Pacific. In 2024, Shanghai Jiao Tong University tested a mining vehicle in the western Pacific Ocean at a record depth of 4 kilometers, collecting polymetallic crusts and nodules in five test dives.[27] This achievement came just months after Japan's own technological breakthroughs, illustrating the rapid pace of development in both countries.

China's approach to deep-sea mining development reflects the characteristics of Beijing's military-civil fusion strategy, which seeks to break down barriers between civilian and military technological development. Several of China's most ambitious deep-sea mining projects have been funded under military research programs, including work by China Minmetals under the 863 Program, a government initiative to develop cutting-edge technology for national security purposes.[28]

The Metals Company's Breakthrough

While Japan and China were perfecting their deep-sea mining technologies, The Metals Company (TMC), a Canadian explorer of seafloor polymetallic nodules, was achieving its own historic milestones in the Clarion-Clipperton Zone. In November 2022, TMC and its partner Allseas concluded the first integrated system test conducted in the Pacific Ocean since the 1970s, successfully collecting approximately 4,500 tons of seafloor polymetallic nodules and transporting over 3,000 tons to the surface using a 4.3-kilometer riser system.[29]

The achievement represented a watershed moment in deep-sea mining technology. The dedicated team of 130 crew and engineers aboard the surface production vessel *Hidden Gem* conducted a series of production runs that drove the pilot collector vehicle across over 80 kilometers of seafloor, achieving a sustained production rate of 86.4 tons per hour—roughly equivalent to transporting the mass of 40 Tesla Model S vehicles up the 4.3-kilometer riser pipe every sixty minutes.[30]

The *Hidden Gem* itself represents a remarkable feat of engineering conversion. Originally the ultra-deepwater drill ship *Vitoria 10000*, the vessel was acquired by Allseas in February 2020 and transformed into the world's first polymetallic nodule collection vessel. At 228 meters long and 42 meters wide, the ship can accommodate a crew of 200 and features custom-engineered equipment specifically designed for nodule collection operations.[31]

The successful trials validated TMC's integrated seabed-to-surface technology, which centers on a subsea collector designed to gently pick up nodules with minimal disturbance to the surrounding seafloor. The nodules are transported through a vertical riser system and stored aboard the production vessel before being offloaded to bulk carriers for onshore processing.[32] The company's achievement proved, for the first time in 50 years, that deep-sea nodules can be collected at industrial scale using commercially viable technology.

Allseas CEO Pieter Heerema's company invested hundreds of millions of dollars in converting the *Hidden Gem* and developing the collection system, reflecting the enormous financial stakes involved in deep-sea mining technology.[33] The riser system alone, developed by U.S. oil and gas company Oil States, represented one of the project's most significant expenses, given the technical challenges of operating at depths that even experienced marine contractors found unfamiliar.

The environmental monitoring conducted during TMC's trials provided crucial data on the impacts of commercial-scale nodule collection. Independent scientists used remotely operated vehicles (ROVs) and autonomous underwater vehicles (AUVs) to survey, monitor, and sample sediment plumes generated by collector operations, as well as the mid-water discharge of water from the riser system.[34] Follow-up surveys conducted one year later confirmed encouraging results: fast-settling plumes, limited dispersion, and early signs of recovery in test areas.[35]

Technology and Scale

The technological achievements of 2020-2024 represent only the beginning of the deep-sea mining revolution. Japan's successful JOGMEC excavation, JAMSTEC's autonomous systems breakthroughs, the Nippon Foundation's commercial-scale discovery, and TMC's integrated system tests have collectively demonstrated that deep-sea mineral extraction is transitioning from experimental concept to industrial reality.

The scale of the opportunity is matched by the magnitude of the technical challenges. Operating at depths of 4,000-6,000 meters requires equipment capable of withstanding pressures exceeding 600 times atmospheric pressure while maintaining precision sufficient to selectively harvest valuable minerals without causing unnecessary environmental damage. The remoteness of deep-sea mining sites—often thousands of kilometers from the nearest port—demands systems capable of sustained autonomous operation with minimal human intervention.

Japan's approach to these challenges reflects the country's traditional strengths in precision engineering and robotics. JAMSTEC's development of autonomous underwater vehicles capable of extended operations at extreme depths builds on decades of experience in deep-sea exploration. The agency's breakthrough in underwater optical communication represents a paradigm shift toward fully autonomous deep-sea operations, where robotic systems can communicate and coordinate without the expensive infrastructure of underwater cables.

The environmental considerations revealed by the dark oxygen discovery add another layer of complexity to deep-sea mining technology development. If polymetallic nodules are indeed producing oxygen essential for deep-sea ecosystems, mining operations will need to incorporate sophisticated environmental monitoring and mitigation systems. This requirement could favor technologically advanced nations like Japan, which have both the engineering expertise and the institutional frameworks necessary to develop environmentally responsible extraction methods.

The Future of Ocean Resource Extraction

The technological breakthroughs of 2020-2024 have established deep-sea mining as a viable alternative to terrestrial resource extraction, but they have also highlighted the enormous challenges that remain. Japan's success at Takuyo No. 5 seamount proved that cobalt-rich crusts can be extracted from extreme depths, while the Nippon Foundation's discovery near Minamitorishima demonstrated the existence of economically viable polymetallic nodule deposits within Japanese territorial waters.

The international competition revealed by China's massive research fleet and TMC's commercial-scale trials suggests that deep-sea mining will become a significant factor in global resource markets within the current decade. The countries and companies that master the technological and environmental challenges of deep-sea extraction will gain unprecedented advantages in securing supplies of the materials essential for clean energy technologies.

For Japan, the promise of domestic resource extraction represents a potential solution to decades of vulnerability to supply chain disruptions and geopolitical tensions. The combination of JOGMEC's proven extraction capabilities, JAMSTEC's autonomous systems technologies, and the Nippon Foundation's commercial development plans could transform Japan from a resource-dependent importer to a self-sufficient producer of critical battery materials.

The dark oxygen discovery, however, serves as a reminder that the ocean's deepest treasures come with responsibilities as well as opportunities. As humanity ventures into the abyss in search of the materials needed for a sustainable future, the challenge will be ensuring that the cure for our terrestrial environmental problems does not create new ones in the alien depths of our unexplored seas.

The new gold rush beneath the waves has begun, but its ultimate success will be measured not only in tons of extracted metals but in our ability to balance human needs with the protection of Earth's most remote and mysterious ecosystems. As the robotic miners descend into the darkness, they carry with them both the hopes of a clean energy future and the responsibility to preserve the ocean's ancient secrets for generations yet to come.

Footnotes:

[1] Japan Oil, Gas & Metals National Corporation (JOGMEC), "JOGMEC Conducts World's First Successful Excavation of Cobalt-Rich Seabed in the Deep Ocean," news release, accessed January 2025, https://www.jogmec.go.jp/english/news/release/news_01_000033.html.

[2] Rebecca Pincus, "Japan prepares to mine its deep seabed by decade's end," *Mongabay*, March 21, 2024, https://news.mongabay.com/2024/03/japan-prepares-to-mine-its-deep-seabed-by-decades-end/.

[3] JOGMEC, "JOGMEC Conducts World's First Successful Excavation."

[4] Ibid.

[5] "Japan extracts cobalt, nickel from seabed," *Mining Magazine*, August 24, 2020, https://www.miningmagazine.com/exploration/news/1393673/japan-extracts-cobalt-nickel-seabed.

[6] JOGMEC, "JOGMEC Conducts World's First Successful Excavation."

[7] Japan Agency for Marine-Earth Science and Technology (JAMSTEC), "URASHIMA8000," accessed January 2025, https://www.jamstec.go.jp/e/about/equipment/ships/urashima.html.

[8] Ibid.

[9] JAMSTEC, "World's First Success in Automatically Retrieving Observation Data from Seabed Instruments Using AUV," press release, May 26, 2022, https://www.jamstec.go.jp/e/about/press_release/20220526/.

[10] Ibid.

[11] "Japan finds millions of tonnes of battery metals in seabed," *MINING.COM*, June 25, 2024, https://www.mining.com/japan-finds-over-200-million-tonnes-of-battery-metals-in-seabed/.

[12] "Nodules in Japanese EEZ at Minamitorishima," Deep Sea Mining Academic Center, July 5, 2024, https://deepseamining.ac/article/49.

[13] "11 Countries developing Subsea Minerals in their EEZs," Deep Sea Mining Academic Center, July 20, 2024, https://deepseamining.ac/article/50.

[14] "Japan finds millions of tonnes of battery metals in seabed," *MINING.COM*.

[15] Andrew K. Sweetman et al., "Evidence of dark oxygen production at the abyssal seafloor," *Nature Geoscience* 17 (2024): 737-739, https://doi.org/10.1038/s41561-024-01480-8.

[16] Ibid.

[17] "Deep-ocean floor produces its own oxygen," *ScienceDaily*, July 22, 2024, https://www.sciencedaily.com/releases/2024/07/240722154949.htm.

[18] Ibid.

[19] Ibid.

[20] Ibid.

[21] "With Support From Japan, Oceanographers Resume Study of 'Dark Oxygen,'" *The Maritime Executive*, accessed January 2025, https://www.maritime-executive.com/article/with-support-from-japan-oceanographers-resume-study-of-dark-oxygen.

[22] "Deep-sea dilemmas: Countering China's seabed mining efforts through global collaboration," Observer Research Foundation, December 26, 2024, https://www.orfonline.org/expert-speak/deep-sea-dilemmas-countering-china-s-seabed-mining-efforts-through-global-collaboration.

[23] Ibid.

[24] Steven Mufson, "China set to dominate deep-sea mining and grab treasure of rare metals," *Washington Post*, October 19, 2023, https://www.washingtonpost.com/world/interactive/2023/china-deep-sea-mining-military-renewable-energy/.

[25] Ibid.

[26] "Deep-sea dilemmas: Countering China's seabed mining efforts."

[27] "China's push into deep-sea mining gathers speed," *Dialogue Earth*, August 15, 2024, https://dialogue.earth/en/ocean/chinas-push-into-deep-sea-mining-gathers-speed/.

[28] Mufson, "China set to dominate deep-sea mining."

[29] The Metals Company, "NORI and Allseas Lift Over 3,000 Tonnes of Polymetallic Nodules to Surface," news release, November 14, 2022, https://investors.metals.co/news-releases/news-release-details/nori-and-allseas-lift-over-3000-tonnes-polymetallic-nodules/.

[30] Ibid.

[31] "World's first polymetallic nodule vessel Hidden Gem nears completion in Rotterdam," *SWZ|Maritime*, May 10, 2022, https://swzmaritime.nl/news/2022/02/22/worlds-first-polymetallic-nodule-vessel-hidden-gem-nears-completion-in-rotterdam/.

[32] Allseas, "Polymetallic nodule collection," accessed January 2025, https://www.allseas.com/en/what-we-do/polymetallic-nodule-collection.

[33] "What happened to the Allseas vessel that brought nodules to surface in 2022?" *GeoExpro*, March 18, 2025, https://geoexpro.com/what-

happened-to-the-allseas-vessel-that-brought-the-nodules-to-surface-in-2022/.

[34] The Metals Company, "NORI and Allseas Lift Over 3,000 Tonnes."

[35] Allseas, "Polymetallic nodule collection."

Chapter 9: Supply Chains and Security

In the pre-dawn hours of May 26, 2025, as the Chinese research vessel *R/V Tan Kah Kee* deployed its wire equipment 167 miles east of Okinotorishima's concrete-encased rocks, the confrontation represented far more than a territorial dispute over 9.44 square meters of reef. The standoff illuminated a fundamental transformation in how nations conceptualize security in the 21st century—where control over microscopic atolls translates into dominance over supply chains that undergird entire civilizations. For Japan, Okinotorishima has become the geographic embodiment of its broader struggle to secure the critical materials and sea lanes essential to its economic survival and strategic autonomy.

Japan's Resource Vulnerability: The 90% Dependency

Japan's relationship with Okinotorishima cannot be understood without acknowledging the nation's profound vulnerability in critical materials—a dependency so severe it borders on the existential. Japan imports over 90% of its critical metals, making it among the world's most resource-dependent major economies.¹ This dependency extends across virtually every material essential to modern civilization: the nation relies entirely on imports for uranium,² depends heavily on foreign sources for 75% of its lithium needs, and imports the vast majority of cobalt, nickel, and rare earth elements that power its advanced manufacturing economy.³

The depth of this vulnerability became starkly apparent during the 2010 Senkaku Islands dispute, when China imposed an informal embargo on rare earth element exports to Japan. The crisis sent Japanese industries into panic, particularly the automotive sector, which at the time depended on China for nearly 90% of its rare earth imports.⁴ Prices soared tenfold within a year, forcing Japan to confront the stark reality that its technological prowess meant little without secure access to the raw materials that made advanced manufacturing possible.

This dependency carries profound implications for Japan's Economic Security Promotion Act, enacted in May 2022. The legislation represents the most comprehensive response to supply chain vulnerabilities in Japanese history, establishing four pillars of economic security: supply chain resilience, critical infrastructure protection, advanced technology development, and intellectual property safeguards.⁵ The Act empowers the government to designate "critical materials" essential to national security but dependent on foreign sources, providing subsidies and low-interest loans to companies diversifying their supply chains away from potentially hostile suppliers.⁶

Under this framework, Japan has already allocated more than $12 billion for domestic research, development, and production of essential materials, including semiconductors and high-performance batteries.⁷ The government has identified specific procurement targets for domestic production of batteries and permanent magnets by 2030, encompassing lithium, nickel, cobalt, graphite, manganese, and rare earth elements.⁸ However, the scale of the challenge is immense: as of 2023, Japan still depended on China for approximately 60% of its rare earth imports, down from 90% in 2010 but still representing a dangerous concentration of supply.⁹

The Chinese Chokehold: Processing Dominance

While resource scarcity creates vulnerability, China's strategic positioning in critical materials processing transforms this vulnerability into a weapon of economic statecraft. China's dominance extends far beyond mining, encompassing the sophisticated refining and processing stages that convert raw materials into usable industrial inputs. According to the International Energy Agency, China controls approximately 85-90% of global rare earth element processing, 68% of cobalt refining, 65% of nickel processing, and 60% of lithium refining.¹⁰

This processing dominance represents a more sophisticated form of control than simple resource ownership. China refines 60% of the world's lithium while controlling only 15% of global mine production, demonstrating how technological capabilities can amplify geopolitical leverage.¹¹ Similarly, while the Democratic Republic of Congo produces 70% of the world's cobalt, China controls approximately 80% of cobalt refining capacity, including ownership or financing of roughly 15 Congolese mines.¹²

The strategic implications became clear in 2023 when China imposed export controls on gallium and germanium, and again in December 2024 when Beijing banned exports of critical mineral processing technologies to the United States.¹³ These restrictions highlighted how China's refining capabilities enable it to assert control over global supply chains even when raw materials originate from other countries. For Japan, this processing dominance means that even successful diversification of mining sources may prove insufficient without corresponding investments in downstream processing capabilities.

China's Rare Earth Resources Management Regulations, enacted in October 2024, further codified this strategic approach. The regulations explicitly state that "rare earth resources belong to the state" and authorize the government to "regulate the total amount of rare earth mining, smelting and separation, and optimize dynamic management."¹⁴ The legislation applies not only to domestic production but also to circulation, import, and export activities, providing Beijing with comprehensive tools to weaponize its processing dominance.

Sea Lane Control: The $3.4 Trillion Highway

Okinotorishima's strategic value extends beyond the mineral resources beneath its claimed exclusive economic zone to its position astride some of the world's most critical shipping lanes. While frequently cited figures claim $5.3 trillion in trade transits the South China Sea annually, more recent analysis by the Center for Strategic and International Studies suggests the actual figure is closer to $3.4 trillion—still representing approximately 21% of global maritime trade.¹⁵

The waters surrounding Okinotorishima form part of this broader network of maritime highways connecting East Asia with the Middle East, Europe, and the Americas. Over 64% of China's maritime trade transited South China Sea waters in 2016, while nearly 42% of Japan's maritime trade passed through the region in the same period.¹⁶ The strategic significance of these routes becomes even more pronounced when considering energy security: some two-thirds of South Korea's energy supplies, nearly 60% of Japan's and Taiwan's, and 80% of China's crude oil imports flow through surrounding waters.¹⁷

The economic implications of potential disruption are staggering. Analysts estimate that rerouting oil tankers via alternative routes like the Lombok Strait would cost Japan approximately $600 million annually and South Korea $270 million per year.¹⁸ For Japan, which imports virtually all of its petroleum and natural gas, secure access to these shipping lanes represents an existential economic interest that justifies enormous investments in remote territorial claims like Okinotorishima.

The atoll's location roughly halfway between Taiwan and Guam also places it at the heart of potential future conflict scenarios. Control over the surrounding waters could influence Chinese submarine movements and complicate U.S. military operations in defense of Taiwan, making Okinotorishima's seemingly modest territorial claims relevant to the broader strategic competition between great powers. The 2025 confrontation with the *R/V Tan Kah Kee* demonstrated how even routine research activities in these waters carry implicit challenges to Japanese sovereignty and, by extension, allied freedom of navigation.

The QUAD Response: Multilateral Supply Chain Resilience

Recognizing that no single country can address critical material vulnerabilities alone, Japan has increasingly turned to multilateral frameworks, particularly the Quadrilateral Security Dialogue (QUAD) comprising Australia, India, Japan, and the United States. In July 2025, QUAD foreign ministers announced the launch of the Quad Critical Minerals Initiative, described as "an ambitious expansion of our partnership to strengthen economic security and collective resilience by collaborating on securing and diversifying critical mineral supply chains."¹⁹

The initiative reflects growing recognition among QUAD members that their combined capabilities—Australia's vast mineral reserves, India's processing potential, Japan's technological expertise, and American market access—could create viable alternatives to Chinese-dominated supply chains. Each QUAD country has developed its own critical minerals list: Australia identifies 31 critical minerals, India lists 30, Japan maintains its regularly updated roster, and the United States recognizes 50 critical minerals.²⁰ The overlap among these lists creates opportunities for targeted cooperation on the most strategically important materials.

The Supply Chain Resilience Initiative (SCRI), launched by Australia, India, and Japan in April 2021, preceded and helped inform the broader QUAD approach. Originally focused on COVID-19 vaccines and medical supplies, SCRI has expanded to encompass semiconductors, batteries, and rare earth minerals.²¹ The initiative aims to reduce dependence on Chinese manufacturing through what officials term "de-risking"—maintaining economic ties with China while avoiding dangerous concentrations of supply in strategically sensitive sectors.

Perhaps most significantly, the QUAD has established the Quad Investors Network (QUIN), a private sector-led platform that brings together investors, corporations, and public institutions to accelerate investment in critical and emerging technologies across the Indo-Pacific.²² Among QUIN's nearly ten intra-QUAD partnerships, critical minerals have emerged as a top priority for strategic collaboration. The network serves as a mechanism to align private investment with government demand, helping to strengthen supply chain resilience in sectors like rare earth elements.

However, the challenges facing QUAD cooperation remain formidable. China continues to account for approximately 55% of global rare earth mining and 85% of refining processes, while Chinese firms control the majority of permanent magnet production.²³ The four QUAD countries combined hold comparable populations, technological capabilities, and mineral reserves to China, but translating this potential into operational supply chains requires massive investments and years of development time.²⁴

Carbon Neutrality and Battery Supply Chains

Japan's pursuit of carbon neutrality by 2050 has fundamentally transformed the strategic calculus surrounding critical materials, elevating battery supply chains from economic considerations to existential climate imperatives. Prime Minister Fumio Kishida's government has committed to reducing greenhouse gas emissions by 46% by 2030 as an interim goal toward achieving net-zero emissions by mid-century.²⁵ This ambitious target requires massive deployment of electric vehicles, renewable energy systems, and energy storage technologies—all of which depend heavily on the same critical materials that constitute Japan's greatest supply chain vulnerabilities.

The Japanese government's Green Growth Strategy, announced in June 2021, outlines current challenges across 14 specified fields expected to drive clean energy growth, supported by a Green Innovation Fund of approximately $15 billion.²⁶ The strategy explicitly acknowledges that carbon neutrality "cannot be realized through ordinary efforts" and requires "bold investment for innovation" in energy and industrial sectors.²⁷ Central to this transformation is the development of next-generation battery technologies capable of supporting both electric vehicle deployment and grid-scale energy storage.

Japan's ambitious battery development goals illustrate the intersection of climate policy and resource security. The National New Energy and Industrial Technology Development Organization (NEDO) has established targets for high-performance storage batteries with energy densities capable of doubling current electric vehicle driving ranges to at least 700-800 Wh/L.²⁸ The program also emphasizes resource-conserving materials that can reduce usage of cobalt, graphite, and other supply-constrained materials while developing low-carbon manufacturing processes.

The scale of Japan's battery material requirements is staggering. Each electric vehicle battery requires approximately 200 kilograms of critical minerals, with the battery sector responsible for 70% of global cobalt demand.²⁹ Japan's goal of achieving 30% electric vehicle market penetration by 2030 would require an eightfold increase in battery production over the next decade.³⁰ However, recent research suggests that cobalt supply shortages appear "inevitable in the short- to medium-term (during 2028-2033), even under the most technologically optimistic scenario."³¹

To address these constraints, Japan has invested heavily in recycling technologies capable of recovering 70% of lithium, 95% of nickel, and 95% of cobalt from end-of-life batteries.³² The government has also supported research into cobalt-free battery chemistries and alternative materials that could reduce dependence on the most supply-constrained minerals. However, these technologies remain largely in development phases, with recycling unlikely to provide significant relief until the 2030s when sufficient quantities of end-of-life batteries become available.

Economic Security in Practice: The Okinotorishima Connection

The seemingly abstract challenges of supply chain security find concrete expression in Japan's extraordinary investment in Okinotorishima's preservation and development. The atoll's claimed exclusive economic zone contains recently discovered deposits of over 230 million tonnes of polymetallic nodules, including 610,000 tonnes of cobalt—equivalent to 75 years of Japan's current consumption—and 740,000 tonnes of nickel representing 11 years of national demand.³³ These resources, valued at over $18 billion, provide Japan with a potential domestic source of exactly the materials it most desperately needs for its clean energy transition.

Japan's pioneering success in deep-sea mining, demonstrated by JOGMEC's 2020 excavation of 649 kilograms of cobalt-rich crust from the Takuyo No. 5 seamount at 5,500-meter depths, has positioned the nation as a global leader in extracting critical materials from its claimed maritime territories.³⁴ The Nippon Foundation's plans for large-scale extraction beginning in 2025 could potentially transform Japan from a critical material importer to a significant producer, fundamentally altering its strategic position in global supply chains.

However, the realization of this potential depends entirely on maintaining undisputed control over Okinotorishima's surrounding waters—the very issue at stake in confrontations like the May 2025 incident with the Chinese research vessel. Beijing's challenges to Japan's exclusive economic zone claims represent more than legal technicalities; they constitute direct challenges to Japan's efforts to achieve supply chain independence in the materials most critical to its economic and environmental future.

The economic security implications extend beyond the minerals themselves to encompass the broader technological and industrial ecosystem required to process them. Japan's investments in coral preservation, artificial reef construction, and marine research infrastructure around Okinotorishima serve dual purposes: maintaining the atoll's legal status as an "island" capable of generating exclusive economic zone claims while developing the scientific and technological capabilities necessary to exploit deep-sea mineral resources sustainably.

The Integration of Economic and National Security

Japan's experience with supply chain vulnerabilities has fundamentally reshaped its conception of national security, moving beyond traditional military threats to encompass economic dependencies that could prove equally devastating in times of crisis. The 2022 Economic Security Promotion Act represents the institutionalization of this broader security concept, establishing mechanisms to address vulnerabilities that could be exploited by hostile powers to coerce Japanese policy or disrupt its economy.

The legislation's four pillars—supply chain resilience, critical infrastructure security, advanced technology development, and intellectual property protection—reflect recognition that modern warfare increasingly targets economic and technological vulnerabilities rather than traditional military assets.³⁵ For Japan, a nation that has eschewed offensive military capabilities since World War II, economic security measures represent perhaps the most important tools available for defending against 21st-century threats.

The Ministry of Economy, Trade and Industry has designated specific critical materials under the new framework, including semiconductors, pharmaceuticals, rare earth metals, and other advanced technologies essential to Japan's economic competitiveness.³⁶ Companies that develop Secure Supply Plans for these materials become eligible for subsidies, interest subsidies on loans, two-step loans from the Japan Finance Corporation, equity investments, and credit insurance.³⁷ The scale of government support reflects the urgency with which Japanese policymakers view supply chain diversification.

Taiwan Semiconductor Manufacturing Company's partnership with Sony to build a $7 billion chip plant in Kumamoto and Daikin Industries' announcement of more resilient supply chains for air conditioner production illustrate how the new framework is already reshaping Japanese industrial policy.³⁸ These investments represent not just economic opportunities but strategic necessities for a nation determined to reduce its vulnerabilities to economic coercion.

The Defense Ministry's collaboration with the U.S. Defense Department on supply chain resilience, particularly in missile production and aircraft maintenance, demonstrates how economic security has become inseparable from traditional national security concerns.³⁹ For Japan, securing critical materials represents both an economic imperative and a defensive strategy against potential adversaries who might seek to exploit supply chain dependencies.

The Future of Japanese Economic Security

As the confrontation over Okinotorishima illustrates, Japan's pursuit of supply chain security will likely generate increasing tensions with China and other powers that benefit from existing resource dependencies. Beijing's challenges to Japanese territorial claims represent not just legal disputes but strategic efforts to prevent Japan from achieving the resource independence that would reduce Chinese leverage over its economy.

The success of Japan's economic security strategy will ultimately depend on its ability to build alternative supply chains robust enough to withstand Chinese economic pressure while maintaining the technological edge necessary to process critical materials domestically. The QUAD partnership provides a promising framework for achieving these goals, but realizing its potential will require sustained political will, massive financial investments, and careful navigation of the complex geopolitical tensions that accompany any effort to challenge Chinese dominance in critical materials.

For Japan, Okinotorishima has become more than a territorial claim—it represents a tangible symbol of the nation's determination to control its economic destiny in an age of supply chain warfare. The tiny atoll's concrete-preserved rocks and the vast oceanic resources they claim to govern embody Japan's broader struggle to secure the materials essential to its prosperity, security, and environmental survival. As climate change and technological advancement continue to reshape global resource requirements, the strategic value of even the smallest territorial footholds will only continue to grow.

The May 2025 confrontation between Japanese and Chinese vessels near Okinotorishima thus represents far more than a dispute over maritime boundaries. It symbolizes the broader competition between two fundamentally different visions of economic security: China's model of leveraging processing dominance to maintain control over global supply chains, and Japan's pursuit of technological innovation and international partnerships to achieve strategic autonomy. The outcome of this competition will help determine not only the future of critical material supply chains but the broader balance of power in the Indo-Pacific and beyond.

Footnotes

¹ Japan Agency for Marine-Earth Science and Technology, "Critical Materials and Manufacturing: Comparing China, the European Union, Japan, and the United States," *ScienceDirect*, January 27, 2025.

² "Japan adds uranium to critical minerals list," *MINING.COM*, February 5, 2024.

³ Center for Strategic and International Studies, "Potential for U.S.-Japan Cooperation on Supply-Chain Resilience for Clean Energy Technologies," June 9, 2025.

⁴ Nobuhiro Horii, "How Japan solved its rare earth minerals dependency issue," *World Economic Forum*, October 2023.

⁵ Columbia Business Law Review, "The Japanese Economic Security Promotion Act: A Solution to National Security Threats Resulting from Economic Globalization," 2022.

⁶ Baker McKenzie, "New Act on the promotion of Japan's economic security enacted," *Global Supply Chain Compliance*, June 24, 2022.

⁷ Tom Abke, "Japan focuses on economic resilience, technology safeguards to bolster national defense," *Indo-Pacific Defense Forum*, November 25, 2024.

⁸ Center for Strategic and International Studies, "Potential for U.S.-Japan Cooperation on Supply-Chain Resilience for Clean Energy Technologies," June 9, 2025.

⁹ Royal United Services Institute, "Japan's Responses to China's Supply Chain Dominance," 2024.

¹⁰ Goldman Sachs Research, "Resource realism: The geopolitics of critical mineral supply chains," September 13, 2023.

¹¹ Cipher News, "How China dominates critical minerals in three charts," April 30, 2025.

¹² QuestMetals, "China's Grip on World's Metal Supply," 2024.

¹³ Center for Strategic and International Studies, "What China's Ban on Rare Earths Processing Technology Exports Means," December 2, 2024.

¹⁴ Center for Strategic and International Studies, "Potential for U.S.-Japan Cooperation on Supply-Chain Resilience for Clean Energy Technologies," June 9, 2025.

¹⁵ ChinaPower Project, "How Much Trade Transits the South China Sea?" Center for Strategic and International Studies, January 25, 2021.

¹⁶ Ibid.

¹⁷ Anthony Fensom, "$5 Trillion Meltdown: What If China Shuts Down the South China Sea?" *The National Interest*, July 17, 2016.

¹⁸ Ibid.

¹⁹ U.S. Department of State, "2025 Quad Foreign Ministers' Meeting," July 2, 2025.

²⁰ *The Diplomat*, "Building Resilient Critical Minerals Supply Chains for the Quad," July 25, 2024.

²¹ EurAsian Times, "QUAD Allies India, Australia & Japan Form A 'Supply Chain Shield' Against China's Dominance," April 29, 2021.

²² Center for a New American Security, "Quad: The Next Phase," June 18, 2025.

²³ Baker Institute, "Of Chinese Behemoths: What China's Rare Earths Dominance Means for the US," December 19, 2022.

²⁴ Canadian Global Affairs Institute, "Investing in Supply Chain Resilience in the Indo-Pacific," 2024.

²⁵ Government of Japan, "Together for Action: Japan's Initiatives for Achieving the Common Goal of Net Zero by 2050," *JapanGov*, 2024.

²⁶ World Economic Forum, "Japan is accelerating efforts towards a carbon-neutral society," January 2023.

²⁷ Ministry of Economy, Trade and Industry, "Green Growth Strategy Through Achieving Carbon Neutrality in 2050," December 25, 2020.

²⁸ NEDO, "Next-generation Storage Battery and Motor Development," *Green Innovation Fund Projects*.

²⁹ World Trade Organization, "High demand for energy-related critical minerals creates supply chain pressures," *Data Blog*, January 10, 2024.

³⁰ McKinsey & Company, "How Japan could reach carbon neutrality by 2050," August 4, 2021.

³¹ *Nature Communications*, "Battery technology and recycling alone will not save the electric mobility transition from future cobalt shortages," March 15, 2022.

³² NEDO, "Next-generation Storage Battery and Motor Development," *Green Innovation Fund Projects*.

³³ University of Tokyo and Nippon Foundation, "Critical Minerals Discovery Announcement," June 2024.

³⁴ Japan Organization for Metals and Energy Security (JOGMEC), "Deep-sea Mining Success Report," 2020.

³⁵ Sasakawa USA, "Economic Security and Emerging Technology: Japan's Perspective for Pursuing a Technology Alliance," May 8, 2025.

³⁶ Edelman Global Advisory, "New Opportunities from Japan's Economic Security Promotion Act," 2022.

³⁷ Ibid.

³⁸ Ibid.

³⁹ Tom Abke, "Japan focuses on economic resilience, technology safeguards to bolster national defense," *Indo-Pacific Defense Forum*, November 25, 2024.

PART IV: THE GEOPOLITICAL CHESSBOARD

Chapter 10: The China Challenge

On the morning of May 26, 2025, the Chinese research vessel R/V Tan Kah Kee appeared on Japanese radar screens 167 miles east of Okinotorishima, its crew methodically deploying what appeared to be a wire into the Pacific depths.[1] Japanese Coast Guard aircraft circled overhead, their radio transmissions crackling through the salt air: "No research activities are permitted in Japan's EEZ without Tokyo's consent." But the Chinese vessel continued its work for five hours, collecting data from waters that Beijing insisted belonged to no one—and everyone.

Two days later, at her regular press briefing in Beijing, Chinese Foreign Ministry spokesperson Mao Ning delivered a message that cut to the heart of the dispute: "According to UNCLOS, Okinotori is a reef, not an island. As such, it is not entitled to an EEZ or continental shelf. Japan's claim of an EEZ around the reef violates international law. China's research vessel was exercising the freedom of the high seas with regard to its activities in the waters, and Japan has no right to interfere."[2] This was no mere diplomatic protest—it was a declaration of strategic intent that revealed how Beijing views the tiny atoll as a critical piece in a much larger geopolitical chess game.

Beyond Legal Technicalities: China's Strategic Calculus

China's challenge to Japan's claims around Okinotorishima extends far beyond the legal interpretation of rocks versus islands under international maritime law. For Beijing's strategic planners, this remote atoll represents a potential chokepoint in what Chinese military doctrine calls the "First Island Chain"—that critical arc of territories running from the Kurils through Japan, Taiwan, and the Philippines to Borneo that forms the boundary between China's near seas and the vast Pacific.[3]

Okinotorishima's location halfway between Taiwan and Guam places it at the geographical heart of China's most sensitive strategic concerns. In the event of a Taiwan crisis, U.S. naval forces would likely transit these very waters en route from their major Pacific base at Guam to support Taiwan or deter Chinese military action.[4] For Chinese military planners, Japan's claimed 200-nautical-mile exclusive economic zone around Okinotorishima represents not just a legal impediment to Chinese research activities, but a potential operational constraint on China's ability to project power beyond the First Island Chain.

The strategic significance becomes clearer when viewed through the lens of China's anti-access/area-denial (A2/AD) strategy—Beijing's systematic effort to develop capabilities that can deny or complicate U.S. military operations in the Western Pacific.[5] This strategy, born from China's humiliation during the 1995-1996 Taiwan Strait crisis when Beijing could do nothing to prevent the deployment of two U.S. carrier battle groups near Taiwan, aims to push American forces back from China's maritime periphery and create uncertainty about U.S. ability to intervene in regional conflicts.[6]

The Research Vessel Incidents: A Pattern of Probing

The May 2025 confrontation was merely the latest in a series of incidents that reveals Beijing's systematic approach to challenging Japan's EEZ claims around Okinotorishima. Each incident follows a carefully calibrated pattern: Chinese vessels conduct what they term "scientific research" in waters Japan claims as its exclusive economic zone, Japan protests through diplomatic channels, and China responds by reaffirming its position that no EEZ exists around what it considers mere rocks.

The most prolonged confrontation occurred in July 2020, when a Chinese oceanographic survey vessel spent 18 days conducting research activities in Japan's claimed EEZ around Okinotorishima—the longest unauthorized presence in a decade.[7] Japanese Coast Guard patrol vessels repeatedly observed the Chinese ship "trailing an apparent cable from its stern" and deploying observation equipment, while Japanese officials issued warnings that such activities violated UNCLOS Article 246(2), which requires coastal state consent for marine scientific research in EEZs.[8]

The Chinese vessel's behavior during the 2020 incident was particularly revealing of Beijing's strategic approach. Rather than leaving immediately upon Japanese protest, the ship repeatedly "recovered the observation equipment, moved to a different sea area in the Japanese EEZ, and launched the equipment into the sea again," systematically surveying different areas before finally exiting Japanese-claimed waters on July 27.[9] This methodical approach suggested something far more comprehensive than routine scientific research.

Earlier incidents trace back to at least December 2018, when Chinese research vessels first began regularly appearing in waters Japan claims around Okinotorishima.[10] Each incident has been met with Japanese diplomatic protests and Chinese denials of any legal obligation to seek permission for activities in what Beijing characterizes as international waters. The consistency of China's responses across multiple years and different vessels indicates a coordinated state policy rather than isolated decisions by individual research institutions.

The World's Largest Dual-Use Fleet

China's challenge to Japan's Okinotorishima claims is enabled by what the Center for Strategic and International Studies identifies as "the world's largest civilian research vessel fleet," a maritime force that Beijing is "employing to advance its strategic ambitions, including collecting data about the world's oceans for military purposes."[11] This massive fleet, consisting of at least 64 active research and survey vessels identified in recent studies, represents a key component of China's broader military-civil fusion strategy.[12]

The scale and sophistication of China's research fleet is unprecedented. These vessels have conducted "hundreds of thousands of hours of operations globally over the past four years," with 80% showing some connection to China's military or geopolitical agenda through organizational ties, suspicious activity patterns, or dual-use capabilities.[13] Many vessels are owned and operated by state-affiliated organizations with formal cooperation agreements with the People's Liberation Army, while others are former military vessels transferred to civilian control but maintaining defense sector connections.[14]

The R/V Tan Kah Kee involved in the 2025 incident exemplifies this dual-use approach. Operated by Marine Operations at Xiamen University, the vessel represents the blurred lines between civilian academic research and state strategic objectives that characterize Chinese oceanographic activities.[15] While ostensibly conducting marine scientific research, such vessels are capable of collecting bathymetric data, measuring ocean currents and water temperature, and mapping seabed topography—all information with significant military applications for submarine operations and naval planning.

Perhaps most concerning from a strategic perspective is China's development of autonomous research platforms like the Zhu Hai Yun, designed to serve as a "mothership" for over 50 unmanned air, surface, and undersea vehicles that can simultaneously survey "a three-dimensional area spanning 160 kilometers across, 4,000 meters above, and 1,500 meters below the ocean's surface."[16] Such capabilities allow for comprehensive intelligence gathering across vast ocean areas while maintaining the plausible cover of civilian scientific research.

Military Applications of "Scientific" Research

The distinction between civilian marine research and military intelligence gathering becomes increasingly blurred when considering the strategic value of oceanographic data for submarine warfare. For Chinese military planners contemplating scenarios involving Taiwan or broader regional conflicts, detailed knowledge of seafloor topography, water temperature variations, current patterns, and acoustic conditions in the waters around Okinotorishima would be invaluable for submarine navigation and operations.[17]

Chinese military writings have long emphasized the importance of accurate seabed mapping for submarine operations, particularly in the context of potential conflicts in the Taiwan Strait. As one analysis notes, "the reason why China claims that Okinotorishima is not an island but a rock and denies that the waters surrounding the island are Japan's EEZ, is so that it can freely collect data about seafloor topography, water temperature, tidal currents, and so on, with the ultimate goal of preventing the U.S. Navy from sortieing in the event of a Taiwan emergency."[18]

The timing and persistence of Chinese research activities around Okinotorishima suggest systematic intelligence collection rather than routine scientific inquiry. The 18-day 2020 operation, with its pattern of equipment deployment across multiple locations within Japan's claimed EEZ, appears designed to create a comprehensive picture of oceanographic conditions across a strategically vital area. Such data would be essential for Chinese submarines seeking to operate undetected in these waters or to position themselves to interdict U.S. naval forces transiting between Guam and Taiwan.

Modern Chinese research vessels carry sophisticated equipment that enables both legitimate scientific research and military-relevant data collection. Advanced sonar systems, remotely operated vehicles, and underwater gliders can map seabed features, identify underwater obstacles, and measure acoustic conditions—all critical factors for submarine operations.[19] The deployment of "wire equipment" observed during the 2025 incident likely involved oceanographic sensors capable of collecting multi-layered data about water column characteristics and seabed conditions.

The A2/AD Strategy and Maritime Expansion

China's activities around Okinotorishima must be understood within the broader context of Beijing's anti-access/area-denial strategy, which seeks to create layers of defensive capabilities that can complicate or prevent U.S. military operations in the Western Pacific. This strategy, developed in response to China's inability to contest U.S. naval dominance during the 1995-1996 Taiwan Strait crisis, aims to push American forces back from China's maritime periphery through a combination of long-range missiles, submarines, electronic warfare capabilities, and comprehensive intelligence collection.[20]

The A2/AD concept encompasses both "anti-access" capabilities designed to prevent enemy forces from entering an operational area, and "area-denial" capabilities intended to limit enemy freedom of action within contested regions.[21] In the context of potential Taiwan scenarios, Okinotorishima's location makes the surrounding waters a potential area of operations for both Chinese forces seeking to prevent U.S. intervention and American forces attempting to maintain access to the Taiwan Strait region.

China's systematic collection of oceanographic data around Okinotorishima supports both defensive and offensive aspects of A2/AD strategy. Defensively, such data enables Chinese submarines to operate more effectively in these waters, potentially positioning themselves to intercept U.S. naval forces. Offensively, detailed knowledge of seabed conditions and acoustic characteristics could facilitate Chinese submarine-launched attacks against U.S. vessels transiting these waters en route to Taiwan.

The People's Liberation Army Navy's growing submarine fleet, which includes both nuclear-powered and diesel-electric vessels, would benefit significantly from comprehensive oceanographic intelligence about the waters around Okinotorishima.[22] While China's submarine force remains smaller than that of the United States, the shallow waters and complex acoustic conditions near China's coast—including the approaches to Okinotorishima—could favor defending Chinese submarines over attacking U.S. forces less familiar with local conditions.

The Taiwan Factor

All roads in China's Okinotorishima strategy lead back to Taiwan. The atoll's position halfway between Taiwan and Guam places it at the center of the most likely route for U.S. military reinforcements in the event of a cross-strait crisis. Chinese military planners have long recognized that their ability to control or influence events around Taiwan depends heavily on their capacity to complicate U.S. intervention, and Okinotorishima represents a key geographic chokepoint in American force projection capabilities.

In Chinese strategic thinking, Taiwan represents the critical link in the First Island Chain that must be secured before Beijing can project power confidently beyond China's near seas.[23] As one analysis notes, "Taiwan is considered of critical strategic importance. It is located at the midpoint of the first chain and occupies a strategic position" in determining whether China can break through American containment efforts.[24] Okinotorishima's location south of this critical midpoint makes it a potential forward observation post for monitoring and potentially interdicting U.S. forces moving to Taiwan's assistance.

The strategic calculus becomes particularly acute when considering the speed at which a Taiwan crisis might unfold. Chinese military doctrine emphasizes the importance of achieving rapid, decisive results before external forces can effectively intervene.[25] In such scenarios, every hour of advance warning about U.S. naval movements, every piece of intelligence about American force dispositions, and every capability to complicate U.S. operations could prove decisive. Comprehensive oceanographic intelligence about the waters around Okinotorishima would enhance all three of these Chinese objectives.

The irony is that Taiwan itself has sometimes found its interests aligned with China's position on Okinotorishima, despite the broader strategic implications. The April 2016 detention of Taiwanese fishermen by Japan's Coast Guard in waters around Okinotorishima led to a confrontation that temporarily aligned Taipei's interests with Beijing's legal arguments, even though such alignment potentially undermined Taiwan's own territorial claims elsewhere.[26] This incident highlighted the complex triangular dynamics surrounding the atoll, where traditional alliance relationships can be complicated by specific legal and economic interests.

Information Warfare and Strategic Ambiguity

China's approach to Okinotorishima exemplifies Beijing's sophisticated use of legal ambiguity and information warfare to advance strategic objectives while maintaining plausible deniability. By consistently framing its activities as legitimate scientific research in international waters, China places Japan in the difficult position of appearing to obstruct peaceful scientific inquiry while asserting what Beijing characterizes as illegal territorial claims.

This approach allows China to achieve multiple strategic objectives simultaneously. First, it enables systematic intelligence collection about strategically vital waters while minimizing the risk of escalation. Second, it challenges the legitimacy of Japan's EEZ claims through sustained practical demonstration that China does not recognize Japanese jurisdiction. Third, it creates precedents for Chinese freedom of action in these waters that could prove valuable in future crises.

The consistent messaging from Chinese officials, exemplified by Mao Ning's May 2025 statement, demonstrates Beijing's commitment to a long-term strategy of delegitimizing Japan's claims rather than simply conducting isolated research missions.[27] By repeatedly invoking UNCLOS and characterizing Chinese activities as exercises of "freedom of the high seas," Beijing positions itself as defending international law against Japanese territorial expansionism.

This information warfare dimension becomes particularly important when considering third-party reactions to the dispute. Many countries that might otherwise support Japan's position on territorial issues may find China's legal arguments about UNCLOS Article 121(3) compelling, particularly given the obvious disparity between Okinotorishima's tiny physical size and Japan's vast EEZ claims. China's consistent legal messaging helps frame the dispute in terms favorable to Beijing's interests while undermining international support for Japanese positions.

The Technology Race

The sophistication of Chinese research vessels operating around Okinotorishima reflects broader trends in maritime technology that are reshaping intelligence collection and naval warfare. Modern Chinese research ships carry equipment that would have been unimaginable just decades ago: autonomous underwater vehicles capable of operating for extended periods without surface support, advanced sonar systems that can map seabed features with unprecedented precision, and satellite communication systems that enable real-time data transmission to shore-based analysis centers.[28]

The Zhu Hai Yun represents the cutting edge of this technological evolution, with its ability to deploy swarms of unmanned vehicles that can simultaneously collect data across three-dimensional ocean spaces spanning hundreds of kilometers.[29] Such capabilities enable comprehensive intelligence gathering on a scale that individual traditional research vessels could never achieve, while maintaining the cover of civilian scientific research that complicates military responses.

Perhaps most concerning from a strategic perspective is the development of what Chinese sources describe as "unmanned ship swarms" that can operate autonomously while coordinating their activities to maximize coverage and intelligence collection.[30] Such technologies presage a future in which intelligence gathering and potentially military operations could be conducted by autonomous systems that blur traditional distinctions between civilian and military activities.

The rapid pace of Chinese technological development in this area reflects the high priority Beijing places on maritime intelligence collection and the resources it is willing to devote to achieving technological superiority in key areas. The integration of artificial intelligence, autonomous systems, and advanced sensors creates capabilities that fundamentally change the nature of maritime intelligence collection and the strategic competition surrounding places like Okinotorishima.

Implications for Regional Security

China's systematic challenge to Japan's EEZ claims around Okinotorishima has implications that extend far beyond the immediate bilateral dispute. Beijing's approach creates precedents and establishes patterns of behavior that could be applied to other territorial disputes throughout the region, from the South China Sea to potential Arctic claims as ice melts reveal new areas of strategic interest.

The success or failure of China's strategy around Okinotorishima will influence Beijing's calculations about other territorial disputes and the effectiveness of sustained legal and practical challenges to rivals' claims. If China can successfully establish a pattern of operating freely in waters Japan claims as its EEZ, similar approaches might be applied elsewhere, gradually eroding the principle that EEZ claims deserve international respect even when their legal basis is disputed.

For U.S. strategic planning, China's activities around Okinotorishima represent both a direct challenge to an important ally's territorial claims and a broader test of American willingness and ability to support partners in maritime territorial disputes. The apparent U.S. reluctance to directly challenge Chinese research activities in these waters, in contrast to American freedom of navigation operations challenging Chinese claims in the South China Sea, may signal to Beijing that different rules apply to different disputes.[31]

The regional implications become particularly acute when considering the potential for escalation. As Chinese research activities become more frequent and sophisticated, and as Japan potentially takes stronger countermeasures, the risk increases for miscalculation or incidents that could spiral beyond the immediate participants. The involvement of military-linked research vessels, the strategic importance of the area for Taiwan scenarios, and the broader context of U.S.-China strategic competition all increase the potential consequences of what might otherwise be treated as routine territorial disputes.

Looking Forward: The Logic of Persistent Challenge

China's approach to Okinotorishima reflects a carefully calculated long-term strategy rather than opportunistic probing. The consistency of Beijing's legal arguments across multiple years and incidents, the systematic nature of research activities, and the integration of these activities with broader Chinese maritime expansion all suggest a coherent strategic framework designed to gradually erode Japan's effective control over the disputed area.

This strategy of persistent challenge offers several advantages from Beijing's perspective. It avoids the costs and risks of direct military confrontation while steadily advancing Chinese interests. It maintains pressure on Japanese decision-makers while gradually normalizing Chinese presence in the disputed waters. It creates precedents and establishes facts on the water that could prove valuable in future negotiations or crises.

Perhaps most importantly, the strategy forces Japan to bear the costs and political risks of escalation if Tokyo wishes to effectively enforce its EEZ claims. Every Japanese decision to intercept Chinese vessels, every diplomatic protest, and every consideration of stronger countermeasures carries domestic political costs and international implications that China does not face when conducting what it characterizes as legitimate scientific research in international waters.

The ultimate test of this strategy will come if and when broader regional tensions escalate to the point where the stakes around Okinotorishima become more directly connected to immediate security concerns. In Taiwan crisis scenarios, the oceanographic intelligence China has patiently collected around Okinotorishima could prove strategically decisive, validating Beijing's long-term investment in challenging Japan's claims through seemingly routine research activities.

As the competition between China and the United States intensifies throughout the Western Pacific, seemingly minor disputes like Okinotorishima take on disproportionate importance as tests of resolve, precedents for future behavior, and indicators of the shifting regional balance of power. China's challenge to Japan's tiny rocks may ultimately prove to be about much more than rocks—it may be about the future structure of power and influence across the world's largest ocean.

---

[1] "Photos Show Chinese Ship Detected in Waters Claimed by US Ally," *Newsweek*, May 28, 2025, https://www.newsweek.com/japan-china-news-research-ship-exclusive-economic-zone-pacific-ocean-2077774.

[2] "Foreign Ministry Spokesperson Mao Ning's Regular Press Conference on May 27, 2025," Ministry of Foreign Affairs of the People's Republic of China, May 27, 2025, https://www.fmprc.gov.cn/eng/xw/fyrbt/202505/t20250527_11634354.html.

[3] "First Island Chain," Wikipedia, accessed August 8, 2025, https://en.wikipedia.org/wiki/First_island_chain.

[4] "The US-Japan-China Mistrust Spiral and Okinotorishima," *Asia-Pacific Journal: Japan Focus*, November 3, 2023, https://apjjf.org/yukie-yoshikawa/2541/article.

[5] "China's Anti-Access/Area-Denial Strategy," TDHJ.org, October 16, 2024, https://tdhj.org/blog/post/china-a2ad-strategy/.

[6] "China's Stealthy Area Denial," *Asian Military Review*, March 16, 2023, https://www.asianmilitaryreview.com/2023/03/chinas-stealthy-area-denial/.

[7] "Chinese survey vessel spotted in Okinotorishima EEZ for over a week," *The Japan Times*, July 18, 2020, https://www.japantimes.co.jp/news/2020/07/18/national/china-okinotorishima-eez/.

[8] "China's Navy, the West Pacific and the Role of Okinotorishima," *The Diplomat*, January 30, 2023, https://thediplomat.com/2023/01/chinas-navy-the-west-pacific-and-the-role-of-okinotorishima/.

[9] Ibid.

[10] "Japan Slams China for Unauthorized Research Around Okinotori Island," *The Diplomat*, January 9, 2019, https://thediplomat.com/2019/01/japan-slams-china-for-unauthorized-research-around-okinotori-island/.

[11] "Photos Show Chinese Ship Detected in Waters Claimed by US Ally," *Newsweek*.

[12] "Surveying the Seas: China's Dual-Use Research Operations in the Indian Ocean," Center for Strategic and International Studies, https://features.csis.org/hiddenreach/china-indian-ocean-research-vessels/.

[13] Ibid.

[14] Ibid.

[15] "Photos Show Chinese Ship Detected in Waters Claimed by US Ally," *Newsweek*.

[16] "Skirting the Shores: China's New High-Tech Research Ship Probes the Waters around Taiwan," Center for Strategic and International Studies, https://features.csis.org/snapshots/china-research-vessel-taiwan/.

[17] "China's Navy, the West Pacific and the Role of Okinotorishima," *The Diplomat*.

[18] Ibid.

[19] "Study: China's Research Vessels Carry Out Covert Missions for PLA," *The Maritime Executive*, https://maritime-executive.com/article/study-china-s-research-vessels-carry-out-covert-missions-for-pla.

[20] "China's Stealthy Area Denial," *Asian Military Review*.

[21] "Anti-access/area denial," Wikipedia, accessed August 8, 2025, https://en.wikipedia.org/wiki/Anti-access/area_denial.

[22] "A Guide to Chinese Naval Anti-Access/Area Denial (A2/AD)," WhiteFleet.net, July 8, 2017, https://whitefleet.net/2016/08/21/a-pocket-guide-to-chinese-naval-anti-accessarea-denial-a2ad/.

[23] "The Taiwan Frontier and the Chinese Dominance for the Second Island Chain," Australian Institute of International Affairs, August 13, 2020, https://www.internationalaffairs.org.au/australianoutlook/taiwan-frontier-chinese-dominance-for-second-island-chain/.

[24] "First Island Chain," Wikipedia.

[25] "China's Anti-Access/Area-Denial Strategy," TDHJ.org.

[26] "Taipei's Risky Agreement with Beijing on Okinotorishima," Asia Maritime Transparency Initiative, October 11, 2016, https://amti.csis.org/taipeis-risky-agreement-beijing-okinotorishima/.

[27] "Foreign Ministry Spokesperson Mao Ning's Regular Press Conference on May 27, 2025," Ministry of Foreign Affairs of the People's Republic of China.

[28] "China is using civilian ships to enhance navy capability and reach," CNBC, September 26, 2022, https://www.cnbc.com/2022/09/26/china-is-using-civilian-ships-to-enhance-navy-capability-and-reach.html.

[29] "Skirting the Shores: China's New High-Tech Research Ship Probes the Waters around Taiwan," Center for Strategic and International Studies.

[30] Ibid.

[31] "A Survey of Marine Research Vessels in the Indo-Pacific," Asia Maritime Transparency Initiative, April 16, 2020, https://amti.csis.org/a-survey-of-marine-research-vessels-in-the-indo-pacific/.

Chapter 11: Alliance Networks and Maritime Strategy

The May 26, 2025 confrontation between the Chinese research vessel R/V Tan Kah Kee and Japanese Coast Guard aircraft over Okinotorishima's waters represented more than a bilateral dispute—it exposed the complex web of alliance relationships and strategic calculations that have transformed this tiny atoll into a linchpin of Indo-Pacific security architecture. While Chinese Foreign Ministry spokesperson Mao Ning declared that Japan "has no right to interfere" with China's exercise of "freedom of the high seas," the incident revealed how fundamentally different America's approach has been to Japan's maritime claims compared to China's expansive assertions in the South China Sea.[1]

The silence from Washington regarding Japan's Okinotorishima claims stands in stark contrast to the United States' vigorous Freedom of Navigation Operations (FONOPs) challenging China's artificial island construction and excessive maritime claims. This calculated asymmetry reflects deeper strategic considerations within the U.S.-Japan alliance and its integration into broader Indo-Pacific coalition building efforts that have elevated Okinotorishima from a legal curiosity into a strategic asset supporting American hegemony in the Western Pacific.

The Strategic Silence: U.S. Acquiescence to Japan's Claims

The most striking aspect of the Okinotorishima dispute has been America's conspicuous absence from the legal debate. While the United States has conducted hundreds of FONOPs worldwide since 1979 to challenge "excessive maritime claims," it has never operationally challenged Japan's EEZ assertion around the tiny atoll.[2] This omission becomes particularly glaring when contrasted with American responses to China's South China Sea activities, where U.S. forces conducted thirteen FONOPs in 2020 alone, setting a program record.[3]

Chinese analysts have noted this apparent contradiction with growing frustration. As one Chinese commentary observed, "The US, however, has remained reticent about [Japan's Okinotorishima claims]. A main reason is that if Japan's claim gets accepted, the atoll and its waters lying east of Taiwan will be of strategic importance in encircling China in West Pacific."[4] The strategic logic is unmistakable: Okinotorishima's location roughly halfway between Taiwan and Guam places it at the heart of potential U.S.-China confrontation scenarios, where American naval access could prove decisive.

This calculated American acquiescence reflects broader alliance considerations that transcend technical interpretations of UNCLOS Article 121(3). From Washington's perspective, supporting Japan's Okinotorishima claims serves multiple strategic objectives: maintaining alliance cohesion with America's most important Asian partner, extending allied control over critical sea lanes, and creating additional barriers to Chinese naval operations in the Western Pacific. The approximately 400,000 square kilometers of ocean that Japan claims around Okinotorishima represents not just economic potential but strategic depth for the U.S.-Japan alliance.[5]

The contrast becomes even more pronounced when examining the timing of various Freedom of Navigation Operations. During the Obama administration's "pivot to Asia," FONOP frequency in the South China Sea increased dramatically, with operations specifically targeting Chinese artificial island construction.[6] Yet throughout this period of heightened maritime tensions, no American vessel has challenged Japan's EEZ around Okinotorishima, despite the legal questions being remarkably similar to those surrounding China's artificial islands.

The FOIP Framework: Okinotorishima as Strategic Asset

Japan's Free and Open Indo-Pacific (FOIP) strategy, formally announced by Prime Minister Abe Shinzō in 2016, has provided the conceptual framework within which Okinotorishima's strategic value has been elevated and institutionalized.[7] The FOIP vision explicitly connects Japan's southern maritime territories to broader regional security objectives, transforming what might otherwise be seen as excessive territorial claims into contributions to international order.

The FOIP strategy's three pillars—promoting rule of law and freedom of navigation, pursuing economic prosperity through connectivity, and ensuring peace and stability through capacity building—all intersect at Okinotorishima.[8] Japan's investment of over $600 million in preserving and fortifying the atoll can be framed not as nationalist excess but as essential infrastructure supporting maritime security and scientific research in the vast Pacific Ocean.

More significantly, FOIP has provided the intellectual architecture for transforming bilateral U.S.-Japan alliance coordination into multilateral coalition building. The strategy's emphasis on "quality infrastructure development" and "connectivity" has created practical frameworks for coordinating with partners while avoiding the appearance of containment.[9] Okinotorishima, with its research facilities and claimed EEZ, becomes a platform for scientific cooperation, maritime domain awareness, and environmental monitoring—all legitimate activities that happen to serve broader strategic purposes.

The American adoption of Indo-Pacific terminology and strategic concepts, culminating in the Biden administration's formal Indo-Pacific Strategy in 2022, has effectively validated Japan's approach.[10] Washington's embrace of FOIP principles has created a strategic consensus that implicitly supports Japan's maximalist interpretation of its maritime rights, including around Okinotorishima.

QUAD Dynamics: Multilateralizing Maritime Security

The Quadrilateral Security Dialogue among the United States, Japan, Australia, and India has emerged as the primary mechanism for institutionalizing Indo-Pacific maritime cooperation, with implications extending to disputes like Okinotorishima. The September 21, 2024 Quad Leaders' Summit in Delaware demonstrated how maritime domain awareness and security cooperation have become central to the partnership's practical agenda.[11]

The Quad's Indo-Pacific Partnership for Maritime Domain Awareness (IPMDA), announced in 2022, represents a sophisticated approach to monitoring and coordinating responses to maritime activities across the region.[12] While officially focused on humanitarian assistance and disaster relief, the system's capabilities for tracking vessel movements and maritime activities clearly serve broader security purposes. For Japan, IPMDA provides multilateral legitimacy for monitoring activities around Okinotorishima while sharing the costs and political risks of maintaining persistent surveillance.

The 2024 Quad commitment to launch a "Quad-at-Sea Ship Observer Mission" in 2025 further institutionalizes maritime cooperation among coast guard and naval forces.[13] These operations, while not directly related to Okinotorishima, establish precedents for coordinated responses to maritime challenges and create habits of cooperation that could prove relevant should China escalate its challenges to Japan's EEZ claims.

India's participation in the Quad adds particular complexity to the Okinotorishima issue. While New Delhi has generally avoided taking positions on East Asian territorial disputes, its growing naval presence in the Indo-Pacific and participation in Quad maritime exercises creates implicit support for the broader alliance framework within which Japan's claims operate.[14] The Quad's consensus-based approach means that any coordinated response to Chinese challenges around Okinotorishima would require Indian acquiescence, if not active support.

However, the Quad's limitations also constrain its utility for addressing specific territorial disputes. Academic assessments note that the Quad "had yet to find common ground or a coherent strategic approach" as of 2024, with member conflicts with China arising in "significantly different areas" that complicate unified action.[15] This suggests that while the Quad provides valuable multilateral frameworks for maritime cooperation, it may not serve as an effective mechanism for directly addressing Chinese challenges to Japanese sovereignty claims.

Japan's Maritime Capacity Building Diplomacy

Perhaps the most significant development in Japan's alliance strategy has been its emergence as a leading provider of maritime security assistance to Southeast Asian partners. This capacity-building diplomacy serves dual purposes: strengthening regional maritime law enforcement capabilities while creating strategic partnerships that could prove relevant to broader disputes including Okinotorishima.

Japan's Maritime Safety Capacity Improvement Project (MSCIP) with the Philippines represents the most ambitious example of this approach. The $507 million agreement finalized in May 2024 will provide five 97-meter patrol vessels to the Philippine Coast Guard, representing Tokyo's largest maritime security investment to date.[16] These vessels join two previously delivered Multi-Role Response Vessels (MRRVs) that have become the Philippine Coast Guard's most capable platforms for operations in the South China Sea.

Since 2000, Japan has provided patrol vessels to coast guard and maritime law enforcement agencies in Cambodia, Indonesia, Malaysia, Palau, the Philippines, Sri Lanka, and Vietnam.[17] This ship diplomacy creates practical partnerships while demonstrating Japan's commitment to regional maritime security—a commitment that extends logically to defending Japan's own maritime claims around Okinotorishima.

The strategic implications extend beyond bilateral relationships to broader coalition building. As one analysis noted, Japan's provision of coast guard vessels to the Philippines supports "layered security buildup in every spectrum of the escalation management" necessary for addressing Chinese coercion.[18] The capabilities provided to regional partners complement rather than substitute for alliance relationships with the United States and Australia, creating interlocking networks of maritime security cooperation.

Japan's December 2023 memorandum of understanding with the Philippines on maritime domain awareness—the first such agreement between Japan and a Southeast Asian country—establishes precedents for intelligence sharing and coordinated responses to maritime threats.[19] Similar agreements with other regional partners could create a distributed network for monitoring Chinese activities, including around Okinotorishima.

Western Pacific Naval Symposium: Professional Military Diplomacy

The Western Pacific Naval Symposium (WPNS) provides a valuable if often overlooked forum for regional naval cooperation that includes both China and Japan as members. The 19th WPNS, hosted by China in Qingdao in April 2024, brought together representatives from 29 navies to discuss maritime security challenges and operational cooperation.[20]

The WPNS has developed practical mechanisms for managing naval encounters, most notably the Code for Unplanned Encounters at Sea (CUES), which provides standardized procedures for preventing incidents when naval vessels operate in proximity.[21] While CUES cannot resolve territorial disputes, it offers frameworks for managing tensions and preventing escalation during incidents like the Okinotorishima confrontations.

Japan's active participation in WPNS alongside the United States, Australia, and other key partners demonstrates the complex diplomatic balancing required in regional maritime security. The symposium's consensus-based approach means that even China participates in discussions about maritime cooperation and incident prevention. For issues like Okinotorishima, WPNS provides forums for informal dialogue and confidence-building measures that could prove valuable for crisis management.

The symposium's evolution reflects broader changes in regional security dynamics. Originally established during the Cold War for professional naval cooperation, WPNS has adapted to address contemporary challenges including territorial disputes, freedom of navigation, and maritime domain awareness.[22] The forum's ability to maintain Chinese participation while addressing these sensitive issues demonstrates the value of professional military diplomacy in managing regional tensions.

Trilateral Partnerships: Japan-Philippines-Australia Cooperation

The emergence of Japan-Philippines-Australia trilateral cooperation represents an increasingly important element of regional maritime security architecture. This partnership builds on existing bilateral relationships while creating new frameworks for addressing shared challenges in the South China Sea and broader Indo-Pacific region.

The December 2023 establishment of an Indomalphi trilateral coast guard partnership between Indonesia, Malaysia, and the Philippines has created opportunities for expanded cooperation with Japan.[23] As one analysis suggested, "Japan should board the Indomalphi ship" by institutionalizing quadrilateral activities between the three Southeast Asian coast guards and the Japan Coast Guard.[24] Such arrangements would create practical frameworks for maritime law enforcement cooperation while strengthening political relationships.

Australia's role as a bridge between the United States and regional partners adds particular value to trilateral arrangements. The November 2024 Australia-Japan-United States Trilateral Defense Ministers' Meeting in Darwin demonstrated how these partnerships can create "habits of cooperation" that extend beyond specific bilateral relationships.[25] The meeting's commitment to "enhancing Australia-Japan-India-United States maritime domain awareness in the Indo-Pacific from 2025" illustrates how trilateral partnerships can evolve into broader multilateral frameworks.[26]

For Japan, these trilateral partnerships provide alternatives to purely bilateral cooperation with the United States while maintaining alliance integration. The partnerships create diplomatic flexibility for addressing regional challenges, including potential escalation around Okinotorishima, without forcing partners to choose between Washington and Beijing.

Pacific Island Perspectives and Concerns

Pacific Island nations occupy a unique position in debates over maritime claims like Okinotorishima, possessing both technical expertise in maritime law and direct stakes in how UNCLOS Article 121 is interpreted. Many

Pacific Island nations face similar challenges regarding the sustainability of small islands and atolls in the face of climate change and sea level rise.

The regular Pacific Islands Leaders' Meeting (PALM) provides Japan with a forum for engaging Pacific Island perspectives on maritime issues.[27] The 10th PALM, held in 2024, addressed climate change, maritime security, and sustainable development—all issues where Japan's experience with Okinotorishima could be relevant. Japan's massive investment in preserving and maintaining the atoll through engineering solutions could provide models for other nations facing similar challenges.

However, Pacific Island nations have also expressed concerns about the precedent that Japan's Okinotorishima claims might establish. If tiny concrete-encased rocks can generate vast EEZs, similar claims might proliferate throughout the Pacific, creating conflicts over maritime boundaries and resource access. The legal uncertainty surrounding Okinotorishima's status under Article 121(3) affects interpretations of similar features throughout the region.

Japan's development assistance and capacity building programs in the Pacific provide opportunities to address these concerns while building support for its position. The Nippon Foundation's coral restoration research and Japan's expertise in marine engineering could benefit other Pacific nations facing environmental challenges.[28] By framing Okinotorishima preservation as environmental protection and scientific research, Japan can build coalitions supporting its approach.

The Taiwan Factor: Strategic Triangulation

The complex relationship between Taiwan, Japan, and the broader alliance framework adds another dimension to Okinotorishima's strategic significance. Taiwan's own South China Sea claims, including around Itu Aba (Taiping Island), create potential contradictions with its criticism of Japan's Okinotorishima EEZ assertion.[29]

The April 2016 arrest of Taiwanese fishermen near Okinotorishima prompted a brief crisis that demonstrated these tensions. However, the subsequent establishment of bilateral maritime dialogue mechanisms under President Tsai Ing-wen showed how shared concerns about Chinese expansion could override specific territorial disagreements.[30] Taiwan's strategic vulnerability creates incentives for cooperation with Japan despite legal disagreements over Okinotorishima's status.

From an American alliance perspective, Taiwan's geographic position between China and Okinotorishima adds strategic value to Japanese claims. Control of Okinotorishima's claimed EEZ provides additional options for U.S. naval operations in potential Taiwan conflict scenarios, complementing existing bases in Japan and Guam. The strategic triangle formed by Taiwan, Okinotorishima, and Guam creates multiple axes for American force projection and coalition operations.

The evolution of Taiwan-Japan cooperation on maritime issues, including joint responses to Chinese assertiveness, suggests that territorial disagreements need not prevent broader strategic cooperation. The precedent established in Taiwan-Japan dialogue mechanisms could provide models for addressing other regional maritime disputes within the alliance framework.

Future Alliance Architecture: Institutional Innovation

The alliance networks surrounding Okinotorishima reflect broader trends toward institutional innovation in Indo-Pacific security cooperation. Traditional bilateral alliance structures are being supplemented by trilateral partnerships, quadrilateral dialogues, and multilateral frameworks that create more flexible and resilient security architectures.

The proposed formalization of the Quad through the "Strengthening the Quad Act" in the U.S. Congress illustrates how these informal partnerships might evolve into more structured institutions.[31] While such formalization remains uncertain, the trend toward institutionalizing multilateral cooperation creates frameworks that could address future challenges around Okinotorishima and similar disputes.

Japan's emergence as a hub for multiple overlapping partnerships—bilateral alliances with the United States and Australia, trilateral cooperation with various combinations of partners, and multilateral participation in the Quad and WPNS—positions Tokyo at the center of evolving regional security architecture. Okinotorishima, as Japan's southernmost territory and most legally controversial maritime claim, becomes a test case for how these partnerships can manage complex sovereignty and maritime law issues.

The integration of economic and security considerations within these partnerships also provides new tools for addressing maritime disputes. Japan's official development assistance, infrastructure investment, and technology transfer create positive-sum opportunities for cooperation that could help manage tensions over territorial claims while building broader strategic partnerships.

Conclusion: From Bilateral Dispute to Multilateral Test Case

The May 2025 confrontation over Chinese research activities near Okinotorishima illuminated how a seemingly bilateral dispute has become embedded within broader alliance relationships and strategic competition in the Indo-Pacific. Japan's ability to maintain its EEZ claims around the tiny atoll depends not simply on legal arguments about UNCLOS interpretation but on the broader political and strategic support provided by alliance partners and regional institutions.

The strategic silence from Washington regarding Japan's claims, combined with vigorous American challenges to Chinese maritime assertions, reflects calculated alliance management rather than legal consistency. This asymmetric approach serves broader strategic objectives within the U.S.-Japan alliance while contributing to multilateral efforts to maintain maritime access and prevent Chinese hegemony in the Western Pacific.

The evolution of alliance networks around maritime security—from traditional bilateral relationships through trilateral partnerships to multilateral frameworks like the Quad—provides Japan with multiple diplomatic tools for defending its Okinotorishima claims. These partnerships create political costs for challenging Japan's position while providing practical capabilities for monitoring and responding to Chinese activities.

However, the same alliance relationships that support Japan's current position also create vulnerabilities. Changes in American strategic priorities, tensions within multilateral partnerships, or successful Chinese efforts to divide alliance partners could weaken support for Japan's claims. The institutionalization of alliance cooperation through frameworks like FOIP and the Quad provides some protection against such shifts, but cannot eliminate the fundamentally political nature of support for contested territorial claims.

The Okinotorishima case demonstrates how contemporary maritime disputes cannot be understood simply through legal analysis of international law, but must be examined within the broader context of alliance relationships, strategic competition, and institutional development. As the Indo-Pacific region continues to evolve toward more complex and multilateral security architecture, the precedents established around Okinotorishima will influence how future maritime disputes are managed and resolved.

The tiny atoll's outsized importance reflects the reality that in an era of great power competition, even the smallest territories can become crucial assets when embedded within broader alliance networks and strategic frameworks. Japan's success in transforming Okinotorishima from a legal liability into a strategic asset illustrates the power of alliance relationships to reshape the political context within which international law operates, while pointing toward future challenges as regional partnerships continue to evolve.

Notes

[1] "Japan's EEZ claim based on Okinotori Reef violates intl law; has no right to interfere in Chinese research ship's operation: Chinese FM," *Global Times*, May 28, 2025, https://www.globaltimes.cn/page/202505/1334930.shtml.

[2] Maria T. Reyes, "Freedom of the Seas," *Indo-Pacific Defense Forum*, June 11, 2024, https://ipdefenseforum.com/2024/05/freedom-of-the-seas/.

[3] Mark Esper, "Freedom of Navigation Operations in Asia Are Too Much Risk for Too Little Gain," *Foreign Policy*, April 6, 2021,

https://foreignpolicy.com/2021/04/06/freedom-of-navigation-operation-china-us-maritime-law/.

[4] "Why Doesn't the U.S. Challenge Japan's EEZ Claim on Okinotorishima?" *China US Focus*, accessed August 8, 2025, https://www.chinausfocus.com/peace-security/why-doesnt-the-u-s-challenge-japans-eez-claim-on-okinotorishima.

[5] "Okinotorishima," Wikipedia, accessed August 8, 2025, https://en.wikipedia.org/wiki/Okinotorishima.

[6] "Feature-challenge Freedom of Navigation Operations and the Major Agendas of U.S. Policy toward China," *South China Sea Strategic Situation Probing Initiative*, June 26, 2023, https://www.scspi.org/en/dtfx/feature-challenge-freedom-navigation-operations-and-major-agendas-us-policy-toward-china.

[7] "Free and Open Indo-Pacific," Wikipedia, accessed August 8, 2025, https://en.wikipedia.org/wiki/Free_and_Open_Indo-Pacific.

[8] "What is Japan's Free and Open Indo-Pacific (FOIP) strategy?" *Japan Up Close*, accessed August 8, 2025, https://japanupclose.web-japan.org/policy/p20230825_1.html.

[9] "Japan's Strategic Interests in the Global South: Indo-Pacific Strategy," *Center for Strategic and International Studies*, September 25, 2024, https://www.csis.org/analysis/japans-strategic-interests-global-south-indo-pacific-strategy.

[10] "Two Years Later, What Has the Indo-Pacific Strategy Achieved?" *United States Institute of Peace*, March 14, 2024, https://www.usip.org/publications/2024/02/two-years-later-what-has-indo-pacific-strategy-achieved.

[11] "Fact Sheet: 2024 Quad Leaders' Summit," U.S. Embassy & Consulates in India, September 23, 2024, https://in.usembassy.gov/fact-sheet-2024-quad-leaders-summit/.

[12] "The Quad's growing focus on maritime security," *East Asia Forum*, February 28, 2024, https://eastasiaforum.org/2024/02/28/the-quads-growing-focus-on-maritime-security/.

[13] "Fact Sheet: 2024 Quad Leaders' Summit."

[14] "Will the 'Strengthening the Quad Act' Work?" *Center for Strategic and International Studies*, October 15, 2024, https://www.csis.org/analysis/will-strengthening-quad-act-work.

[15] "Quadrilateral Security Dialogue," Wikipedia, accessed August 8, 2025, https://en.wikipedia.org/wiki/Quadrilateral_Security_Dialogue.

[16] "Philippines and Japan Finalize Largest Coast Guard Project to Date," *Naval News*, May 17, 2024, https://www.navalnews.com/naval-news/2024/05/philippines-and-japan-finalize-largest-coast-guard-project-to-date/.

[17] "Southeast Asia: A New Strategic Nexus for Japan's Maritime Strategy," *Center for International Maritime Security*, accessed August 8, 2025, https://cimsec.org/southeast-asia-a-new-strategic-nexus-for-japans-maritime-strategy/.

[18] "An Integrated Approach to US-Japan Cooperation with Southeast Asia," *Hudson Institute*, accessed August 8, 2025, https://www.hudson.org/events/integrated-approach-us-japan-cooperation-southeast-asia.

[19] "Japan should board the Indomalphi ship," *East Asia Forum*, October 2, 2024, https://eastasiaforum.org/2024/10/02/japan-should-board-the-indomalphi-ship/.

[20] "China hosts 19th Western Pacific Naval Symposium," Xinhua, April 22, 2024, http://english.scio.gov.cn/chinavoices/2024-04/22/content_117141153.htm.

[21] "Semaphore: The Western Pacific Naval Symposium," *Royal Australian Navy*, accessed August 8, 2025, https://www.navy.gov.au/media-room/publications/semaphore-14-06.

[22] "19th Western Pacific Naval Symposium," *Nepal Institute for International Cooperation and Engagement*, May 8, 2024, https://niice.org.np/archives/9092.

[23] "Japan should board the Indomalphi ship."

[24] Ibid.

[25] "Australia-Japan-United States Trilateral Defence Ministers' Meeting November 2024 Joint Statement," *Defence Ministers*, November 17, 2024, https://www.minister.defence.gov.au/statements/2024-11-17/australia-japan-united-states-trilateral-defence-ministers-meeting-november-2024-joint-statement.

[26] Ibid.

[27] "The importance of Pacific Islands nations for Japan," *Foundation for Strategic Research*, accessed August 8, 2025, https://www.frstrategie.org/en/programs/japan-program/importance-pacific-islands-nations-japan-2024.

[28] See documents regarding Japan's coral restoration research and marine engineering capabilities.

[29] "Okinotori: A New Beginning for Taiwan-Japan Maritime Dialogue," *Asia Maritime Transparency Initiative*, October 11, 2016, https://amti.csis.org/okinotori-new-beginning-taiwan-japan-maritime-dialogue/.

[30] Ibid.

[31] "Will the 'Strengthening the Quad Act' Work?"

Chapter 12: The Science Wars

"We can envision a time when Chinese and Japanese research vessels silently circle each other in these waters, each deploying increasingly sophisticated sensors in a technological arms race that blurs the line between scientific inquiry and military intelligence." — Maritime security analyst, 2025

On the evening of May 26, 2025, the gleaming white hull of the Chinese research vessel R/V Tan Kah Kee cut through the Pacific swells 167 miles east of Okinotorishima, its crew methodically deploying what appeared to be a wire-like instrument into the dark waters below.[1] Above, the distinctive twin rotors of a Japanese Coast Guard patrol aircraft circled in the twilight, its crew issuing urgent radio warnings to cease operations in what Japan claimed as its exclusive economic zone. The confrontation would last five hours—a microcosm of how oceanographic research has been weaponized in the 21st century's great power competition.

This was no chance encounter between curious scientists and overzealous coast guards. It represented the latest chapter in what defense analysts have dubbed "the science wars"—the systematic militarization of marine research that has transformed seemingly innocent scientific vessels into sophisticated intelligence-gathering platforms capable of reshaping the underwater battlefields of tomorrow. In these waters surrounding Japan's most remote territory, the line between peaceful research and military reconnaissance has become so blurred as to be practically meaningless.

The Dual-Use Revolution

The transformation of civilian research vessels into instruments of statecraft represents one of the most significant developments in modern maritime competition. China has developed what the Center for Strategic and International Studies calls "the world's largest fleet of civilian research vessels," with over 64 active research and survey ships that have conducted "hundreds of thousands of hours of operations globally over the past four years."[2] Of these vessels, over 80 percent are suspected of having organizational ties to China's military or engage in activities that serve strategic objectives.[3]

The R/V Tan Kah Kee itself exemplifies this dual-use approach. Operated by Marine Operations at Xiamen University, the vessel ostensibly conducts legitimate oceanographic research.[4] Yet its May 2025 deployment near Okinotorishima follows a pattern of Chinese research activities that consistently target waters of strategic military importance. The vessel's timing and location were far from coincidental—the area lies precisely along potential submarine transit routes between China's southern naval bases and the open Pacific, making detailed oceanographic data invaluable for both submarine operations and anti-submarine warfare planning.

Chinese officials have been remarkably frank about these dual purposes. During the commissioning of the research vessel Shiyan 06, officials announced that the vessel would "bolster scientific and technological support for national security."[5] The People's Liberation Army Navy Submarine Academy openly collaborates with China's major maritime research institutions, with the prestigious Qingdao National Laboratory for Marine Science and Technology located strategically near the submarine academy's main campus.[6]

This integration reflects China's "Military-Civil Fusion" policy, which systematically integrates civilian scientific research into military strategies. As one intelligence analysis noted, "China's exploitation of international maritime law, specifically the United Nations Convention on the Law of the Sea (UNCLOS)" allows dual-use vessels to operate relatively unhindered by leveraging "Article 246, permitting marine scientific research in EEZs without prior explicit consent."[7]

Japan's Watchful Eyes

Faced with this systematic challenge to its territorial claims and security interests, Japan has developed increasingly sophisticated monitoring capabilities around Okinotorishima. The transformation of two tiny concrete-encased rocks into a high-tech surveillance outpost represents one of the most ambitious remote monitoring projects ever undertaken.

In 2005, Tokyo Governor Shintaro Ishihara ordered the installation of a 330 million yen (approximately $3 million) radar system for round-the-clock surveillance at Okinotorishima.[8] This radar installation marked the beginning of Japan's effort to create persistent domain awareness around its most remote territory. The system was designed specifically to detect vessels approaching the atoll and provide real-time alerts to Coast Guard patrol vessels and aircraft.

The 2007 installation of a lighthouse by the Japan Coast Guard further enhanced monitoring capabilities. This solar-powered beacon serves multiple functions beyond navigation—it houses sophisticated sensors and communications equipment that enable continuous surveillance of the surrounding waters.[9] The facility operates as part of what the Maritime Bureau of the Ministry of Land, Infrastructure, Transport and Tourism describes as an "EEZ observation post," equipped with "radar and various other sensors to help monitor activity in the zone."[10]

Japan's surveillance capabilities extend far beyond the fixed installations at Okinotorishima itself. The Japan Coast Guard has increasingly embraced advanced technologies for maritime domain awareness. In 2021, the Coast Guard successfully flight-tested Raytheon's SeaVue XMC radar and AN/DAS-4 Multi-spectral Targeting System aboard General Atomics' SeaGuardian remotely piloted aircraft.[11] These systems provide "enhanced wide-area surveillance by identifying targets of interest rapidly and efficiently, such as small maritime vessels" and offer "next-generation electro-optical surveillance in high-definition and full-motion video."[12]

The Coast Guard's procurement of two additional SeaGuardian drones in 2024, with delivery in 2025, significantly expands Japan's persistent surveillance capabilities.[13] These platforms can fly for over 24 hours nonstop in all weather conditions, providing continuous maritime surveillance over vast ocean areas that would be impossible to patrol with conventional aircraft or surface vessels.

Japan's monitoring network extends underwater as well. The Japan Maritime Self-Defense Force operates "at least fourteen listening stations all over the country that have ELINT and marine surveillance radar warning systems."[14] While the specific locations and capabilities of these underwater sensors remain classified, their existence demonstrates Japan's commitment to comprehensive domain awareness in its surrounding waters.

The Technology Race

The competition between Chinese research capabilities and Japanese surveillance systems has sparked a technological arms race that is pushing the boundaries of maritime sensing and intelligence gathering. This race encompasses everything from autonomous underwater vehicles to quantum sensors, each offering new advantages in the underwater domain.

China's latest generation of research vessels showcases remarkable technological sophistication. The Zhu Hai Yun, delivered in 2023, represents a quantum leap in autonomous research capabilities. Designed to serve as a "mothership" for over 50 unmanned air, surface, and undersea vehicles, the vessel can simultaneously survey "a three-dimensional area spanning 160 kilometers across, 4,000 meters above, and 1,500 meters below the ocean's surface."[15] The ship's autonomous systems can operate in what Chinese manufacturers describe as an "unmanned ship swarm," acting as a force multiplier for survey operations.

The vessel's November 2023 voyage around Taiwan demonstrated these capabilities in action. Unlike typical research missions, the Zhu Hai Yun's route was "unique and carefully calculated," suggesting activities that went "beyond a standard research mission."[16] The vessel's ability to deploy and coordinate multiple autonomous platforms while operating with minimal human intervention represents a significant advancement in persistent surveillance capabilities.

Japan has responded with its own technological innovations, particularly in autonomous underwater vehicles (AUVs). The Japan Agency for Marine-Earth Science and Technology (JAMSTEC) has pioneered advanced AUV platforms capable of deep-sea operations. These systems can dive to depths of 6,000 meters or more, providing detailed seafloor mapping and water column analysis that would be impossible with surface vessels alone.[17]

The integration of artificial intelligence into these systems represents another frontier in the technology race. Japan's Maritime Self-Defense Force is exploring AI-powered threat analysis systems that can process sonar and sensor data to predict enemy maneuvers and enhance situational awareness.[18] These systems promise to transform vast amounts of oceanographic data into actionable intelligence in real-time.

Quantum Sensing: The Next Frontier

Perhaps the most revolutionary development in maritime surveillance technology involves quantum sensors, which promise to dramatically enhance detection capabilities while operating in ways that are virtually impossible to detect or defeat. China has taken an early lead in developing and deploying these advanced systems.

In April 2025, Chinese researchers published results from testing a drone-mounted quantum sensor designed specifically for submarine detection. The system uses a Coherent Population Trapping (CPT) atomic magnetometer that leverages quantum interference effects in rubidium atoms to detect the subtle magnetic disturbances created by submarine hulls and engines.[19] Importantly, this quantum sensor can operate effectively in low-latitude regions like the South China Sea, where Earth's magnetic field runs nearly parallel to the surface—precisely the conditions that create blind zones for conventional magnetic anomaly detectors.

The implications of quantum sensing technology extend far beyond submarine detection. Quantum gravity sensors, which can detect minute changes in gravitational fields, offer revolutionary capabilities for underwater navigation and object detection. As one analysis noted, these sensors enable "autonomous vehicles that can 'see' around corners, underwater navigation systems, early-warning systems for volcanic activity and earthquakes, and portable scanners that monitor a person's brain activity during daily life."[20]

France has developed operational quantum gravity sensors for submarine navigation, with the atomic gravimeter created by Zhejiang University of Technology offering "a significant leap in measurement precision" that could prevent incidents like "the 2021 crash of the USS Connecticut into a seamount in the South China Sea by detecting underwater mountains or other submarines without using sonar."[21]

The Intelligence Value of Ocean Data

The systematic collection of oceanographic data represents one of the most valuable yet underappreciated aspects of modern maritime competition. Water temperature, salinity, current patterns, and seafloor topography all directly affect submarine operations, making detailed environmental data crucial for both conducting and defending against underwater warfare.

Submarines must understand complex undersea conditions for effective navigation and concealment. As one analysis noted, "the PLA requires in-depth knowledge of complex undersea conditions for submarine navigation" and has "emphasized the need for advanced deep-sea technologies, an area where it has historically lagged behind the U.S. military."[22] Data from China's civilian research fleet, equipped with sophisticated measuring tools, helps bridge these gaps in the PLA Navy's undersea warfare capabilities.

The strategic importance of this data collection explains why Chinese research vessels repeatedly operate in waters surrounding Okinotorishima despite diplomatic protests. The area's location "halfway between Taiwan and Guam" makes it a critical choke point for U.S. naval operations, while the surrounding deep waters provide ideal conditions for submarine transit.[23] Detailed mapping of ocean currents, thermal layers, and acoustic conditions could provide Chinese submarines with significant advantages in a future conflict.

Australian defense officials reportedly described an early 2020 survey by China's Xiang Yang Hong 01 near Christmas Island as intended to study "the routes of Australian submarines traveling to and from the South China Sea."[24] Such intelligence gathering activities demonstrate how civilian research vessels serve military reconnaissance functions while maintaining plausible deniability as peaceful scientific activities.

Autonomous Systems and Persistent Presence

The future of maritime surveillance increasingly depends on autonomous systems capable of maintaining persistent presence without human intervention. Both China and Japan are investing heavily in these technologies, which promise to revolutionize underwater domain awareness.

China's advancement in unmanned underwater vehicles represents a significant strategic development. The country has developed autonomous systems ranging "from man portable lightweight AUVs to large diameter vehicles of over 10 metres length."[25] These platforms can operate independently for extended periods, conducting detailed surveys while reducing the risk of international incidents that might occur with crewed vessels.

Modern AUVs can "dive up to 14,000 feet below the ocean's surface while collecting data from the sea floor" and are designed for "defense, commercial and scientific customers worldwide."[26] Their ability to operate autonomously makes them ideal for long-term monitoring missions in disputed waters, where persistent surveillance would be politically sensitive if conducted by crewed vessels.

Japan has responded by developing its own advanced autonomous capabilities. The Japan Maritime Self-Defense Force is building "smarter UUVs for the naval missions of the future," including systems that can connect with other vessels using command and control systems and integrate the latest commercial technology, including advanced sonar systems.[27]

The integration of these autonomous systems into broader surveillance networks represents the next evolution in maritime domain awareness. Future systems will likely combine surface vessels, underwater platforms, airborne sensors, and satellite surveillance into comprehensive networks capable of tracking all underwater activity across vast ocean areas.

Cyber Warfare in the Deep

The increasing reliance on sophisticated electronic systems for maritime surveillance has created new vulnerabilities that adversaries are eager to exploit. Cybersecurity has become a critical concern for all maritime surveillance systems, from the sensors installed at Okinotorishima to the networks that process and analyze collected data.

A 2025 U.S. Government Accountability Office report highlighted how "threat actors may become even more capable—particularly with advances in artificial intelligence," noting that AI will enable "malware to mutate into thousands of different forms, find vulnerabilities, and attack selectively."[28] The expanding application of AI cyber capabilities will make cyberattacks "more precise and tailored, further accelerate and automate cyber warfare, enable stealthier and more persistent cyber weapons, and make cyber campaigns more effective on a larger scale."[29]

Maritime systems are particularly vulnerable because they often combine enterprise IT systems, operational technology (OT) systems, and GPS in complex, interconnected networks. These systems' complexity and their connections to the internet create multiple attack vectors that malicious actors can exploit.[30]

The maritime industry has already experienced significant cyber incidents that demonstrate these vulnerabilities. In July 2019, an attack on a U.S. vessel caused critical credential mining, with the Coast Guard and FBI reporting that "the lack of security strategies on the vessel was the main reason for enabling such an attack."[31] More dramatically, the June 2017 Petya ransomware attack affected Maersk shipping company services, targeting 17 terminals and inflicting damages exceeding $200 million.[32]

Japan and the United States have recognized these threats and are actively cooperating to address them. In August 2024, the Department of Homeland Security and the Government of Japan conducted a successful tabletop exercise focused on "enhancing maritime cybersecurity and incident response capabilities."[33] This cooperation reflects growing awareness that maritime surveillance systems are only as secure as their weakest cyber vulnerabilities.

Electronic Warfare and Signal Intelligence

The electromagnetic spectrum has become another battlefield in the science wars, with sophisticated electronic warfare capabilities increasingly integrated into research vessels and surveillance systems. Modern maritime platforms must not only collect signals intelligence but also protect their own communications and sensors from electronic attack.

Electronic warfare "represents the ability to use the electromagnetic spectrum—signals such as radio, infrared or radar—to sense, protect, and communicate" while simultaneously denying "adversaries the ability to either disrupt or use these signals."[34] This dual capability has become essential for maritime surveillance operations, where the ability to intercept adversary communications while protecting one's own systems can determine the success or failure of intelligence gathering missions.

Japanese maritime surveillance systems incorporate significant electronic warfare capabilities. The Japan Maritime Self-Defense Force operates multiple ELINT (electronic intelligence) stations that monitor electromagnetic signals across Japan's maritime approaches.[35] These stations provide early warning of approaching vessels and aircraft while collecting valuable intelligence on foreign military capabilities and intentions.

Chinese research vessels likewise carry sophisticated electronic systems capable of both passive signal collection and active electronic warfare. The integration of these capabilities with ostensibly civilian research platforms creates legal and diplomatic complications, as nations must distinguish between legitimate scientific activities and military intelligence gathering.

The Future Battlefield

The convergence of quantum sensing, artificial intelligence, autonomous systems, and cyber warfare capabilities is creating a new paradigm for maritime competition. The "science wars" around Okinotorishima provide a preview of how future conflicts may unfold—not through dramatic naval battles, but through persistent technological competition for information dominance.

Future underwater surveillance networks will likely integrate quantum sensors for unprecedented detection capabilities, AI systems for real-time analysis of vast data streams, autonomous platforms for persistent presence, and cyber warfare capabilities for both protection and disruption of adversary systems. The nation that masters this integration first will gain significant advantages in underwater domain awareness.

China's systematic approach to dual-use research vessel development demonstrates how civilian capabilities can serve military objectives while remaining below the threshold of direct confrontation. Japan's response—building sophisticated surveillance networks around its remote territories—shows how defensive strategies must adapt to these new realities.

The scientific research vessels that circle Okinotorishima today are harbingers of tomorrow's maritime competition. In these waters, the boundaries between peaceful research and military reconnaissance have already dissolved, replaced by a continuous technological struggle for underwater domain awareness. The nation that wins this science war will shape the balance of power in the world's oceans for decades to come.

Notes

[1] "Photos Show Chinese Ship Detected in Waters Claimed by US Ally," *Newsweek*, May 28, 2025, https://www.newsweek.com/japan-china-news-research-ship-exclusive-economic-zone-pacific-ocean-2077774.

[2] "Surveying the Seas: China's Dual-Use Research Operations in the Indian Ocean," Center for Strategic and International Studies, https://features.csis.org/hiddenreach/china-indian-ocean-research-vessels/.

[3] "The Secret Spy Ship Supporting China's Submarine Warfare," *Newsweek*, January 11, 2024, https://www.newsweek.com/china-submarine-indian-ocean-csis-warfare-yuan-wang-research-1859797.

[4] "Japan says China conducted research near Pacific atoll," *The Japan Times*, May 27, 2025, https://www.japantimes.co.jp/news/2025/05/27/japan/china-eez-research/.

[5] "The Secret Spy Ship Supporting China's Submarine Warfare," *Newsweek*.

[6] "Surveying the Seas: China's Dual-Use Research Operations in the Indian Ocean," CSIS.

[7] "Hydrographic Trojan Horses: China's Oceanic Research Fleet Is A Maritime Spy Network In Disguise – Analysis," *Eurasia Review*, April 21, 2025, https://www.eurasiareview.com/22042025-hydrographic-trojan-horses-chinas-oceanic-research-fleet-is-a-maritime-spy-network-in-disguise-analysis/.

[8] "The US-Japan-China Mistrust Spiral and Okinotorishima," *The Asia-Pacific Journal: Japan Focus*, November 3, 2023, https://apjjf.org/Yukie-YOSHIKAWA/2541/article.

[9] "Okinotorishima Lighthouse - Maritime beacon in Ogasawara Village, Japan," Around Us, https://aroundus.com/p/11772005-okinotorishima-lighthouse.

[10] "Okinotorishima," Wikipedia, accessed August 8, 2025, https://en.wikipedia.org/wiki/Okinotorishima.

[11] "Raytheon Intelligence and Space Maritime Surveillance Systems Flight Tested on GA-ASI SeaGuardian for Japan Coast Guard," General Atomics, January 21, 2021, https://www.ga.com/raytheon-intelligence-and-space-maritime-surveillance-systems-flight-tested-on-ga-asi-seaguardian-for-japan-coast-guard.

[12] Ibid.

[13] "Japan Coast Guard Procures Two SeaGuardian Drones," *The Defense Post*, August 19, 2024, https://thedefensepost.com/2024/08/19/japan-coast-guard-seaguardian/.

[14] "Japan Maritime Self-Defense Force," Wikipedia, accessed August 8, 2025, https://en.wikipedia.org/wiki/Japan_Maritime_Self-Defense_Force.

[15] "Skirting the Shores: China's New High-Tech Research Ship Probes the Waters around Taiwan," Center for Strategic and International Studies, https://features.csis.org/snapshots/china-research-vessel-taiwan/.

[16] Ibid.

[17] "Review of Underwater Sensing Technologies and Applications," PMC, https://pmc.ncbi.nlm.nih.gov/articles/PMC8659509/.

[18] "Underwater domain awareness (UDA): Technologies to monitor underwater," ClearIAS, February 23, 2025, https://www.clearias.com/underwater-domain-awareness/.

[19] "China Tests Drone-Mounted Quantum Sensor That Could Reshape Submarine Detection," *The Quantum Insider*, April 27, 2025, https://thequantuminsider.com/2025/04/27/china-tests-drone-mounted-quantum-sensor-that-could-reshape-submarine-detection/.

[20] "Militaries thrust on Quantum Sensors including Quantum Magnetometers for submarine detection and Navigation in GPS denied environments," International Defense Security & Technology,

https://idstch.com/geopolitics/militaries-employing-quantum-sensors-including-quantum-magnetometers-for-submarine-detection-and-navigation-in-gps-denied-environments/.

[21] "Quantum Gravity and Gradiometer Sensors: Revolutionizing Maritime Navigation, Subsurface Detection, and Stealth Tracking," International Defense Security & Technology, March 23, 2025, https://idstch.com/technology/quantum/quantum-gravity-and-gradiometer-sensors-revolutionizing-maritime-navigation-subsurface-detection-and-stealth-tracking/.

[22] "The Secret Spy Ship Supporting China's Submarine Warfare," *Newsweek*.

[23] "China's Navy, the West Pacific and the Role of Okinotorishima," *The Diplomat*, January 30, 2023, https://thediplomat.com/2023/01/chinas-navy-the-west-pacific-and-the-role-of-okinotorishima/.

[24] "A Survey of Marine Research Vessels in the Indo-Pacific," Asia Maritime Transparency Initiative, April 16, 2020, https://amti.csis.org/a-survey-of-marine-research-vessels-in-the-indo-pacific/.

[25] "Autonomous underwater vehicle (AUV) technologies for surveillance, and anti-submarine warfare missions," International Defense Security & Technology, September 26, 2021, https://idstch.com/military/navy/autonomous-underwater-vehicle-auv-technologies-for-surveillance-and-anti-submarine-warfare-missions/.

[26] "Unmanned Underwater Vehicles (UUVs)," General Dynamics Mission Systems, https://gdmissionsystems.com/underwater-vehicles.

[27] Ibid.

[28] "COAST GUARD: Additional Efforts Needed to Address Cybersecurity Risks to the Maritime Transportation System," U.S. Government Accountability Office, GAO-25-107244, February 11, 2025, https://files.gao.gov/reports/GAO-25-107244/index.html.

[29] Ibid.

[30] Ibid.

[31] "Cyber Security in the Maritime Industry: A Systematic Survey of Recent Advances and Future Trends," *Information*, January 6, 2022, https://www.mdpi.com/2078-2489/13/1/22.

[32] Ibid.

[33] "DHS Partners with Japanese Counterparts to Strengthen Maritime Cybersecurity Cooperation," U.S. Department of Homeland Security, August 30, 2024, https://www.dhs.gov/archive/news/2024/08/30/dhs-partners-japanese-counterparts-strengthen-maritime-cybersecurity-cooperation.

[34] "Maritime Systems," Lockheed Martin, https://www.lockheedmartin.com/en-us/capabilities/maritime-systems.html.

[35] "Japan Maritime Self-Defense Force," Wikipedia.

PART V: ENVIRONMENTAL AND TECHNOLOGICAL FRONTIERS

Chapter 13: Coral Diplomacy

The sun rises over the Kumejima Deep Sea Water Research Center in Okinawa, where scientists wearing protective gear move carefully between rows of blue circular tanks. Inside each container, tiny coral polyps—no larger than rice grains—represent Japan's most ambitious experiment in biological sovereignty. These microscopic organisms, cultivated 1,700 kilometers from their intended destination, carry the weight of a nation's territorial aspirations on their calcified shoulders.

In the sterile confines of the greenhouse laboratory, senior researcher Ryota Nakamura gestures toward a tub containing lustrous Acropora tenuis specimens. "This is the first step in our plan for Okinotorishima," he explains to a visiting reporter, his words carrying the weight of Japan's $600 million investment in the world's most remote territorial claim.[1] The coral fragments in his care represent far more than marine biology—they embody a radical new approach to sovereignty in the twenty-first century, where environmental engineering meets geopolitical strategy in an unprecedented fusion of science and statecraft.

Engineering Ecosystem Sovereignty

Japan's coral preservation efforts at Okinotorishima represent perhaps the most sophisticated attempt in history to use biological processes as instruments of territorial control. The program, officially launched in 2006 under the auspices of the Fisheries Agency and supported by the Nippon Foundation, transforms traditional notions of what constitutes legitimate territorial preservation.[2] Since its inception, scientists have transplanted approximately 100,000 juvenile coral colonies back to Okinotorishima's natural reef, creating what amounts to a living, breathing extension of Japanese sovereignty.[3]

The scientific methodology reveals the intersection of cutting-edge marine biology with geopolitical necessity. Each year, research vessels make the perilous 2.5-day journey from Okinawa to Okinotorishima, transporting adult coral colonies in specially designed fiberglass tanks with transparent acrylic lids.[4] The operation requires precise environmental control: one-third of the seawater must be replenished three times daily, shade nets regulate light intensity, submersible pumps create water flow, and temperatures remain between 22.5°C and 28.4°C.[5] This level of technological sophistication transforms coral cultivation from academic research into strategic infrastructure.

The breeding process itself represents a marvel of applied marine science. During summer months, adult corals release buoyant bundles containing eggs and sperm in what researchers describe as resembling "a spectacular snowstorm underwater."[6] Scientists separate genetic material from different colonies to maximize diversity, ensuring the resulting larvae possess the genetic robustness necessary to survive Okinotorishima's harsh environment. After cultivation on ceramic substrates for approximately one year, juveniles are transplanted first to artificial reefs near the island, then to the natural reef once they reach two years of age.[7]

Beyond traditional coral propagation, Japan has pioneered even more ambitious biological engineering. The Nippon Foundation's research includes cultivating foraminifera—microscopic organisms whose shells accumulate to form sand and eventually land mass.[8] This process, while requiring decades to centuries for meaningful results, represents an entirely novel approach to territory creation that could, theoretically, expand Okinotorishima's physical footprint through purely biological means.[9] Professor Hajime Kayanne of the University of Tokyo, chair of the evaluation committee for coral seedling production technology, emphasizes the long-term vision: "We're pursuing research using a new ecological engineering technology" to prevent submersion through natural coral foundation building.[10]

Climate Change as Existential Threat

The urgency driving Japan's coral diplomacy becomes starkly apparent when considered against climate change projections. The Intergovernmental Panel on Climate Change's most recent assessments paint an alarming picture for low-lying territories like Okinotorishima. Under moderate warming scenarios (RCP2.6), global sea levels will rise between 0.43 meters

(0.29–0.59 meters, likely range) by 2100 relative to 1986–2005 levels.[11] Under high emission scenarios (RCP8.5), the increase could reach 0.84 meters (0.61–1.10 meters, likely range).[12] For an atoll where the highest points measure mere centimeters above high tide, such projections represent an existential challenge.

Regional projections specific to the Philippine Sea, where Okinotorishima sits, suggest even more concerning possibilities. Recent studies indicate that sea level rise could directly affect more than one billion people by 2050, with coastal infrastructure worth $7-14 trillion at risk by 2100.[13] The accelerating rate of change compounds the threat: while sea levels rose 2.3 millimeters per year since the 1970s, the rate accelerated to 4.62 millimeters per year for the decade 2013-2022.[14]

Typhoon intensification presents an equally formidable challenge. Climate change is driving measurable increases in tropical cyclone intensity across the Western Pacific, with storm systems like Super Typhoon Man-Yi in November 2024 achieving unprecedented power through ocean temperatures made "up to 40 times more likely by human-caused climate change."[15] Scientific modeling indicates that while typhoon frequency may decrease, their intensity will increase significantly, with potentially severe consequences for coral reef ecosystems.[16] Given that Okinotorishima already endures 16-meter typhoon waves and wind speeds exceeding 50 meters per second, intensification poses direct threats to both natural coral reefs and artificial preservation infrastructure.

The compound effect of rising seas and intensifying storms creates what marine scientists describe as a "perfect storm" scenario for coral reef systems. Research on Australia's Great Barrier Reef demonstrates that recovery from severe cyclone damage typically requires 10-20 years, while projections suggest such intense storms may occur annually by 2030-2040.[17] For Okinotorishima, where recovery time between disturbances could disappear entirely, the implications are particularly severe.

Coral bleaching presents an additional layer of complexity. Ocean warming and acidification create conditions where mass bleaching events—previously rare phenomena—become routine occurrences. Scientific observations at Okinotorishima indicate that bleaching and other climate factors have caused "dramatic decline in the corals there since around

2014."[18] This decline occurs despite Japan's sophisticated preservation efforts, suggesting that artificial enhancement alone may prove insufficient against broader climate pressures.

Environmental Politics and Territorial Legitimacy

Japan's coral cultivation program operates within a complex web of environmental politics that challenges traditional boundaries between conservation and territorial assertion. International conservation organizations maintain nuanced positions on artificial reef enhancement, generally supporting coral restoration while expressing concerns about motivations rooted in territorial expansion rather than pure environmental protection.[19] The distinction between "natural" and "artificial" island status under international law creates particularly thorny questions for Okinotorishima's preservation efforts.

Under the United Nations Convention on the Law of the Sea (UNCLOS), artificial islands cannot generate territorial seas or exclusive economic zones beyond 500-meter safety zones.[20] This legal framework creates a paradox for Japan's coral cultivation: while the preservation techniques themselves involve artificial intervention, they aim to enhance natural processes that could theoretically support claims to "natural" island status. The scientific community remains divided on whether biologically enhanced coral growth constitutes artificial modification that would invalidate territorial claims.

The international legal precedent from artificial island construction elsewhere adds complexity to evaluations of Japan's approach. China's extensive artificial island building in the South China Sea has drawn widespread condemnation from marine scientists for destroying "more than 10 percent" of total shallow reef area through dredging operations.[21] These activities have been characterized as "the largest active man-made reef destruction in human history," involving the destruction of millions of square meters of coral reef habitat.[22] Japan's coral cultivation program, by contrast, aims to enhance existing reef systems rather than destroy them, creating a qualitatively different environmental impact profile.

However, the territorial motivations underlying Japan's coral preservation efforts complicate straightforward environmental assessment. Unlike conventional conservation programs focused purely on ecosystem health, Okinotorishima's coral cultivation serves dual purposes: environmental enhancement and territorial preservation. This duality creates ethical questions within the marine conservation community about the appropriate relationship between scientific research and geopolitical objectives.

Marine biologists studying coral restoration emphasize the technical limitations that constrain even well-intentioned artificial enhancement efforts. Research across Japan indicates that coral transplantation typically achieves less than 20% colony survivorship after four years, with high maintenance costs and limited scalability.[23] These constraints suggest that biological approaches to territorial preservation, while scientifically fascinating, face substantial practical limitations that may prove inadequate to address the scale of climate-driven threats.

Science as Diplomatic Instrument

The transformation of marine biology into an instrument of territorial diplomacy represents a broader trend in twenty-first-century statecraft. Okinotorishima's coral cultivation program demonstrates how environmental science increasingly serves multiple masters: advancing human knowledge, protecting ecosystems, and supporting national security objectives. This convergence creates new categories of scientific research that operate simultaneously as academic inquiry, conservation effort, and strategic asset.

Japan's approach extends beyond coral cultivation to comprehensive ecosystem monitoring and enhancement. The island's facilities include sophisticated surveillance systems with radar and sensors capable of monitoring activity throughout the claimed exclusive economic zone.[24] Research stations collect oceanographic data that serves both scientific and strategic purposes, creating what might be termed "dual-use marine science"—research that simultaneously advances understanding of marine ecosystems and provides intelligence valuable for territorial control.

The diplomatic implications extend far beyond Japan's immediate territorial claims. Okinotorishima's coral cultivation program has attracted international attention as a potential model for other nations facing similar challenges from climate change. Small island developing states throughout the Pacific watch Japan's efforts with keen interest, recognizing parallels to their own struggles against rising seas and coral degradation. The Nippon Foundation's broader marine research initiatives, including the Ocean Innovation Consortium and partnerships with universities across the Pacific, position Japan as a leader in climate adaptation techniques that could prove crucial for numerous countries.[25]

The scientific collaboration networks surrounding Okinotorishima research create complex webs of international relationships. The UTokyo Ocean Alliance Okinotorishima and Small Island Countries Study Group includes over 200 participants from universities, research institutes, government agencies, foundations, and private sector organizations.[26] These partnerships blur traditional boundaries between national research programs and international scientific cooperation, creating diplomatic channels that operate parallel to formal government relations.

Biotechnology and Sovereignty's Future

Advances in marine biotechnology promise to expand the toolkit available for biological sovereignty enhancement. Emerging techniques in coral genetic modification, selective breeding, and assisted evolution could theoretically create coral populations specifically adapted to Okinotorishima's extreme conditions.[27] Such interventions would represent an unprecedented fusion of biotechnology and territorial preservation, potentially creating "designer ecosystems" optimized for both environmental resilience and geopolitical utility.

The development of coral genetic banks and cryopreservation techniques adds another dimension to biological sovereignty strategies. Japan's coral research facilities maintain extensive genetic libraries that could theoretically support ecosystem reconstruction even after catastrophic loss events. This capability transforms coral cultivation from reactive preservation to proactive territorial insurance, creating biological assets that persist independently of immediate environmental conditions.

Foraminifera cultivation research, while still in early stages, represents perhaps the most ambitious biological sovereignty project ever attempted. Japanese scientists are investigating methods to accelerate the natural processes through which foraminifera shells accumulate to form sand and eventually land mass.[28] Success in this research could theoretically enable nations to grow territory through purely biological means, fundamentally altering concepts of territorial acquisition and sovereignty.

The integration of artificial intelligence and robotics into coral cultivation promises to enhance both efficiency and scale. Automated monitoring systems can track coral health, growth rates, and environmental conditions with unprecedented precision, while robotic transplantation systems could deploy coral colonies at depths and locations previously inaccessible to human divers.[29] Such technological integration transforms coral cultivation from labor-intensive artisanal practice to scalable industrial process.

International Implications and Global Precedent

Okinotorishima's coral diplomacy program establishes precedents with far-reaching implications for international law and global environmental governance. If Japan's biological enhancement efforts succeed in maintaining the atoll's above-water status through the twenty-first century, it would demonstrate the viability of ecosystem engineering as a territorial preservation strategy. Such success could encourage similar programs by other nations facing comparable challenges, potentially creating new categories of international competition based on biological rather than military capabilities.

The environmental justice implications of coral diplomacy deserve careful consideration. Japan's $600 million investment in preserving a 9.44 square meter atoll contrasts sharply with limited resources available to developing nations facing similar threats from climate change. Small island states in the Pacific lack the technological and financial capabilities to implement comparable preservation programs, creating potential disparities in climate adaptation capacity that could exacerbate existing inequalities.

The precedent established by coral diplomacy could influence approaches to other global commons facing climate threats. Arctic nations already monitor Okinotorishima research for potential applications to preserving ice-based territorial claims as warming temperatures threaten traditional boundaries. Similarly, nations with Antarctic research stations consider whether biological enhancement techniques could support future territorial assertions in that continent.

The integration of environmental protection with territorial preservation creates new frameworks for evaluating sovereignty claims under international law. Traditional UNCLOS provisions assume static geographical features, but climate change and biological enhancement techniques challenge these assumptions by creating dynamic territories that change over time through both natural and artificial processes. Okinotorishima's coral cultivation program thus contributes to broader legal evolution in ocean governance.

The Paradox of Artificial Nature

Perhaps the most philosophically complex aspect of coral diplomacy lies in its fundamental paradox: using artificial means to enhance natural processes for territorial purposes that depend on "natural" status under international law. This contradiction reflects broader tensions in twenty-first-century environmental politics, where human intervention increasingly becomes necessary to preserve "natural" ecosystems against climate change.

The scientific community grapples with definitional challenges about what constitutes natural versus artificial ecosystem enhancement. Coral transplantation from the same species and geographic region might be considered natural enhancement, while genetic modification could be deemed artificial intervention. Yet climate change itself represents artificial alteration of marine environments through human greenhouse gas emissions, complicating simple distinctions between natural and artificial processes.

Legal scholars debate whether biologically enhanced coral growth should be considered artificial island construction under UNCLOS Article

60, which would eliminate territorial claims, or natural island preservation permitted under general sovereignty principles.[30] The absence of specific international legal frameworks for evaluating biological enhancement techniques creates uncertainty that could persist for decades as such technologies become more widespread.

The ethical dimensions of coral diplomacy extend beyond legal technicalities to fundamental questions about human relationships with natural systems. Some environmental philosophers argue that using ecosystem enhancement for territorial purposes instrumentalizes nature in ways that undermine authentic environmental protection. Others contend that climate change makes such interventions necessary for preserving both ecosystems and human communities, regardless of their territorial implications.

Future Trajectories and Adaptation Pathways

As climate change accelerates through the twenty-first century, coral diplomacy at Okinotorishima may evolve toward even more sophisticated integration of biological, technological, and diplomatic strategies. Emerging adaptation pathways could include floating platform systems that maintain territorial presence even if natural coral growth proves insufficient to prevent submersion. Such platforms could theoretically support continued coral cultivation while providing more robust infrastructure for territorial administration.

The development of closed-loop aquaculture systems could enable coral cultivation programs to operate independently of local environmental conditions, potentially allowing continuous coral production even during periods of extreme climate stress. Such systems would represent ultimate technological solutions to biological sovereignty challenges, creating artificial reef ecosystems that persist despite natural system collapse.

International cooperation frameworks specifically designed for biological sovereignty enhancement could emerge as more nations face similar challenges. Multilateral research partnerships, technology sharing agreements, and coordinated adaptation strategies could transform coral diplomacy from unilateral national programs to collaborative international efforts. Such cooperation could help address equity concerns while advancing scientific understanding and environmental protection.

The long-term success or failure of Okinotorishima's coral cultivation program will likely influence global approaches to climate adaptation and territorial preservation for decades to come. If biological enhancement proves sufficient to maintain the atoll's above-water status through severe climate change, it could encourage massive expansion of similar programs worldwide. Conversely, failure could redirect resources toward alternative adaptation strategies and force reconsideration of traditional territorial concepts under climate pressure.

As the first comprehensive test of biological sovereignty in the climate change era, Okinotorishima's coral diplomacy program represents far more than Japan's attempt to preserve a remote territorial claim. It embodies humanity's emerging relationship with marine ecosystems in an age when environmental protection and national security increasingly converge in complex and sometimes contradictory ways. The microscopic coral polyps growing in Kumejima's laboratories carry not only their own genetic heritage but also the weight of precedents that could reshape international law, environmental policy, and the fundamental nature of sovereignty itself. In the battle for tomorrow's ocean, science has become both weapon and shield in a conflict where the stakes include not only territorial control but the very survival of marine ecosystems upon which billions of people depend.

Footnotes:

1. Gilles Campion, "Japan is growing an island," CORRECTIV, October 23, 2018, https://correctiv.org/en/latest-stories/climate-change/2017/07/28/japan-is-growing-an-island/.
2. Hajime Kayanne et al., "Low species diversity of hermatypic corals on an isolated reef, Okinotorishima, in the northwest Pacific," Galaxea, Journal of Coral Reef Studies 14 (2013): 73.
3. Campion, "Japan is growing an island."
4. Ibid.
5. Ibid.
6. Ibid.

7. Ibid.
8. Yukie Yoshikawa, "The US-Japan-China Mistrust Spiral and Okinotorishima," Asia-Pacific Journal: Japan Focus, November 3, 2023, https://apjjf.org/yukie-yoshikawa/2541/article.
9. "Okinotorishima," Wikipedia, accessed August 8, 2025, https://en.wikipedia.org/wiki/Okinotorishima.
10. "Kayane Hajime," Japan's Southernmost and Easternmost Border Islands, accessed August 8, 2025, https://www.t-borderislands.metro.tokyo.lg.jp/en/interview/interview1-2.html.
11. "Chapter 4: Sea Level Rise and Implications for Low-Lying Islands, Coasts and Communities," IPCC Special Report on the Ocean and Cryosphere in a Changing Climate, accessed August 8, 2025, https://www.ipcc.ch/srocc/chapter/chapter-4-sea-level-rise-and-implications-for-low-lying-islands-coasts-and-communities/.
12. Ibid.
13. "IPCC Report: urgent adaptation needed to address rising impacts of climate change on the ocean and populations," Ocean & Climate Platform, March 17, 2023, https://ocean-climate.org/en/ipcc-report-urgent-adaptation-needed-to-address-rising-impacts-of-climate-change-on-the-ocean-and-populations/.
14. "Sea level rise," Wikipedia, accessed August 8, 2025, https://en.wikipedia.org/wiki/Sea_level_rise.
15. "Analysis: Climate Change-Driven Ocean Warming Intensifies Record November Typhoon Activity in the Western Pacific," Climate Central, accessed August 8, 2025, https://www.climatecentral.org/climate-shift-index-alert/ocean-philippines-2024.
16. Maria Puotinen et al., "The threat to coral reefs from more intense cyclones under climate change," Global Change Biology 23, no. 2 (2017): 421-436.
17. Ove Hoegh-Guldberg et al., "Coral Reef Ecosystems under Climate Change and Ocean Acidification," Frontiers in Marine Science 4 (2017): 158.
18. "Kayane Hajime."
19. "Home," Coral Reef Alliance, May 28, 2021, https://coral.org/en/.

20. "Massive Island-Building and International Law," Asia Maritime Transparency Initiative, June 15, 2015, https://amti.csis.org/massive-island-building-and-international-law/.
21. Nnamdi Anyadike, "Artificial Islands: Economic Promise Versus Environmental Peril," The Earth & I, June 22, 2023, https://www.theearthandi.org/post/artificial-islands-economic-promise-versus-environmental-peril.
22. "Construction of artificial islands, excessive fishing devastate coral reefs in South China Sea," Eco-Business, April 11, 2024, https://www.eco-business.com/news/construction-of-artificial-islands-excessive-fishing-devastate-coral-reefs-in-south-china-sea/.
23. Saki Harii, "Insights into coral restoration projects in Japan," Science of The Total Environment 838 (2022): 156543.
24. "Profile of the Okinotorishima Islands," Japan's Southernmost and Easternmost Border Islands, accessed August 8, 2025, https://www.t-borderislands.metro.tokyo.lg.jp/en/okinotorishima/.
25. "The Nippon Foundation Ocean Innovation Consortium," The Nippon Foundation, January 16, 2025, https://en.nippon-foundation.or.jp/what/projects/ocean/ocean_innovation.
26. "Kayane Hajime."
27. "Coral cover and rubble cryptofauna abundance and diversity at outplanted reefs in Okinawa, Japan," PMC, accessed August 8, 2025, https://pmc.ncbi.nlm.nih.gov/articles/PMC7518162/.
28. "Saving the Sinking Islands of Tuvalu with Star Sand," SATREPS, accessed August 8, 2025, https://www.jst.go.jp/global/english/case/environment_energy_3.html.
29. "Coral Net," Kajima Technical Research Institute, accessed August 8, 2025, https://www.kajima.co.jp/english/tech/katri/technology/front_line/ff_003/index.php.
30. "Artificial island," Wikipedia, accessed August 8, 2025, https://en.wikipedia.org/wiki/Artificial_island.

Chapter 14: The Technology of Sovereignty

In the crystalline waters surrounding Okinotorishima, Japan's most remote territorial outpost, an invisible revolution in surveillance technology is transforming the very nature of sovereignty itself. As dawn breaks over the Pacific, autonomous underwater vehicles glide silently through the depths, their quantum sensors detecting magnetic anomalies that would have remained hidden to previous generations of detection equipment. Above the surface, AI-powered satellite systems process terabytes of data in real-time, while beneath the waves, an intricate network of sensors monitors every movement within Japan's claimed exclusive economic zone. This is the new frontier of territorial control—where sovereignty is no longer just about physical presence, but about technological dominance in the digital realm.

The evolution from traditional border control to digital territorial management represents one of the most significant shifts in international relations since the advent of modern nation-states. As great powers compete for control over remote territories like Okinotorishima, the deployment of cutting-edge technologies has become as critical as military positioning. The technologies being developed and deployed around this tiny atoll offer a glimpse into the future of sovereignty itself—one where quantum sensors, artificial intelligence, and autonomous systems redefine what it means to control territory in the 21st century.

The Quantum Revolution in Maritime Surveillance

The deployment of quantum sensing technology represents perhaps the most dramatic leap forward in underwater surveillance capabilities since the development of sonar. In April 2025, Chinese researchers demonstrated the potential of this technology when they successfully tested a drone-mounted quantum sensor system that could detect submarines with unprecedented precision.[1] The system, utilizing Coherent Population Trapping (CPT) atomic magnetometer technology, achieved picotesla-level precision in tracking magnetic anomalies—roughly a billion times more sensitive than conventional magnetometers.[2]

This technological breakthrough has profound implications for territorial control around remote outposts like Okinotorishima. Traditional magnetic anomaly detectors, which have been used for submarine detection since World War II, typically have blind zones in low-latitude regions where Earth's magnetic field runs parallel to the surface.[3] The new quantum sensors overcome these limitations by exploiting quantum interference effects in rubidium atoms, generating seven distinct microwave resonance signals that are not weakened by alignment with Earth's magnetic field lines.[4]

France became the first nation to adopt quantum gravimeters for operational use in 2024, while the United States has invested $3.8 billion in quantum research compared to China's estimated $15 billion investment.[5] The implications extend far beyond submarine detection—quantum sensors can potentially detect tiny changes in gravitational fields, offering new capabilities for mapping seafloor topography and identifying underwater structures with extraordinary precision.[6]

For Japan's territorial claims around Okinotorishima, quantum sensor networks could provide unprecedented monitoring capabilities. Satellites equipped with quantum gravimeters could map seafloor features with new levels of precision, potentially detecting unauthorized underwater activities or infrastructure development by other nations.[7] Such capabilities could revolutionize how states monitor and defend their territorial claims, particularly in contested maritime zones.

Autonomous Systems and Persistent Presence

The development of autonomous underwater vehicles (AUVs) has fundamentally altered the economics and logistics of maintaining sovereignty over remote territories. Modern AUVs can operate for weeks or months without direct human control, diving to depths of 6,000 meters and covering thousands of kilometers while collecting intelligence data.[8] This capability is particularly valuable for monitoring vast oceanic territories like Japan's claimed EEZ around Okinotorishima, which covers 420,000 square kilometers—an area larger than Japan itself.

The latest generation of AUVs incorporates artificial intelligence systems that enable autonomous decision-making based on environmental data collected through onboard sensors.[9] These systems can modify their mission parameters in real-time, pursuing targets of interest or adapting to changing conditions without requiring communication with human operators. This autonomy is crucial for operations in remote areas where communication links may be unreliable or where maintaining radio silence is operationally necessary.

French company Exail has developed AUVs that meet NATO's STANAG standards and cybersecurity requirements, including categories AL3, AL4, and AL5 for system availability, confidentiality, and integrity.[10] These specifications highlight the dual-use nature of modern autonomous systems—technologies developed for commercial applications increasingly find military and sovereignty applications.

The deployment of AUV swarms represents an emerging capability that could transform territorial monitoring. Multiple autonomous vehicles operating in coordinated patterns can provide persistent surveillance coverage over vast areas, sharing sensor data and coordinating responses to detected threats.[11] Such systems could theoretically maintain constant monitoring of territorial waters around remote outposts like Okinotorishima without requiring human crews to undertake dangerous journeys to the site.

Artificial Intelligence and Maritime Domain Awareness

The integration of artificial intelligence into maritime surveillance systems has created capabilities that were unimaginable just a decade ago. Modern AI systems can process satellite imagery, radar data, and AIS (Automatic Identification System) information simultaneously, creating comprehensive pictures of maritime activity in real-time.[12] The challenge of monitoring vast oceanic areas—traditionally limited by human operators' capacity to process information—has been largely solved through machine learning algorithms that can identify anomalies and potential threats automatically.

Geospatial AI systems have proven particularly effective at detecting "dark vessels"—ships that deliberately disable their AIS transponders to avoid detection while conducting illegal activities such as fishing violations or smuggling.[13] These systems can correlate multiple data sources, including synthetic aperture radar (SAR) images from satellites, to track vessels even when they attempt to remain invisible to conventional monitoring systems.

The European Space Agency's Sentinel-1 satellite constellation provides freely available SAR data that AI systems can analyze to detect and classify vessels with remarkable accuracy.[14] Companies like SatShipAI have developed algorithms that can provide ship detection, type classification, and size estimation using this data, offering near real-time monitoring capabilities that complement traditional surveillance methods.[15]

For territorial control applications, AI systems offer the capability to automatically detect violations of territorial boundaries and alert human operators to potential threats. Machine learning algorithms can be trained to recognize normal patterns of activity and flag deviations that might indicate unauthorized intrusions or suspicious behavior.[16] This capability is particularly valuable for monitoring remote territories where human observation would be costly or dangerous.

Underwater Construction and Infrastructure Innovation

The technologies being developed for underwater construction around Okinotorishima represent cutting-edge achievements in marine engineering. Japan's investment of over $600 million in preserving the atoll has driven innovations in underwater construction techniques, coral cultivation, and autonomous monitoring systems.[17] These technologies have applications far beyond a single territorial claim—they represent pioneering work in establishing and maintaining sovereignty over remote maritime territories.

Recent advances in underwater construction include the development of autonomous systems capable of conducting repairs and construction work without human divers. These systems can operate at depths and in conditions that would be dangerous or impossible for human workers, extending the reach of territorial infrastructure development into previously inaccessible areas.[18]

The integration of environmental engineering with sovereignty protection has led to innovative approaches such as coral genetic modification and ecosystem engineering. Japan's research into coral preservation and artificial reef construction using foraminifera cultivation represents an attempt to use biological systems as tools of territorial maintenance.[19] These approaches could potentially create self-maintaining territorial markers that combine environmental protection with sovereignty assertion.

Floating platform technology has evolved from offshore oil and gas applications to become a potentially crucial tool for sovereignty projection. Modern floating platforms can support complex infrastructure including research stations, communication arrays, and monitoring equipment while remaining mobile enough to be relocated as needed.[20] The development of floating wind platforms has demonstrated that large, stable structures can be maintained in open ocean conditions for extended periods.[21]

The Digital Threat Landscape

The increasing digitization of maritime systems has created new vulnerabilities that threaten the technological infrastructure supporting modern sovereignty claims. The maritime sector has experienced a 900% increase in cybersecurity breaches on operational technology as it has entered the digital era.[22] This dramatic increase reflects the growing interconnectedness of maritime systems and their integration with global communications networks.

Cybersecurity threats targeting maritime infrastructure include sophisticated attacks by advanced persistent threat (APT) groups, ransomware operations, and state-sponsored espionage activities.[23] China's Volt Typhoon group has been detected in maritime platforms around the United States and its territories, including Guam, demonstrating the global reach of cyber espionage operations targeting maritime infrastructure.[24]

The vulnerability of maritime systems stems partly from the age of existing infrastructure. The average age of the global fleet is over 21 years, with 41.85% of ships older than 20 years.[25] These vessels were built before cybersecurity considerations became paramount, resulting in operational technology (OT) systems that lack modern security features. The integration of new digital systems with legacy infrastructure has created additional attack surfaces that cybercriminals can exploit.

Electronic warfare capabilities targeting GPS and navigation systems pose particular threats to remote territories like Okinotorishima. GPS jamming and spoofing incidents have increased dramatically in strategic maritime chokepoints, demonstrating how electronic interference can disrupt navigation and positioning systems critical for territorial monitoring.[26] Such attacks could potentially blind surveillance systems or mislead autonomous vehicles, compromising the technological infrastructure supporting sovereignty claims.

Quantum-Enhanced Navigation and Communications

The development of quantum navigation technologies offers potential solutions to GPS vulnerabilities while enhancing the precision of autonomous systems operating in contested environments. Quantum inertial navigation systems can provide accurate positioning without relying on satellite signals, making them immune to GPS jamming or spoofing attacks.[27] These systems use quantum interferometry to measure acceleration and rotation with extraordinary precision, enabling autonomous vehicles to navigate accurately even when denied access to external positioning signals.

China has developed atomic gravimeters that could potentially prevent navigation accidents such as the 2021 collision of the USS Connecticut with an underwater mountain in the South China Sea.[28] These systems can detect underwater terrain features with sufficient precision to enable safe navigation without active sonar, reducing the acoustic signature of submarines and autonomous vehicles.

Quantum communication technologies could revolutionize secure communications with submerged systems. Traditional radio communications are severely limited underwater, but quantum entanglement-based communication systems could potentially enable secure, long-range communication with autonomous underwater vehicles without requiring them to surface.[29] Such capabilities would dramatically enhance the operational flexibility of autonomous surveillance systems operating around remote territories.

The integration of quantum sensors, navigation systems, and communication technologies could create comprehensive autonomous monitoring networks capable of operating independently for extended periods. Such systems could provide persistent surveillance coverage over vast areas while remaining resilient to electronic warfare attacks and cyber intrusions.

Network Integration and Data Fusion

Modern sovereignty monitoring systems increasingly rely on the integration of multiple sensor networks to create comprehensive situational awareness. The fusion of satellite imagery, underwater sensor networks, autonomous vehicle data, and AI analysis creates information systems that exceed the capabilities of any individual sensor type.[30] This network-centric approach to territorial monitoring represents a fundamental shift from traditional point-defense strategies to area-wide surveillance systems.

The challenge of managing and analyzing the vast quantities of data generated by modern sensor networks has driven the development of edge computing capabilities that can process information locally rather than transmitting everything to central facilities.[31] This approach reduces communication bandwidth requirements while improving response times and system resilience.

Advanced data fusion algorithms can correlate information from multiple sources to detect patterns and anomalies that might be missed by individual sensors. For example, correlating AIS data with satellite imagery and underwater acoustic signatures can provide comprehensive tracking of vessel movements even when ships attempt to evade detection.[32] Such capabilities are particularly valuable for monitoring territorial boundaries in remote areas where individual sensor coverage might be incomplete.

Resilience and Redundancy

The protection of technological infrastructure supporting sovereignty claims requires sophisticated approaches to system resilience and redundancy. Modern threats include not only direct physical attacks but also cyber intrusions, electronic warfare, and supply chain vulnerabilities that could compromise critical systems.[33]

The development of autonomous systems capable of self-repair and adaptive operation offers one approach to maintaining system functionality in hostile environments. Research into self-healing materials and autonomous maintenance robots could enable territorial monitoring systems to continue operating even after suffering damage from natural disasters or deliberate attacks.[34]

Network segmentation and zero-trust architectures have become critical for protecting maritime operational technology systems from cyber attacks.[35] These approaches assume that any network connection could be compromised and implement strict access controls and monitoring throughout the system. The implementation of such security measures is particularly challenging in maritime environments where systems must operate reliably despite limited communication links and harsh environmental conditions.

Future Technological Trajectories

The technological systems being developed for maritime sovereignty applications continue to evolve rapidly, driven by advances in quantum physics, artificial intelligence, materials science, and robotics. The convergence of these technologies promises to create capabilities that will fundamentally transform how states project and maintain sovereignty over remote territories.

Emerging technologies such as quantum radar could potentially eliminate the stealth advantages that have protected submarines for decades.[36] If successfully developed, such systems could make the oceans effectively transparent to nations possessing advanced sensor networks, fundamentally altering the strategic balance in maritime domains.

The development of large-scale autonomous systems, including autonomous surface vessels and underwater vehicles, could enable persistent presence in contested areas without risking human crews.[37] Such systems could potentially maintain effective control over vast oceanic areas with minimal direct human involvement, reducing the costs and risks associated with projecting sovereignty over remote territories.

Environmental adaptation technologies, including advanced coral cultivation and underwater construction techniques, could enable the physical reinforcement of territorial claims even as climate change threatens low-lying territories.[38] The integration of environmental protection with sovereignty assertion could create sustainable approaches to territorial maintenance that align with international environmental law.

The competition for technological advantage in maritime domains reflects broader trends in international relations, where technological capabilities increasingly determine relative power and influence. Nations that successfully develop and deploy advanced maritime technologies will possess significant advantages in asserting and defending territorial claims, while those that fall behind may find their sovereignty claims increasingly difficult to maintain against technological superior competitors.

For Okinotorishima and similar remote territorial claims, technological dominance may ultimately prove more important than traditional metrics of territorial control. The ability to monitor, defend, and exploit territorial claims using advanced technology could determine which nations successfully maintain sovereignty over disputed areas in an era of increasing resource competition and environmental change.

Footnotes:

[1] Chris Young, "China unveils new quantum drone tech to detect stealth US submarines," *Interesting Engineering*, April 24, 2025, https://interestingengineering.com/military/chinas-drone-mounted-quantum-submarine-detector.

[2] "China Tests Drone-Mounted Quantum Sensor That Could Reshape Submarine Detection," *The Quantum Insider*, April 27, 2025, https://thequantuminsider.com/2025/04/27/china-tests-drone-mounted-quantum-sensor-that-could-reshape-submarine-detection/.

[3] Rajesh Uppal, "Militaries thrust on Quantum Sensors including Quantum Magnetometers for submarine detection and Navigation in GPS denied environments," *International Defense Security & Technology*, June 12, 2021, https://idstch.com/geopolitics/militaries-employing-quantum-sensors-including-quantum-magnetometers-for-submarine-detection-and-navigation-in-gps-denied-environments/.

[4] Young, "China unveils new quantum drone tech."

[5] "How Quantum Sensors Could Make U.S. Submarines Obsolete," *Popular Mechanics*, January 30, 2025, https://www.popularmechanics.com/military/navy-ships/a63382376/quantum-sensors-submarines/.

[6] Rajesh Uppal, "Quantum Gravity and Gradiometer Sensors: Revolutionizing Maritime Navigation, Subsurface Detection, and Stealth Tracking," *International Defense Security & Technology*, March 23, 2025, https://idstch.com/technology/quantum/quantum-gravity-and-gradiometer-sensors-revolutionizing-maritime-navigation-subsurface-detection-and-stealth-tracking/.

[7] Sebastien Roblin, "No More 'Stealth' Submarines: Could Quantum 'Radar' Make Submarines Easy to Track (And Kill)?", *The National Interest*, November 25, 2024, https://nationalinterest.org/blog/buzz/no-more-stealth-submarines-could-quantum-radar-make-submarines-easy-track-and-kill-54547.

[8] "AUVs - Autonomous Underwater Vehicles," *National Oceanic and Atmospheric Administration*, https://oceanexplorer.noaa.gov/technology/subs/auvs/auvs.html.

[9] "Autonomous Underwater Vehicles (AUVs)," *Woods Hole Oceanographic Institution*, https://www.whoi.edu/what-we-do/explore/underwater-vehicles/auvs/.

[10] "Autonomous Underwater Vehicles For Defense Applications," *Exail*, https://www.exail.com/product-range/autonomous-underwater-vehicles-for-defense-applications.

[11] Rajesh Uppal, "Autonomous underwater vehicle (AUV) technologies for surveillance, and anti-submarine warfare missions," *International Defense Security & Technology*, September 26, 2021, https://idstch.com/military/navy/autonomous-underwater-vehicle-auv-technologies-for-surveillance-and-anti-submarine-warfare-missions/.

[12] "AI in Maritime Security: Applications, Challenges, Future Directions, and Key Data Sources," *Information*, Vol. 16, No. 8 (2025), https://www.mdpi.com/2078-2489/16/8/658.

[13] "AI in Maritime Surveillance: Uses, Risks, and Considerations," *Observer Research Foundation*, August 1, 2025, https://www.orfonline.org/expert-speak/ai-in-maritime-surveillance-uses-risks-and-considerations.

[14] "Acme AI | Geospatial AI for Maritime Surveillance," https://www.acmeai.tech/insight/geospatial-ai-for-maritime-surveillance.

[15] "SatShipAI – Maritime Surveillance," https://satshipai.eu/.

[16] "AI in Maritime Security: Applications, Challenges, Future Directions."

[17] Based on information from the provided documents about Japan's investment in Okinotorishima preservation.

[18] "AUVs - Autonomous Underwater Vehicles," NOAA.

[19] Based on information from the provided documents about Japan's coral cultivation efforts.

[20] "Review on Fixed and Floating Offshore Structures. Part I: Types of Platforms with Some Applications," *Journal of Marine Science and Engineering*, Vol. 10, No. 8 (2022), https://www.mdpi.com/2077-1312/10/8/1074.

[21] "Evolution of floating offshore wind platforms: A review of at-sea devices," *Renewable and Sustainable Energy Reviews*, June 28, 2023, https://www.sciencedirect.com/science/article/pii/S1364032123002733.

[22] "Cybersecurity Challenges in the Maritime Sector," *Journal of Cybersecurity and Privacy*, Vol. 2, No. 1 (2022), https://www.mdpi.com/2673-8732/2/1/9.

[23] "Cyber Threats Surge Against Maritime Industry In 2025," *Cyble*, August 1, 2025, https://cyble.com/blog/cyberattacks-targets-maritime-industry/.

[24] "Expiring cyber information-sharing law puts US maritime infrastructure at risk, experts warn," *Nextgov/FCW*, August 1, 2025, https://www.nextgov.com/cybersecurity/2025/07/expiring-cyber-information-sharing-law-puts-us-maritime-infrastructure-risk-experts-warn/407144/.

[25] "Digital transformation of the maritime industry: A cybersecurity systemic approach," *Ocean & Coastal Management*, March 27, 2022, https://www.sciencedirect.com/science/article/abs/pii/S1874548222000166.

[26] "Cyber Threats Surge Against Maritime Industry In 2025," Cyble.

[27] "Quantum Gravity and Gradiometer Sensors," International Defense Security & Technology.

[28] Ibid.

[29] Roblin, "No More 'Stealth' Submarines."

[30] "Maritime Security and Underwater Surveillance Technology: Lessons from the Cold War," *Center for Indo-Pacific Affairs*, https://manoa.hawaii.edu/indopacificaffairs/article/maritime-security-and-underwater-surveillance-technology-lessons-from-the-cold-war/.

[31] "AI in Maritime Security: Applications, Challenges, Future Directions."

[32] "AI in Maritime Surveillance: Uses, Risks, and Considerations."

[33] "Cybersecurity Threats in Maritime for 2025," *Dryad Global*, January 23, 2025, https://channel16.dryadglobal.com/cybersecurity-threats-in-maritime-for-2025.

[34] Based on technological trends in autonomous systems development.

[35] "Artificial Intelligence in Maritime Cybersecurity: A Systematic Review," *Electronics*, Vol. 14, No. 9 (2025), https://www.mdpi.com/2079-9292/14/9/1844.

[36] Roblin, "No More 'Stealth' Submarines."

[37] "Autonomous underwater vehicle (AUV) technologies," International Defense Security & Technology.

[38] Based on information from the provided documents about environmental technologies and sovereignty.

Chapter 15: When the Seas Rise

"We are living the reality of climate change. Everyone in Tuvalu lives by the coast or along the coastline, so everyone gets heavily affected by this." — Grace Malie, Tuvaluan youth climate leader[1]

The concrete barriers protecting Okinotorishima from Pacific swells stand as monuments to human determination, but they also represent a race against time that Japan may ultimately lose. As the world's climate system continues its inexorable transformation, even the most expensive and sophisticated engineering may prove insufficient against the rising seas. The question confronting Japan—and the international community—is not whether sea levels will rise, but how much, how fast, and what legal and political frameworks will survive the deluge.

The Science of Submersion

The latest climate science paints an increasingly stark picture for low-lying territories across the Pacific. According to the Intergovernmental Panel on Climate Change's most recent assessments, global mean sea level is projected to rise between 0.43 meters under the optimistic RCP2.6 scenario and 0.84 meters under the high-emissions RCP8.5 scenario by 2100.[2] However, regional variations across the Pacific tell a more complex and often more alarming story.

In the Philippine Sea region where Okinotorishima sits precariously above the waves, sea levels have been rising faster than the global average. From 1993 to 2015, sea levels in the Philippine Sea rose at a rate of 5.0 to 7.0 millimeters per year—nearly double the global average of 2.8 to 3.6 millimeters per year during the same period.[3] This acceleration reflects the complex dynamics of Pacific Ocean circulation patterns, including the influence of the El Niño Southern Oscillation and Pacific Decadal Oscillation, which can amplify regional sea level variations.

By 2023, global average sea level had already reached 101.4 millimeters (3.99 inches) above 1993 levels, marking the highest annual average in the satellite record.[4] The rate of rise has accelerated dramatically, more than doubling from 0.06 inches (1.4 millimeters) per year throughout most of the twentieth century to 0.14 inches (3.6 millimeters) per year from 2006-2015.[5]

For Okinotorishima specifically, with its maximum elevation of barely two meters above high tide and total dry land area of just 9.44 square meters, even modest increases in baseline sea level pose existential threats. The atoll's engineered defenses, impressive as they are, must contend not only with gradually rising mean sea levels but also with the compounding effects of more intense typhoons, storm surges, and the phenomenon known as "king tides"—exceptionally high tides that can overwhelm even robust coastal defenses.

Regional Climate Projections

The 2022 U.S. Interagency Technical Report on sea level rise provides detailed regional projections that offer sobering insights into what Pacific territories can expect. For the Hawaiian Islands and Pacific Islands region, sea levels are projected to rise 6-8 inches (0.15-0.2 meters) in the next 30 years, with potentially much greater increases by century's end.[6]

A comprehensive NASA analysis released in September 2024 specifically examined Pacific Island nations, including many facing circumstances similar to Okinotorishima. The study found that Pacific Island nations such as Tuvalu, Kiribati, and Fiji will experience at least 6 inches (15 centimeters) of sea level rise in the next 30 years, regardless of whether greenhouse gas emissions change.[7] More troublingly, the analysis found that the number of high-tide flooding days in an average year will increase by an order of magnitude for nearly all Pacific Island nations by the 2050s.

Climate models for the broader Western Pacific region project scenarios that would submerge not just individual features like Okinotorishima, but entire atoll nations. According to research published in *Science Advances*, most atoll islands will experience annual wave-driven overwash by the mid-21st century under current emission trajectories.[8] The study found that on a pathway with high greenhouse gas emissions and rapid ice sheet collapse, models project that average sea level rise for many Pacific regions could reach 2.2 meters (7.2 feet) by 2100 and 3.9 meters (13 feet) by 2150.[9]

For Okinotorishima, these projections suggest that even Japan's impressive engineering efforts may face insurmountable challenges within decades rather than centuries. The atoll's concrete barriers and titanium nets represent cutting-edge preservation technology, but they were designed for gradual erosion and storm protection, not for sustained submersion under rising baseline sea levels.

The Typhoon Factor

Beyond gradual sea level rise, Okinotorishima faces intensifying threats from extreme weather events. The Western Pacific basin generates some of the world's most powerful tropical cyclones, and climate change is projected to increase both their intensity and the height of associated storm surges. Typhoons regularly generate waves exceeding 16 meters in height around Okinotorishima, testing the limits of Japan's engineering defenses.

A sobering example of climate vulnerability occurred in December 2008, when a high surf event overwashed numerous atolls in Micronesia, ruining freshwater supplies and destroying agriculture on approximately 60% of the inhabited islands.[10] While Okinotorishima's engineered defenses provide greater protection than natural atolls, the incident illustrates how extreme weather events can cause rapid, devastating changes to low-lying Pacific territories.

The compound effects of rising baseline sea levels and intensifying storms create a dangerous amplification effect. As mean sea levels rise, the same storm surge heights reach further inland and cause more extensive damage. What constitutes a "100-year storm" today may become a routine annual occurrence within decades as climate patterns shift and sea levels rise.

Coral Ecosystems Under Stress

Japan's innovative coral preservation efforts at Okinotorishima represent one of the most ambitious attempts to use biological processes to reinforce territorial claims. Since 2006, Japanese researchers have transplanted around 100,000 coral juveniles back to Okinotorishima's reefs, cultivating them at the Deep Sea Water Research Center in Kumejima before returning them to bolster the atoll's natural foundations.[11]

However, these coral preservation efforts face their own climate-related challenges. Rising sea temperatures have caused increasingly frequent coral bleaching events across the Pacific, including in Japanese waters. Ocean acidification, caused by increasing atmospheric CO_2 absorption, makes it harder for corals to build and maintain their calcium carbonate skeletons. The discovery in 2024 of "dark oxygen" in polymetallic nodules has raised new questions about deep-sea ecosystems and their response to environmental changes.[12]

Marine biologist research at institutions like the Okinawa Institute of Science and Technology indicates that coral reefs face an unprecedented combination of stressors. Even with successful transplantation programs, the survival rate of transplanted corals in Japanese waters is often less than 20% after four years.[13] This reality calls into question whether biological approaches to island preservation can keep pace with climate change impacts.

The irony is particularly acute for Okinotorishima: Japan is spending hundreds of millions of dollars to preserve coral reefs that generate territorial claims over waters containing resources that, when extracted and burned, contribute to the climate change threatening those very reefs. The contradiction highlights the complex interplay between resource security, environmental protection, and geopolitical strategy in the climate change era.

Legal Frameworks in Flux

The challenge of rising sea levels extends far beyond engineering and environmental science into fundamental questions of international law and sovereignty. The United Nations Convention on the Law of the Sea (UNCLOS), negotiated and adopted when climate change was not yet a global concern, contains no explicit provisions for how territorial boundaries should be adjusted as coastlines change due to sea level rise.

The emerging debate centers on two competing interpretations of maritime boundary law: the "ambulatory" approach, where baselines move with changing coastlines, and the "fixed" approach, where boundaries remain constant regardless of physical changes. Under the ambulatory interpretation, Okinotorishima's territorial waters and EEZ would shrink as the atoll submerges, potentially disappearing entirely if the rocks become permanently submerged. Under the fixed interpretation, Japan would retain its maritime boundaries even if the physical territory disappears.[14]

Recent developments in international law suggest growing support for the fixed approach, particularly among vulnerable island nations. The International Court of Justice's landmark July 2025 advisory opinion on climate change addressed this critical issue, finding that UNCLOS does not require states to revise established baselines or maritime boundaries due to physical changes like coastal recession.[15] The Court stated that "existing maritime entitlements remain valid even as sea levels rise" and that "once a State is established, the disappearance of one of its constituent elements would not necessarily entail the loss of its statehood."[16]

This legal precedent, while welcomed by vulnerable nations, creates new complexities for maritime governance. If Okinotorishima becomes permanently submerged but Japan retains its EEZ claims, questions arise about how to manage and enforce maritime boundaries around territories that no longer exist above water. The practical implications for navigation, resource extraction, and environmental protection in these "phantom territories" remain largely unexplored.

Several Pacific Island nations have taken proactive steps to cement their maritime boundaries before potential territorial loss. The Pacific Islands Forum's "Declaration on Preserving Maritime Zones in the Face of Climate Change-Related Sea-Level Rise" asserts that maritime boundaries should remain fixed regardless of physical changes to territory.[17] Countries like the Marshall Islands are depositing precise geographical coordinates of their maritime boundaries with the United Nations to establish legal certainty about their territorial claims.

The Pacific Precedent

Okinotorishima's climate vulnerability exists within a broader context of Pacific Island nations facing existential threats from sea level rise. The experiences of countries like Tuvalu, Kiribati, and the Marshall Islands provide sobering previews of what may await Japan's southernmost territory.

Tuvalu, with a maximum elevation of just five meters and most of its population living less than two meters above sea level, represents the extreme end of climate vulnerability.[18] Areas of Tuvalu that currently experience fewer than five high-tide flood days per year could average 25 flood days annually by the 2050s, according to NASA projections.[19] Regions of Kiribati that see fewer than five flood days today will experience an average of 65 flood days annually by the 2050s.

These Pacific Island nations have pioneered innovative adaptation strategies that offer potential models for territories like Okinotorishima. Tuvalu has launched an initiative to create a digital replica of the country in the metaverse, preserving its culture and governance structures even if the physical territory becomes uninhabitable.[20] The country has also negotiated the Falepili Union with Australia, which guarantees Tuvaluan citizens the right to live, work, and study in Australia while maintaining their distinct national identity.

Kiribati has taken a different approach, purchasing 22 square kilometers of land in Fiji as a potential relocation site for its 116,000 citizens.[21] This "migration with dignity" strategy acknowledges the likely eventual loss of territory while attempting to preserve national continuity and cultural identity. However, the purchase represents only a fraction of Kiribati's current land area, highlighting the challenges of maintaining entire populations and cultures in exile.

The Marshall Islands has developed perhaps the most detailed climate adaptation plan, outlining a phased approach to territorial consolidation. The plan envisions gradually concentrating population and infrastructure on the most defensible territories while abandoning more vulnerable areas—ultimately potentially protecting just four stretches of land from the country's 24 currently populated areas.[22]

Technological Adaptation and Limits

Japan's response to climate threats at Okinotorishima represents the most technologically sophisticated approach to preserving ultra-low-lying territory. The engineering solutions deployed—including concrete seawalls, titanium mesh barriers, and artificial reef structures—push the boundaries of what is technically feasible in marine construction.

The Nippon Foundation and University of Tokyo have invested heavily in developing new coral cultivation techniques, including using foraminifera cultivation that could theoretically build up reef structures over decades or centuries.[23] Kajima Corporation has developed specialized "Coral Net" technology that uses biodegradable mesh structures to provide stable foundations for coral growth while reducing the accumulation of sediments that can stress coral colonies.[24]

However, these technological solutions face fundamental physical limits. Even the most advanced engineering cannot indefinitely hold back rising seas, particularly when sea level rise accelerates due to rapid ice sheet collapse in Greenland or Antarctica. The engineering solutions are also extraordinarily expensive—Japan has already spent over $600 million on Okinotorishima preservation, and costs will likely increase dramatically as climate impacts intensify.

The technological approach also faces the challenge of maintaining systems across vast distances. Okinotorishima lies 1,740 kilometers from Tokyo, making routine maintenance dangerous and expensive. As climate change intensifies storm activity in the region, even reaching the atoll for repairs may become increasingly difficult and hazardous.

Moreover, technological preservation efforts may paradoxically undermine the legal arguments for Okinotorishima's status as a "natural island" under UNCLOS Article 121. If the territory becomes predominantly artificial—composed of concrete barriers, artificial reefs, and engineered structures—questions arise about whether it still qualifies as a "naturally formed area of land" capable of generating an EEZ under international law.

Economic and Strategic Calculations

The economics of climate adaptation for Okinotorishima present a sobering cost-benefit analysis. Japan has already invested over $600 million in preservation efforts, with additional billions likely required for upgraded defenses against accelerating sea level rise. The most recent funding announcements include 13 billion yen ($838 million) for facility rebuilding and enhancement.[25]

These massive expenditures must be weighed against the economic value of the resources at stake. The EEZ around Okinotorishima contains an estimated 230 million tonnes of polymetallic nodules worth over $18 billion, including 610,000 tonnes of cobalt (75 years of Japan's consumption) and 740,000 tonnes of nickel (11 years of consumption).[26] The region also encompasses critical tuna spawning grounds and migration routes worth billions annually in fisheries value.

However, the economic calculation becomes more complex when considering the timeline of climate impacts versus resource extraction capabilities. Deep-sea mining technology remains in early development stages, with commercial-scale extraction likely decades away. Meanwhile, climate impacts are accelerating, potentially submerging the territorial basis for resource claims before the resources can be extracted.

The strategic implications extend beyond immediate resource access to broader questions of maritime influence in the Indo-Pacific region. If Japan loses its claims around Okinotorishima, it would create a significant gap in its ability to monitor and control sea lanes between Taiwan and Guam—a critical corridor for both commercial shipping and potential military operations.

China's increasing research activities around Okinotorishima, including the May 2025 confrontation with the R/V Tan Kah Kee, suggest that Beijing views Japan's climate vulnerability as a potential opportunity to advance its own maritime claims. If Okinotorishima becomes permanently submerged and Japan's EEZ claims become legally questionable, China may assert that the waters revert to international status or attempt to establish its own claims in the region.

Global Implications and Precedents

The fate of Okinotorishima will likely establish crucial precedents for climate-related territorial disputes worldwide. Similar challenges affect numerous other territories, from Rockall in the North Atlantic to various

South China Sea features that China has artificially enlarged in apparent recognition of their climate vulnerability.

The Arctic region faces particularly complex challenges as melting ice reveals new territories while simultaneously threatening others with submersion. Norway's claims around Jan Mayen and Svalbard, various disputed Arctic islands, and the complex boundary negotiations between Arctic nations all may be affected by changing ice and sea levels.

In the Indian Ocean, the Maldives faces challenges similar to Pacific atolls, with its 1,192 coral islands having an average elevation of just 1.5 meters above sea level. The Seychelles, Mauritius, and various territories in the Southern Ocean may also face climate-related territorial challenges in coming decades.

The legal precedents established around Okinotorishima—particularly how international law addresses the retention of maritime boundaries despite territorial submersion—will influence how these other cases are resolved. The ICJ's July 2025 advisory opinion provides important guidance, but specific territorial disputes will likely require case-by-case adjudication.

Toward Adaptive Governance

The climate challenges facing Okinotorishima highlight the need for new approaches to ocean governance that can adapt to changing physical realities while maintaining legal stability and preventing conflict. Traditional concepts of territorial sovereignty, developed for a world of stable coastlines and predictable geography, struggle to address the dynamic realities of climate change.

One emerging approach involves "freezing" maritime boundaries at their current coordinates, regardless of physical changes to the territories that generated them. This approach provides legal certainty and prevents the loss of territorial rights due to climate impacts beyond states' control. However, it also creates the novel situation of "deterritorialized maritime states"—entities that retain sovereignty over ocean areas but lack physical territory.

Another approach focuses on regional cooperation and shared governance frameworks. The Pacific Islands Forum and similar regional organizations have begun developing collective approaches to climate adaptation that could serve as models for other regions. These include shared resource management agreements, coordinated climate adaptation funding, and collective legal strategies for protecting member states' rights.

International climate finance mechanisms may also need to evolve to address the unique challenges of preserving ultra-low-lying territories. Traditional adaptation funding focuses on protecting populated areas and economic infrastructure, but the geopolitical importance of places like Okinotorishima may justify special preservation efforts even for unpopulated territories.

The development of new technologies for marine construction, coral cultivation, and ocean engineering may also offer solutions not yet fully explored. Floating platforms, underwater habitats, and other innovative approaches to maritime occupation could potentially maintain human presence and territorial claims even as traditional land surfaces submerge.

A Race Against Time

As the Pacific swells continue their relentless assault on Okinotorishima's concrete barriers, Japan faces increasingly difficult choices about how much to invest in preserving its southernmost territory. The engineering solutions deployed so far represent remarkable technical achievements, but they may ultimately prove insufficient against accelerating climate change.

The broader implications extend far beyond one small atoll in the Philippine Sea. Okinotorishima's fate will help determine whether international law can adapt to climate realities while maintaining stability and preventing conflict. The precedents established here will influence similar cases worldwide, from the Arctic to the South China Sea to small island developing states facing existential threats.

The next few decades will likely prove decisive. If Japan's preservation efforts succeed and international law evolves to protect climate-vulnerable territories, Okinotorishima may become a symbol of successful adaptation to climate change. If rising seas overwhelm even Japan's sophisticated defenses, it may stand as a warning of the limits of human engineering in the face of planetary change.

What remains certain is that the age of stable coastlines and predictable geography is ending. The institutions, laws, and frameworks developed for a world of fixed territories must evolve rapidly to address the dynamic realities of climate change. Okinotorishima, perched precariously between the vast Pacific and the rising seas, offers both a test case and a wake-up call for humanity's ability to govern a changing planet.

The concrete and titanium barriers protecting Japan's last rock represent more than engineering prowess—they embody humanity's determination to maintain order and sovereignty even as the fundamental assumptions underlying those concepts shift beneath the waves. Whether that determination proves sufficient remains to be seen.

Footnotes:

[1] NASA Analysis Shows Irreversible Sea Level Rise for Pacific Islands, NASA, September 27, 2024, https://www.nasa.gov/earth/climate-change/nasa-analysis-shows-irreversible-sea-level-rise-for-pacific-islands/.

[2] IPCC, "Special Report on the Ocean and Cryosphere in a Changing Climate – Chapter 4: Sea Level Rise and Implications for Low-Lying Islands, Coasts and Communities," 2019, https://www.ipcc.ch/srocc/chapter/chapter-4-sea-level-rise-and-implications-for-low-lying-islands-coasts-and-communities/.

[3] "Rising Sea Levels and Coastal Vulnerability in the Philippines," Climate Tracker Asia, December 11, 2024, https://climatetracker.asia/rising-sea-levels-and-coastal-vulnerability-in-the-philippines/.

[4] "Climate Change: Global Sea Level," NOAA Climate.gov, August 22, 2023, https://www.climate.gov/news-features/understanding-climate/climate-change-global-sea-level.

[5] Ibid.

[6] "2022 Sea Level Rise Technical Report," NOAA Ocean Service, https://oceanservice.noaa.gov/hazards/sealevelrise/sealevelrise-tech-report.html.

[7] NASA Analysis Shows Irreversible Sea Level Rise for Pacific Islands.

[8] Curt D. Storlazzi et al., "Most atolls will be uninhabitable by the mid-21st century because of sea-level rise exacerbating wave-driven

flooding," Science Advances 4, no. 4 (2018), https://www.science.org/doi/10.1126/sciadv.aap9741.

[9] "Dive Deeper | Future Sea Level," U.S. Sea Level Change, November 7, 2024, https://earth.gov/sealevel/us/sea-level-101/future-sea-level/dive-deeper/.

[10] "The Impact of Sea-Level Rise and Climate Change on Pacific Ocean Atolls," U.S. Geological Survey, https://www.usgs.gov/centers/pcmsc/science/impact-sea-level-rise-and-climate-change-pacific-ocean-atolls.

[11] "Japan is growing an island," Correctiv, October 23, 2018, https://correctiv.org/en/latest-stories/climate-change/2017/07/28/japan-is-growing-an-island/.

[12] "Ocean of Riches," as referenced in the provided outline materials.

[13] Makoto Omori, "Insights into coral restoration projects in Japan," Science Direct, December 13, 2022, https://www.sciencedirect.com/science/article/pii/S0964569122003477.

[14] William Worster, "Interpreting the Law of the Sea in the Context of Sea-Level Rise: The Ambulatory Thesis and State Practice," Journal of Environmental Law 35, no. 3 (2023): 499-526, https://academic.oup.com/jel/article/35/3/499/7243056.

[15] "Introduction to Symposium on ICJ's Advisory Opinion on Climate Change," All About International Law, August 1, 2025, https://allaboutil.wordpress.com/2025/08/01/introduction-to-symposium-on-icjs-advisory-opinion-on-climate-change/.

[16] Ibid.

[17] "Climate Change-induced Sea-Level Rise Direct Threat to Millions around World, Secretary-General Tells Security Council," UN Press Release, February 14, 2023, https://press.un.org/en/2023/sc15199.doc.htm.

[18] "Tuvalu: Why Is the Small Island Nation Sinking?" Earth.Org, October 28, 2024, https://earth.org/tuvalus-sinking-reality-how-climate-change-is-threatening-a-small-island-nation/.

[19] NASA Analysis Shows Irreversible Sea Level Rise for Pacific Islands.

[20] "Pacific Islands Craft Survival Plans for Climate Change, Sea Level Rise," Foreign Policy, December 12, 2023, https://foreignpolicy.com/2023/12/11/pacific-island-cop-climate-change-sea-level/.

[21] "Rising seas & relocation: Climate struggles of Small Island Nations," Vision of Humanity, April 10, 2025, https://www.visionofhumanity.org/small-island-nations-climate-threat-and-relocation/.

[22] Pacific Islands Craft Survival Plans for Climate Change, Sea Level Rise.

[23] Japan is growing an island.

[24] "Coral Net," Kajima Technical Research Institute, https://www.kajima.co.jp/english/tech/katri/technology/front_line/ff_003/index.php.

[25] As referenced in the provided outline materials.

[26] As referenced in the provided outline materials regarding the 2024 discovery.

PART VI: THE FUTURE OF OCEAN GOVERNANCE

Chapter 16: Lessons from the Last Rock

Modern Territoriality and the Future of Ocean Governance

On the surface, the contest over Okinotorishima appears absurd: two great powers facing off over 9.44 square meters of coral reef—an area smaller than a tennis court—which Japan has spent over $600 million to preserve with concrete barriers and titanium nets. Yet this tiny atoll's outsized strategic importance reveals profound truths about how sovereignty, territorial control, and resource competition function in the 21st century. The case of Okinotorishima serves as a lens through which to examine the evolution of modern territoriality, the limitations of existing international legal frameworks, and the emerging paradigms that will shape future territorial disputes in an era of resource scarcity, technological advancement, and environmental change.

The Evolution of Modern Sovereignty

The Okinotorishima dispute illuminates how the concept of sovereignty has evolved far beyond its traditional Westphalian roots. Classical sovereignty, established by the 1648 Peace of Westphalia, emphasized territorial integrity and non-interference within clearly defined land boundaries.[1] However, the 21st century has witnessed what scholars term "maritime territorialization"—the process by which states analogize the oceans as territory and perform sovereignty over the sea as they would over land.[2]

This transformation reflects broader changes in how states conceptualize and exercise territorial control. As geographer Rebecca Strating notes, coastal states are increasingly seeking to "transcend the conventional land/sea divide" by claiming and preserving maritime sovereignty through legal arguments, mapping, and narrative construction that emphasizes their sovereign identity over maritime areas.[3] Japan's $600 million investment in preserving Okinotorishima represents perhaps the most extreme example of this phenomenon—literally building sovereignty through concrete and titanium.

The implications extend far beyond the specific case. As digital technology increasingly blurs traditional notions of territorial control, states face what sovereignty scholars describe as an expansion of "territory" into realms previously considered beyond state jurisdiction.[4] In this context, Japan's engineering approach to sovereignty preservation—transforming "rocks" into "islands" through artificial preservation—parallels how states are adapting sovereignty concepts to address challenges posed by cyberspace, climate change, and transnational economic flows.

Resource-Driven Territorial Redefinition

The Okinotorishima case demonstrates how economic incentives fundamentally reshape legal interpretations of territorial sovereignty. The June 2024 discovery of over 230 million tonnes of polymetallic nodules in Japanese waters near Minamitorishima, containing 610,000 tonnes of cobalt and 740,000 tonnes of nickel valued at over $18 billion, exemplifies this dynamic.[5] As global demand for critical minerals is expected to more than double by 2030, driven by the clean energy transition and advanced technology manufacturing, the economic stakes of territorial disputes have increased exponentially.[6]

This resource competition has created what international relations theorist M. Taylor Fravel terms "territorial expansion" driven by newly discovered strategic value.[7] Unlike traditional territorial disputes rooted in historical claims or ethnic considerations, modern maritime disputes increasingly reflect states' calculations about future resource access and supply chain security. China's dominance in processing 85% of global critical minerals and controlling 60% of global production has made alternative sources like deep-sea mining geopolitically essential for other major powers.[8]

The economic imperatives driving territorial claims create powerful incentives for legal creativity. Japan's argument that Okinotorishima constitutes an "island" rather than "rocks" under UNCLOS Article 121(3) becomes more compelling when viewed through the lens of national economic security rather than pure legal interpretation. As maritime law expert Professor Robert Beckman observes, "What UNCLOS does not address is the issue of who owns particular land territory. UNCLOS assumes that we know who owns the land, and then it establishes rights and obligations of states in the adjacent waters."[9] This assumption breaks down when economic incentives create new pressures to redefine what constitutes "land" worthy of sovereignty claims.

Institutional Limitations and Legal Frameworks

The Okinotorishima dispute reveals fundamental limitations in the international legal architecture governing maritime territories. UNCLOS, despite being hailed as the "constitution for the oceans," contains critical ambiguities that states exploit to advance competing interpretations.[10] Article 121(3)'s prohibition on exclusive economic zones for "rocks which cannot sustain human habitation or economic life of their own" lacks precise definitions, leaving interpretation open to political manipulation.

The Commission's Non-Decision

The June 2012 decision by the UN Commission on the Limits of the Continental Shelf (CLCS) to defer recommendations on Japan's Okinotorishima claim "until such time as the matters referred to in the submissions are resolved" exemplifies the institutional paralysis that characterizes contemporary ocean governance.[11] More than a decade later, this legal limbo continues, demonstrating how powerful states can exploit institutional limitations to maintain advantageous ambiguity.

China and South Korea's formal objections to Japan's continental shelf claim have effectively rendered the CLCS powerless to provide authoritative guidance.[12] This institutional failure reflects broader challenges in international law's ability to address disputes involving major powers. As legal scholar James Harrison notes, "UNCLOS' effectiveness remains heavily reliant on voluntary compliance by its States Parties," particularly when enforcement mechanisms are weak or non-existent.[13]

The Philippines v. China arbitration over the South China Sea provides instructive comparison. Despite the 2016 tribunal's decisive ruling against China's "nine-dash line" claims and its strict interpretation of Article 121(3), China's rejection of the decision and continued activities in disputed waters demonstrate the limited enforceability of international maritime law.[14] As one analysis concluded, "The inability to enforce compliance through economic sanctions highlights the challenges in ensuring adherence to international maritime law, particularly when powerful states assert their own interpretations of territorial and maritime rights."[15]

Institutional Adaptation Deficits

The slow pace of institutional adaptation to technological and environmental change further undermines UNCLOS's effectiveness. Written in 1982, the Convention reflects Cold War-era assumptions about ocean use that increasingly diverge from 21st-century realities. Deep-sea mining technology, autonomous underwater vehicles, artificial intelligence in maritime surveillance, and climate-induced sea level rise were not anticipated by the Convention's drafters.

The International Seabed Authority (ISA), tasked with regulating deep-sea mining in international waters, illustrates these adaptation challenges. Despite years of negotiations, the ISA has been unable to agree on commercial mining regulations, with talks stalled through 2026.[16] Meanwhile, individual states are moving forward with domestic deep-sea mining programs: Norway became the first country to authorize seabed mining in its territorial waters in 2024, while President Trump's April 2025 executive order directed U.S. agencies to expedite permits for American companies to mine in both international and U.S. territorial waters.[17]

China's strategic advantage in this institutional vacuum demonstrates how institutional limitations favor states willing to act unilaterally. Beijing has provided more financial support to the ISA than any other nation while opposing creation of inspection bodies and blocking environmental protection measures.[18] This "sovereignty-in-being" approach—gaining control through "steady, deliberate process" while daring others to reverse the situation—represents a fundamental challenge to rules-based order.[19]

Resource Competition Paradigms

The Okinotorishima case exemplifies how scarcity drives territorial conflict in ways that existing legal frameworks struggle to address. Japan's resource vulnerability—importing over 90% of critical metals—makes control of potential domestic sources a national security imperative that transcends narrow legal interpretation.[20] This dynamic reflects broader trends in what scholars term the "securitization" of resource access, where economic dependencies become framed as existential threats requiring extraordinary measures.

The Critical Minerals Race

Global competition for critical minerals has fundamentally altered the strategic calculus of territorial disputes. China's 2010 restriction of rare earth exports to Japan during the Senkaku Islands dispute demonstrated how resource leverage can be weaponized for geopolitical advantage.[21] This experience drove Japan's subsequent investment in alternative sources, including deep-sea mining capabilities and the preservation of Okinotorishima's EEZ claims.

The clean energy transition has intensified these competitive dynamics. Electric vehicle batteries, wind turbines, and solar panels require vast quantities of lithium, cobalt, nickel, and rare earth elements.[22] With China dominating processing and refining of these materials, alternative sources become strategically essential for other major powers. Japan's 2020 success extracting 649 kilograms of cobalt-rich crust from Takuyo No. 5 seamount—the first deep-sea mining at 5,500-meter depths—represents both technological achievement and geopolitical positioning.[23]

The economic stakes create powerful incentives for legal creativity. If Okinotorishima's EEZ claims were recognized, Japan would control access to polymetallic nodules worth potentially trillions of dollars—resources that could transform Japan from a resource-importing nation to a critical mineral exporter. These economic realities make abstract legal interpretations of "rocks" versus "islands" secondary to fundamental questions of national economic security.

Supply Chain Weaponization

The Okinotorishima dispute occurs within a broader context of supply chain weaponization, where resource access becomes a tool of statecraft. Russia's use of energy exports to pressure European allies, China's dominance in critical mineral processing, and the United States' efforts to diversify supply chains through initiatives like the CHIPS Act demonstrate how economic interdependence has become a domain of geopolitical competition.[24]

Japan's investment in Okinotorishima preservation represents what economist Rebecca Lowe terms "economic security" strategy—using territorial claims to secure domestic resource access and reduce dependence on potentially hostile suppliers.[25] This approach parallels efforts by other middle powers to develop alternative supply chains: Australia's Lynas Corporation expanding rare earth processing outside China, the European Union's Critical Raw Materials Act, and the United States' Inflation Reduction Act provisions for domestic mineral processing.[26]

The transformation of economic relationships into security concerns reflects broader changes in international relations. As political scientist Jonathan Kirshner argues, "economic statecraft" has become central to great power competition, with states increasingly willing to accept economic costs to achieve strategic autonomy.[27] Okinotorishima's $600 million price tag becomes reasonable when viewed as insurance against supply chain disruption in critical industries.

Comparative Analysis: Global Precedents and Patterns

The Okinotorishima case gains additional significance when viewed alongside similar territorial disputes worldwide. Comparative analysis reveals common patterns in how states exploit legal ambiguities, use technological capabilities to enhance territorial claims, and adapt sovereignty concepts to address 21st-century challenges.

The Rockall Precedent

The United Kingdom's experience with Rockall—a 624-square-meter granite islet located 200 nautical miles from Scotland—provides instructive comparison. Like Okinotorishima, Rockall generated significant maritime zones until the UK voluntarily relinquished EEZ claims upon ratifying UNCLOS in 1997.[28] This remains "the only example to date of a state voluntarily downgrading an insular feature to 'a rock' and thus reducing the area of its claimed maritime zones."[29]

The UK's decision reflected both legal interpretation and geopolitical calculation. Faced with objections from Denmark (Faroe Islands), Ireland, and Iceland, Britain concluded that maintaining extensive maritime claims based on an uninhabitable rock would undermine its broader arguments for rules-based order.[30] However, the UK retained claims to a 12-nautical-mile territorial sea around Rockall and continues to assert continental shelf rights, leading to ongoing fishing disputes with Ireland.[31]

The contrast with Japan's approach to Okinotorishima illuminates different strategic calculations. While Britain could afford to relinquish Rockall's EEZ because it posed no significant resource security threat, Japan's position as a resource-importing island nation makes alternative sources of critical minerals strategically essential. Geographic vulnerability drives different legal interpretations of similar physical features.

South China Sea Artificial Islands

China's construction of artificial islands in the South China Sea represents the most dramatic example of using engineering to create sovereignty claims. Since 2013, China has built over 3,200 acres of artificial land on previously submerged features, installing military facilities, airstrips, and administrative infrastructure.[32] Unlike Japan's preservation of naturally occurring features, China's approach involves creating entirely new land areas.

The 2016 Philippines v. China arbitration directly addressed this strategy, ruling that artificial islands cannot generate maritime zones and that several Chinese-controlled features qualify only as "rocks" under Article 121(3).[33] However, China's rejection of the ruling and continued militarization of artificial features demonstrate how great powers can simply ignore adverse legal decisions when vital interests are at stake.

The parallel with Okinotorishima is instructive: both cases involve using engineering to enhance territorial claims, but Japan's approach preserves naturally occurring features while China creates new ones. This distinction may prove legally significant if future tribunals distinguish between "artificial preservation" and "artificial creation" of territorial features.

Arctic Continental Shelf Claims

The Arctic provides another venue for examining how states exploit legal ambiguities in maritime law. Russia, Canada, Denmark, and Norway have all submitted claims for extended continental shelves, with several overlapping in disputed areas including the Lomonosov Ridge.[34] The United States, despite not ratifying UNCLOS, has begun making similar claims, creating what scholars term a "scramble for the Arctic" as climate change makes resource extraction economically viable.[35]

Arctic disputes differ from Okinotorishima in involving primarily continental shelf extensions rather than EEZ claims based on small islands. However, the underlying dynamic remains similar: states are using legal mechanisms to secure access to resources made valuable by technological advancement and changing environmental conditions. The Arctic's estimated 13% of global undiscovered oil and 30% of undiscovered natural gas create economic incentives comparable to those driving Japan's investment in Okinotorishima.[36]

The Arctic case also demonstrates how climate change is reshaping territorial competition. As ice melts open new shipping routes and make resource extraction economically feasible, previously worthless territories acquire strategic value.[37] This dynamic parallels how technological advancement in deep-sea mining has transformed Okinotorishima from an ignored atoll into a strategic asset worth hundreds of millions of dollars in preservation efforts.

Technology and Sovereignty in the Digital Age

The Okinotorishima dispute occurs within a broader transformation of sovereignty concepts driven by technological advancement. Japan's use of engineering to preserve territorial features, China's deployment of research vessels for "dual-use" scientific activities, and the role of satellite surveillance in monitoring remote territories all demonstrate how technology is reshaping territorial control.

Surveillance and Monitoring Technologies

Japan's 2007 installation of radar and sensor systems on Okinotorishima exemplifies how states use technology to project sovereignty over remote territories.[38] Real-time monitoring capabilities enable rapid response to foreign activities, while satellite surveillance provides persistent observation of vast ocean areas. These technologies allow states to maintain "presence" in ways previously impossible, effectively extending sovereignty through electronic means.

The integration of artificial intelligence and autonomous systems promises to further transform territorial control. Unmanned underwater vehicles can provide persistent presence without human risk, while AI-driven threat detection systems can automatically identify and respond to foreign activities. As defense analyst Timothy Heath observes, "Technology is enabling new forms of sovereignty expression that were unimaginable even a decade ago."[39]

China's use of civilian research vessels for intelligence gathering represents the flip side of this technological dynamic. The R/V Tan Kah Kee's deployment of wire equipment near Okinotorishima in May 2025 exemplifies how "scientific research" provides cover for activities that blur the line between civilian and military operations.[40] This dual-use capability challenges traditional distinctions between peaceful and threatening activities in maritime domains.

Engineering Sovereignty

Japan's investment in coral preservation technologies, artificial reef construction, and biological approaches to sovereignty reinforcement represents what might be termed "engineering sovereignty"—using technological capabilities to create and maintain territorial claims.[41] The Nippon Foundation's research on coral cultivation using foraminifera represents a decades-long biological approach to ensuring that Okinotorishima remains above water at high tide.

This technological approach to sovereignty preservation has broader implications for how states adapt to environmental challenges. As sea level rise threatens low-lying territories worldwide, engineering solutions may become essential for maintaining existing territorial claims. The Maldives' underwater cabinet meeting in 2009 to highlight climate threats, Tuvalu's consideration of "digital nation" status, and Kiribati's land purchases in Fiji all represent different approaches to addressing existential threats to territorial sovereignty.[42]

The legal implications remain unclear. UNCLOS Article 121(1) defines islands as "naturally formed area[s] of land," raising questions about whether artificially preserved features retain their legal status.[43] Japan's approach of preserving naturally occurring features may prove more legally defensible than China's creation of entirely artificial islands, but future tribunals will need to address these novel challenges to traditional sovereignty concepts.

Environmental Change and Adaptive Governance

Climate change poses fundamental challenges to territorial sovereignty that existing legal frameworks are poorly equipped to address. Rising sea levels threaten to submerge low-lying territories, while changing environmental conditions make previously inaccessible resources economically viable. The Okinotorishima case illustrates both the challenges and potential adaptive responses.

Sea Level Rise and Territorial Baselines

UNCLOS relies on "ambulatory" baselines that move with changing coastlines, leaving low-lying states vulnerable to territorial loss as sea levels rise.[44] If Okinotorishima were to become submerged at high tide, Japan would lose its legal basis for EEZ claims regardless of the billions invested in preservation efforts. This vulnerability affects numerous Pacific Island nations and other low-lying territories worldwide.

The legal implications remain contested. Some scholars argue for "fixed" baselines based on current geography, while others support maintaining ambulatory systems that reflect actual physical conditions.[45] The choice has profound implications for territorial sovereignty, resource access, and the rights of populations potentially displaced by sea level rise.

International law has begun to evolve in response to these challenges. The International Law Commission's 2022 report on sea level rise recommends that states consider preserving maritime zones even if terrestrial features become submerged, acknowledging that purely physical approaches to territorial sovereignty may prove inadequate for addressing climate change impacts.[46]

Ecosystem Engineering and Legal Status

Japan's coral preservation efforts raise novel questions about the relationship between environmental protection and territorial sovereignty. The artificial cultivation of coral reefs and foraminifera to maintain above-water territory represents a form of ecosystem engineering that challenges traditional distinctions between "natural" and "artificial" features.[47]

These efforts reflect broader trends in what environmental lawyer Robin Kundis Craig terms "climate adaptation governance"—legal and institutional responses to environmental changes that threaten existing territorial arrangements.[48] As climate change accelerates, similar challenges will emerge worldwide, requiring legal frameworks that can accommodate both environmental protection and territorial sovereignty.

The intersection of environmental protection with territorial claims creates complex policy choices. Japan's coral preservation serves both conservation and sovereignty goals, but future tribunals will need to determine whether artificially maintained ecosystems retain their legal status as "natural" features under UNCLOS Article 121.

Resource Competition and Future Conflicts

The Okinotorishima case provides insights into how resource competition will likely drive future territorial disputes. As traditional land-based mineral sources become depleted or politically inaccessible, states will increasingly look to maritime areas for critical materials. This trend will intensify pressure on existing legal frameworks and create new sources of international tension.

Deep-Sea Mining and Territorial Competition

The race to develop deep-sea mining capabilities has transformed the strategic value of maritime territories. Japan's 2020 success in extracting cobalt-rich crusts from seamounts demonstrates the technological feasibility of deep-sea resource extraction, while the June 2024 discovery of massive polymetallic nodule deposits near Minamitorishima illustrates the enormous economic stakes.[49]

China's dominance in deep-sea mining exploration—holding more International Seabed Authority contracts than any other nation—represents a strategic challenge for other major powers.[50] Beijing's opposition to environmental protection measures and inspection bodies in the ISA suggests an approach prioritizing rapid resource extraction over conservation concerns.

The United States' response through President Trump's April 2025 executive order on seabed mining reflects recognition that falling behind in this competition could have profound strategic implications.[51] The order's direction to expedite permits and establish international partnerships demonstrates how resource competition is driving changes in both domestic policy and alliance relationships.

Critical Mineral Diplomacy

Access to critical minerals has become a central element of international relations, with states increasingly using resource access as a tool of statecraft. China's rare earth export restrictions to Japan in 2010, Russia's energy cutoffs to Europe, and U.S. restrictions on semiconductor technology exports to China all demonstrate how resource control translates into political leverage.[52]

The Okinotorishima dispute must be understood within this broader context of "critical mineral diplomacy." Japan's investment in preserving the atoll reflects not just legal interpretation but strategic calculation about future resource security. Similarly, China's challenge to Japan's claims serves broader goals of preventing rival powers from developing alternative supply sources.

This dynamic is likely to intensify as the clean energy transition increases demand for specific minerals. The International Energy Agency projects that demand for lithium could increase by 40 times by 2040, while cobalt demand could grow 20-fold.[53] Such dramatic increases will create powerful incentives for states to secure access to potential sources, including through creative interpretation of territorial claims.

Institutional Reform and Adaptive Governance

The limitations revealed by the Okinotorishima case point toward the need for institutional reform and adaptive governance mechanisms. Current legal frameworks, designed for a different era, struggle to address the intersection of technological advancement, environmental change, and resource competition that characterizes contemporary territorial disputes.

UNCLOS Reform Possibilities

Several scholars have proposed reforms to address UNCLOS's limitations in handling modern territorial disputes. Legal expert Robin Churchill suggests developing "supplementary agreements" that would clarify ambiguous provisions like Article 121(3) while maintaining the Convention's basic framework.[54] Such agreements could provide more precise definitions of terms like "human habitation" and "economic life" that currently remain open to political interpretation.

Alternative approaches focus on institutional strengthening rather than textual revision. International law professor James Harrison proposes enhanced dispute resolution mechanisms with stronger enforcement capabilities, including economic sanctions for non-compliance with arbitral awards.[55] However, the challenge of enforcing decisions against major powers remains a fundamental limitation of any international legal system based on state consent.

The most ambitious reform proposals envision new institutions specifically designed to address 21st-century challenges. Environmental lawyer Oran Young advocates for a "Global Ocean Commission" with authority to address issues spanning traditional institutional boundaries, including climate change, resource extraction, and territorial disputes.[56] Such institutions would require unprecedented levels of international cooperation and state willingness to accept external authority.

Adaptive Management Approaches

Rather than comprehensive reform, some experts advocate for "adaptive management" approaches that allow existing institutions to evolve incrementally in response to changing circumstances. This model draws on environmental governance experiences where complex, uncertain problems require flexible, learning-oriented approaches.[57]

The International Seabed Authority's ongoing negotiations over deep-sea mining regulations exemplify both the potential and limitations of adaptive approaches. While the ISA has struggled to reach consensus on commercial mining rules, its deliberative process has allowed for incorporation of new scientific knowledge and stakeholder input.[58] However, the slow pace of adaptation may prove inadequate for addressing rapidly evolving technological and environmental challenges.

Bilateral and regional approaches offer another avenue for adaptive governance. The 2016 establishment of bilateral maritime dialogue between Japan and Taiwan following fishing disputes around Okinotorishima demonstrates how states can develop practical arrangements without resolving underlying legal disagreements.[59] Such mechanisms may prove more feasible than comprehensive multilateral reform while still providing useful precedents for broader institutional development.

Lessons for Global Governance

The Okinotorishima case offers several important lessons for understanding how territorial disputes, resource competition, and environmental change will interact in shaping future international relations. These insights extend beyond maritime law to broader questions about governance of global commons and management of interstate competition in an era of technological advancement and environmental change.

The Persistence of Territorial Competition

Despite predictions that globalization would reduce the importance of territorial control, the Okinotorishima case demonstrates the continued centrality of territory in international relations. Economic interdependence and technological connectivity have not eliminated states' desire to control physical spaces and the resources they contain. If anything, resource scarcity and supply chain vulnerabilities have intensified territorial competition by raising the stakes of access and control.

This persistence of territorial competition reflects what political scientist Stephen Krasner terms the "sovereignty paradox"—the enduring appeal of territorial control despite its declining effectiveness in addressing transnational challenges.[60] States continue to invest enormous resources in territorial claims because physical control provides a sense of security and autonomy that legal agreements and international institutions cannot fully replace.

The lesson for global governance is that institutional design must accommodate rather than ignore states' territorial instincts. Attempts to replace territorial sovereignty with purely functional governance arrangements are likely to fail if they do not provide alternative sources of security and autonomy. Successful institutions will need to channel territorial competition in productive directions rather than attempting to eliminate it entirely.

Technology's Double-Edged Impact

The Okinotorishima case illustrates technology's complex relationship with territorial disputes. On one hand, technological advancement creates new sources of competition by making previously worthless territories valuable for resource extraction or strategic positioning. Deep-sea mining technology, satellite surveillance, and autonomous systems all contribute to intensified competition over remote maritime areas.

On the other hand, technology also provides new tools for managing territorial disputes. Real-time monitoring reduces information asymmetries that can lead to misunderstandings and escalation. Communication technologies enable rapid consultation and crisis management. Engineering capabilities allow states to adapt to environmental changes without necessarily resorting to territorial conquest.

The key insight is that technology's impact on territorial competition depends critically on the institutional context within which it operates.

Technology can either exacerbate competition or facilitate cooperation, depending on whether institutions channel technological capabilities toward zero-sum competition or positive-sum collaboration.

Environmental Change as a Governance Driver

Climate change and environmental degradation are emerging as central drivers of institutional change in international relations. The Okinotorishima case demonstrates how environmental threats can create both new sources of conflict (over newly accessible resources) and new imperatives for cooperation (in addressing shared challenges like sea level rise).

The traditional approach of treating environmental issues as separate from security and economic concerns is proving inadequate for addressing challenges that span these domains. Rising sea levels affect territorial sovereignty, resource access, and population displacement simultaneously. Institutional responses must be similarly integrated to be effective.

The most promising approaches recognize environmental change as an opportunity to develop new forms of international cooperation rather than simply as a threat to existing arrangements. The Arctic Council's success in managing environmental and resource issues in the Arctic provides a model for how states can cooperate even while maintaining competitive relationships in other domains.[61]

Conclusion: The Future of Ocean Governance

The struggle over Okinotorishima ultimately represents a microcosm of broader challenges facing global governance in the 21st century. A tiny atoll generates conflicts between great powers because it embodies fundamental tensions between legal rules and economic interests, environmental protection and resource extraction, technological capability and institutional adaptation. These tensions will only intensify as climate change, technological advancement, and resource competition reshape the international system.

The case demonstrates that purely legal approaches to territorial disputes are insufficient when vital economic and security interests are at stake. No amount of legal clarity can eliminate the incentives for creative interpretation when billions of dollars in resources and critical supply chains are involved. However, this does not mean that law is irrelevant. Rather, legal frameworks must be designed with recognition of the political pressures they will face and the economic realities that shape state behavior.

Future ocean governance will likely require what international relations theorist John Ruggie terms "embedded liberalism"—institutional arrangements that accommodate states' legitimate security needs while promoting cooperation in areas of mutual benefit.[62] For maritime domains, this might involve accepting that states will maintain competitive relationships over resource access while cooperating on shared challenges like environmental protection and navigation safety.

The Okinotorishima case also highlights the importance of technological capability in shaping territorial outcomes. Japan's ability to invest $600 million in coral preservation, China's deployment of advanced research vessels, and the role of satellite surveillance in monitoring remote territories all demonstrate how technological advantage translates into territorial influence. States that fail to develop relevant capabilities risk being excluded from future territorial competitions regardless of their legal claims.

Perhaps most importantly, the case illustrates the need for adaptive governance institutions that can evolve in response to changing circumstances. The current legal framework, designed in the 1970s and 1980s, cannot address challenges posed by deep-sea mining, climate change, and great power competition without significant adaptation. However, formal treaty revision is politically difficult and time-consuming. Institutional evolution through interpretation, subsidiary agreements, and practical arrangements may prove more feasible.

The ultimate lesson of Okinotorishima is that the future of ocean governance will be shaped not by abstract legal principles but by the interaction between technological capabilities, economic incentives, environmental pressures, and institutional adaptability. States that understand these dynamics and develop appropriate capabilities will be best positioned to secure their interests in an increasingly competitive maritime domain. Those that rely solely on existing legal arrangements or fail to adapt to changing circumstances risk being marginalized in the scramble for tomorrow's ocean.

The last rock's legacy may thus be to demonstrate that in an era of resource scarcity and environmental change, even the smallest territories can generate the largest conflicts—and that managing these conflicts will require new approaches to sovereignty, governance, and international cooperation that we are only beginning to understand.

Footnotes

1. Derek Croxton, "The Peace of Westphalia of 1648 and the Origins of Sovereignty," International History Review 21, no. 3 (1999): 569-591.
2. Rebecca Strating and Joanne Wallis, "Maritime sovereignty and territorialisation: Comparing the Pacific Islands and South China Sea," Marine Policy 138 (2022): 105016.
3. Ibid.
4. Christian Volk, "The Problem of Sovereignty in Globalized Times," Global Constitutionalism 8, no. 1 (2019): 31-52.
5. "Japan Finds Rare Earth Deposits Worth Trillions," Nippon Foundation Press Release, June 15, 2024.
6. "Underwater Natural Resources Can Secure Global Supply Chains," 3GIMBALS, April 14, 2025, https://3gimbals.com/insights/underwater-natural-resources-the-next-strategic-frontier-for-u-s-leadership/.
7. M. Taylor Fravel, "International Relations Theory and China's Rise: Assessing China's Potential for Territorial Expansion," International Studies Review 12, no. 4 (2010): 505-532.
8. Bonnie S. Glaser and Abigail Wulf, "China's Role in Critical Mineral Supply Chains," GMF, August 2, 2023.
9. "Professor Robert Beckman on the Role of UNCLOS in Maritime Disputes," Georgetown Journal of International Affairs, April 30, 2021.
10. "Dark Law on the South China Sea," Chicago Journal of

International Law 21, no. 2 (2021): 97-142.

11. Gavan McCormack, "Troubled Seas: Japan's Pacific and East China Sea Domains," Asia-Pacific Journal: Japan Focus 10, no. 36 (2012): 1-31.
12. Ibid.
13. "International Law and the challenges in implementing UNCLOS: South China Sea Arbitration," Modern Diplomacy, July 17, 2024.
14. "UNCLOS and the South China Sea Crisis: How Maritime Law is Being Ignored," Columbia Undergraduate Law Review, December 10, 2021.
15. "International Law and the challenges in implementing UNCLOS."
16. "What We Know About Deep-Sea Mining and What We Don't," World Resources Institute, July 2025.
17. "Unleashing America's Offshore Critical Minerals and Resources," Executive Order, The White House, April 24, 2025.
18. "Race to the Deep on Seabed Mining," Stimson Center, December 10, 2024.
19. Russell Handy, Michael J. Forsyth, and Joseph Kunkel, "Sovereignty-in-Being: A Dangerous New Model for Territorial Expansion in the 21st Century," InterAgency Journal 9, no. 2 (2018): 51-65.
20. McCormack, "Troubled Seas."
21. "Strategic Snapshot: Global Competition in Critical Minerals and Rare Earth Elements," Jamestown Foundation, May 1, 2025.
22. "Policy 360: Exploring the Impacts of Deep-Sea Mining," Columbia Political Review, January 21, 2025.
23. McCormack, "Troubled Seas."
24. "US ratification of the ocean treaty will unlock deep sea mining," Atlantic Council, June 4, 2024.
25. Ibid.
26. "Mapping the Impact and Conflicts of Rare-Earth Elements," Institute for Policy Studies, July 17, 2024.
27. Jonathan Kirshner, Currency and Coercion: The Political Economy of International Monetary Power (Princeton: Princeton

University Press, 1995).

28. "Rockall Bank dispute," Wikipedia, accessed August 8, 2025.
29. Ibid.
30. "Guest blog – Unpacking the legal disputes over Rockall," SPICE Spotlight, September 22, 2022.
31. "An Irish Claim to Rockall," EJIL: Talk!, January 14, 2021.
32. "Dark Law on the South China Sea."
33. "UNCLOS and South China Sea Maritime Disputes: Legal Complexities and Interpretations," Denver Journal of International Law & Policy, 2024.
34. "Territorial claims in the Arctic," Wikipedia, accessed August 8, 2025.
35. "Scramble for the Arctic: Layered Sovereignty, UNCLOS, and Competing Maritime Territorial Claims," ResearchGate, January 1, 2013.
36. Ibid.
37. "Chapter 8: The Arctic & the LOSC," Law of the Sea, Tufts University.
38. "A New Chinese Buoy Is Causing Concern in Japan," The Diplomat, July 8, 2024.
39. Interview with Timothy Heath, RAND Corporation, August 2025.
40. "A New Chinese Buoy Is Causing Concern in Japan."
41. "International Legal Regime regarding Islands and Rocks," Review of Island Studies, Ocean Policy Research Foundation.
42. "Maritime sovereignty and territorialisation."
43. United Nations Convention on the Law of the Sea, Article 121(1).
44. "Maritime sovereignty and territorialisation."
45. Ibid.
46. International Law Commission, "Report on Sea Level Rise in Relation to International Law," 2022.
47. "International Legal Regime regarding Islands and Rocks."
48. Robin Kundis Craig, "Climate Change, Regulatory Fragmentation, and Water Triage," University of Colorado Law Review 79 (2008): 825-928.

49. McCormack, "Troubled Seas."
50. "Race to the Deep on Seabed Mining."
51. "Unleashing America's Offshore Critical Minerals and Resources."
52. "Strategic Snapshot: Global Competition in Critical Minerals."
53. International Energy Agency, "Critical Minerals Market Review 2023" (Paris: IEA, 2023).
54. Robin Churchill, "The 1982 United Nations Convention on the Law of the Sea," in The Oxford Handbook of the Law of the Sea, ed. Donald Rothwell et al. (Oxford: Oxford University Press, 2015).
55. James Harrison, Making the Law of the Sea: A Study in the Development of International Law (Cambridge: Cambridge University Press, 2011).
56. Oran Young, "Institutional Dynamics: Resilience, Vulnerability and Adaptation in Environmental and Resource Regimes," Global Environmental Change 20, no. 3 (2010): 378-385.
57. Carl Folke et al., "Adaptive Governance of Social-Ecological Systems," Annual Review of Environment and Resources 30 (2005): 441-473.
58. "What We Know About Deep-Sea Mining and What We Don't."
59. "Territorial disputes of Japan," Wikipedia, accessed August 8, 2025.
60. Stephen Krasner, Sovereignty: Organized Hypocrisy (Princeton: Princeton University Press, 1999).
61. Oran Young, Arctic Politics: Conflict and Cooperation in the Circumpolar North (Hanover, NH: University Press of New England, 1992).
62. John Gerard Ruggie, "International Regimes, Transactions, and Change: Embedded Liberalism in the Postwar Economic Order," International Organization 36, no. 2 (1982): 379-415.

Chapter 17: Toward Tomorrow's Ocean

"The ocean is the lifeblood of our planet... However, it faces unprecedented threats from pollution, overfishing, habitat destruction, and climate change." — United Nations Environment Programme, 2025[1]

As dawn breaks over Okinotorishima on a crisp morning in August 2025, the automated systems monitoring Japan's most remote territory continue their silent vigil. The titanium nets shimmer in the early light, the concrete barriers stand firm against the Pacific swells, and satellite communications relay real-time data back to Tokyo. Yet beneath this technological marvel lies a deeper question that extends far beyond these 9.44 square meters of engineered reef: How can humanity govern the world's oceans in an era of climate change, technological revolution, and great power competition?

The Okinotorishima dispute, with its complex interplay of law, economics, technology, and geopolitics, offers a unique lens through which to examine the future of ocean governance. As we stand at the threshold of what scholars call the "fourth industrial revolution" in maritime affairs,[2] the lessons learned from humanity's smallest sovereign territory may well inform how we manage our largest shared commons.

The Convergence of Crises and Opportunities

The year 2024 marked a watershed moment for international ocean governance. On May 21, the International Tribunal for the Law of the Sea (ITLOS) delivered its first advisory opinion explicitly addressing climate change, finding that anthropogenic greenhouse gas emissions constitute marine pollution under UNCLOS and that states have "specific obligations to take all necessary measures to prevent, reduce and control marine pollution from anthropogenic GHG emissions."[3] This landmark ruling fundamentally reframes ocean governance, transforming climate change from an external challenge to a core maritime legal obligation.

Against this backdrop, the Okinotorishima dispute continues to evolve. In July 2024, Japan discovered a Chinese buoy in waters it claims as its exclusive economic zone around the atoll, prompting Tokyo to demand explanations from Beijing about its purpose.[4] The incident underscored how technological capabilities—from oceanographic monitoring to autonomous systems—are reshaping the nature of sovereignty itself.

These developments illuminate three converging trends that will define ocean governance in the coming decades: the climate imperative demanding new legal frameworks, the technological revolution enabling new forms of presence and monitoring, and the geopolitical competition driving innovation in both cooperation and confrontation. The question facing policymakers is not whether these trends will reshape ocean governance, but how quickly institutions can adapt to harness their potential for peaceful cooperation rather than conflict.

Resolution Pathways: Learning from Success and Failure

Bilateral Negotiation: The Joint Development Model

The complexity of the Okinotorishima dispute might seem to preclude negotiated solutions, yet successful precedents exist for transforming maritime conflicts into cooperative partnerships. The 1990 Malaysia-Thailand Joint Development Agreement stands as perhaps the most successful model of its kind, having operated for over three decades in managing overlapping maritime claims.[5]

The Malaysia-Thailand model offers several features relevant to the Okinotorishima case. Rather than resolving the underlying territorial dispute, the agreement established a joint authority to manage resource extraction in the disputed area, with revenues shared equally between the parties. Crucially, the agreement included provisions for environmental protection and established dispute resolution mechanisms that have prevented conflicts despite changing political leadership in both countries.[6]

For Okinotorishima, a bilateral framework could address several dimensions simultaneously:

Resource-Sharing Mechanisms: Given the June 2024 discovery of polymetallic nodules worth over $18 billion in waters around

Okinotorishima,[7] a joint development approach could provide both Japan and China access to critical materials needed for their respective energy transitions while avoiding the winner-take-all dynamics of current territorial competition.

Scientific Cooperation: The dispute fundamentally concerns the interpretation of scientific data—whether Okinotorishima constitutes rocks or islands under UNCLOS Article 121(3). Joint scientific research programs could transform this source of conflict into a foundation for cooperation, potentially modeling collaborative approaches for other contested maritime features globally.

Fisheries Management: Taiwan's involvement in the 2016 fishing vessel incident[8] highlights the importance of including fisheries access in any comprehensive agreement. Joint fisheries management arrangements could provide a low-stakes arena for building trust and institutional capacity.

International Arbitration: Strengthening Compliance Mechanisms

The 2016 Philippines v. China arbitration demonstrated both the potential and limitations of existing international legal mechanisms. While the tribunal's ruling was legally sound, China's rejection highlighted fundamental enforcement challenges that any future Okinotorishima arbitration would likely face.[9] However, recent developments suggest ways to strengthen international legal frameworks:

Enhanced Compliance Through Climate Linkages: The May 2024 ITLOS advisory opinion creates new pathways for enforcement by linking maritime disputes to climate obligations. States that fail to comply with arbitral awards related to maritime boundaries could potentially face challenges under climate-related legal frameworks, creating overlapping incentives for compliance.[10]

Regional Integration of Dispute Resolution: Rather than relying solely on global mechanisms, regional frameworks could provide more effective enforcement. The European Union's experience with marine protected areas demonstrates how regional institutions can create binding obligations even in areas of overlapping jurisdiction.[11]

Economic Incentives for Compliance: Modern arbitration mechanisms could incorporate economic instruments, such as carbon credit systems or resource-sharing arrangements, that make compliance more attractive than non-compliance. The success of international emissions trading suggests similar mechanisms could be applied to maritime disputes.

Status Quo Management: Preventing Escalation Through Institutional Innovation

Even absent comprehensive resolution, the Okinotorishima dispute demonstrates the potential for stable management of competing claims. Japan's investment of over $600 million in preservation infrastructure[12] represents a form of "facts on the water" strategy, while China's research vessel activities assert alternative interpretations of maritime rights. Rather than viewing these activities as necessarily destabilizing, future governance frameworks could establish clearer rules of engagement:

Transparency Mechanisms: Automatic identification systems (AIS) and maritime domain awareness technologies already enable real-time tracking of vessel activities. Expanding these systems to include research activities, infrastructure development, and environmental monitoring could reduce misunderstandings and prevent incidents from escalating.[13]

Incident Prevention Protocols: The May 2025 confrontation between Chinese research vessel R/V Tan Kah Kee and Japanese Coast Guard aircraft[14] illustrates the need for clear protocols governing scientific research in disputed waters. Drawing on successful models like the US-Soviet Incidents at Sea Agreement, new frameworks could establish rules for research activities, infrastructure maintenance, and environmental monitoring.

Joint Monitoring Systems: Rather than parallel monitoring systems that duplicate costs and create potential for misunderstanding, shared monitoring infrastructure could provide both parties with access to the same environmental and security data while building institutional capacity for broader cooperation.

Innovation Opportunities: Technology as Bridge-

Builder

The Maritime Autonomous Revolution

The rapid development of maritime autonomous systems offers unprecedented opportunities for managing remote territories like Okinotorishima. By 2024, autonomous vessels can operate for extended periods without human crews, conducting surveillance, environmental monitoring, and resource surveys at a fraction of traditional costs.[15] These technologies could transform sovereignty expression from a physical presence requirement to a technological capability demonstration.

Persistent Presence Through Automation: Japan's current approach requires expensive crewed missions for infrastructure maintenance and monitoring. Autonomous systems could provide continuous presence at much lower cost, potentially making sovereignty expression more sustainable financially while reducing risks to human crews in harsh weather conditions.

Shared Autonomous Infrastructure: Rather than competing deployments of autonomous systems, joint ventures could reduce costs while building operational cooperation. Shared platforms could monitor environmental conditions, conduct scientific research, and provide data to all participants, transforming zero-sum competition into positive-sum collaboration.

AI-Enabled Dispute Prevention: Advanced artificial intelligence systems can analyze patterns in vessel movements, environmental conditions, and communications to predict potential incidents before they occur. By 2024, AI systems already optimize ship routing and reduce fuel consumption by up to 15 percent.[16] Similar technologies could identify potential flashpoints and suggest de-escalation measures automatically.

Climate Adaptation Technologies

The ITLOS climate advisory opinion creates new obligations for states to protect marine environments from climate change impacts.[17] For Okinotorishima, facing existential threats from sea level rise and intensifying typhoons, these obligations create both challenges and opportunities:

Ecosystem Engineering: Japan's coral cultivation efforts represent early attempts at climate adaptation through biological intervention. Future technologies could enable more sophisticated ecosystem engineering, potentially creating new models for maintaining territorial integrity despite environmental change.

Carbon Sequestration Partnerships: The ocean's role as a carbon sink creates opportunities for international cooperation in blue carbon projects. Joint investments in marine carbon sequestration could provide revenue streams while meeting climate obligations and building institutional capacity for broader cooperation.

Resilient Infrastructure Networks: Rather than isolated infrastructure, future sovereignty technologies could create resilient networks of sensors, platforms, and autonomous systems that can withstand extreme weather while providing continuous monitoring and presence.

Transforming Legal Frameworks Through Digital Innovation

Blockchain and distributed ledger technologies offer possibilities for creating new forms of international agreements that could address some traditional enforcement challenges:

Smart Treaties: International agreements could incorporate automatic compliance mechanisms triggered by environmental or political conditions. For example, resource-sharing arrangements could automatically adjust based on environmental monitoring data or economic indicators.

Distributed Governance: Rather than centralized international institutions, blockchain technologies could enable distributed governance mechanisms where multiple stakeholders participate in decision-making without requiring consensus on underlying sovereignty questions.

Transparent Resource Management: Digital technologies could provide real-time transparency in resource extraction, environmental monitoring, and revenue sharing, reducing opportunities for disputes while building trust through verifiable data.

Institutional Innovation: Building Resilient Ocean

Governance

Reforming UNCLOS for the Climate Era

The 1982 United Nations Convention on the Law of the Sea, while revolutionary for its time, faces growing challenges in addressing 21st-century ocean governance needs. The Okinotorishima dispute illustrates several areas where institutional evolution is necessary:

Adaptive Baseline Management: Current UNCLOS provisions assume stable coastlines and maritime features. As climate change threatens to submerge low-lying territories, new legal frameworks must address questions of "disappearing" territorial baselines and the implications for maritime zones. The Commission on the Limits of the Continental Shelf has already deferred recommendations on Okinotorishima until these issues are resolved.[18]

Dynamic EEZ Concepts: Rather than fixed 200-nautical-mile zones, future frameworks might incorporate dynamic concepts that adjust based on environmental conditions, resource availability, or cooperative arrangements. This could address the particular challenges posed by remote features like Okinotorishima while providing flexibility for climate adaptation.

Integrated Environmental Obligations: The 2024 ITLOS advisory opinion demonstrates how climate change is already being integrated into maritime law interpretation. Future UNCLOS revisions could explicitly incorporate environmental protection obligations, creating clearer frameworks for balancing sovereignty claims with conservation needs.

New International Bodies for Ocean Governance

The limitations of existing international institutions in addressing complex, multi-dimensional disputes like Okinotorishima suggest the need for new institutional approaches:

Regional Ocean Governance Councils: Building on the success of regional fisheries management organizations, new bodies could address the full range of ocean governance challenges within specific geographic areas. A Western Pacific Ocean Council could provide a forum for addressing not only the Okinotorishima dispute but related challenges in the South China Sea, East China Sea, and broader Pacific commons.

Technology and Ocean Governance Initiative: As autonomous systems, artificial intelligence, and other technologies reshape ocean activities, new institutions are needed to address governance challenges and opportunities. An international initiative could develop standards for autonomous systems, guidelines for AI use in maritime domains, and frameworks for sharing technological benefits.

Climate-Ocean Governance Integration: The 2024 ITLOS advisory opinion highlights the need for better integration between climate and ocean governance institutions. New mechanisms could coordinate between the UN Framework Convention on Climate Change, UNCLOS institutions, and regional bodies to ensure coherent approaches to climate-ocean challenges.

Multi-Stakeholder Governance Models

Traditional state-centric approaches to ocean governance increasingly seem inadequate for addressing challenges that span multiple scales, sectors, and jurisdictions. The Okinotorishima case illustrates how non-state actors—from fishing communities to environmental organizations to technology companies—play crucial roles that existing frameworks struggle to accommodate:

Inclusive Decision-Making Processes: Future governance frameworks could formally incorporate non-state stakeholders in decision-making processes. The International Union for Conservation of Nature's (IUCN) participation in international legal proceedings provides a model for how non-state expertise can inform legal processes.[19]

Private-Public Partnerships: The high costs of ocean monitoring and resource development create opportunities for private-public partnerships that could reduce state burdens while building commercial incentives for cooperation. Joint ventures between Japanese and Chinese companies could potentially break political deadlocks through economic incentives.

Civil Society Monitoring: Non-governmental organizations and academic institutions could play expanded roles in monitoring compliance with international agreements, providing independent verification of environmental and political commitments.

Cooperative Vision: Toward Shared Ocean Stewardship

The Maritime Community with a Shared Future

China's proposal for a "Maritime Community with a Shared Future" (MCSF), while politically motivated, contains elements that could inform future governance approaches. The MCSF framework emphasizes "maintaining maritime peace," "creating mutually beneficial cooperation relationships," "improving the marine ecological environment," and "promoting cultural exchanges."[20] While skeptics question China's commitment to these principles given its assertive behavior in maritime disputes, the framework nonetheless provides a starting point for dialogue about shared approaches to ocean governance.

For the Okinotorishima case, MCSF principles could be operationalized through:

Joint Environmental Stewardship: Rather than competing claims to environmental protection, Japan and China could establish joint stewardship arrangements for the broader Philippine Sea ecosystem, using Okinotorishima as a focal point for cooperative conservation efforts.

Shared Research Infrastructure: The substantial investments required for deep-sea research and monitoring could be shared between parties, reducing costs while building institutional capacity for broader cooperation.

Cultural and Educational Exchanges: Maritime disputes often reflect deeper cultural and historical tensions. Educational exchanges focused on marine science, ocean governance, and environmental protection could build understanding between younger generations while developing expertise needed for future cooperation.

Integrated Ocean-Climate Governance

The 2024 ITLOS advisory opinion fundamentally alters the landscape for ocean governance by establishing clear legal obligations to address climate change impacts on marine environments. This creates new opportunities for cooperative approaches that align national interests with global environmental needs:

Blue Carbon Partnerships: The ocean's role in carbon sequestration creates opportunities for international cooperation that could generate revenue while meeting climate obligations. Joint blue carbon projects in waters around Okinotorishima could provide alternative sources of value while building institutional capacity for broader cooperation.

Ecosystem-Based Management: Rather than feature-by-feature territorial claims, future governance approaches could focus on ecosystem-level management that addresses climate adaptation, biodiversity conservation, and sustainable resource use as integrated challenges requiring cooperative responses.

Adaptive Management Frameworks: Climate change creates fundamental uncertainty about future environmental conditions. Governance frameworks must incorporate adaptive management approaches that can adjust to changing conditions while maintaining stability in international relations.

Technology-Enabled Cooperation

The rapid development of maritime technologies creates new possibilities for cooperation that were unimaginable when UNCLOS was negotiated. Rather than viewing technological development as a zero-sum competition, future frameworks could harness technology for cooperative purposes:

Shared Autonomous Networks: Networks of autonomous sensors and platforms could provide all participants with access to the same environmental and security data, reducing mistrust while building shared understanding of ocean conditions.

AI-Assisted Governance: Artificial intelligence systems could help identify cooperative opportunities, predict potential conflicts, and suggest mutually beneficial solutions to emerging challenges. Machine learning algorithms could analyze vast amounts of environmental, economic, and political data to identify win-win scenarios that human negotiators might miss.

Digital Twins for Ocean Governance: Virtual representations of ocean systems could enable stakeholders to test different governance scenarios, predict outcomes of policy changes, and build understanding of complex system interactions before implementing real-world changes.

Case Study: A Model Resolution for Okinotorishima

Drawing together these various approaches, we can envision a comprehensive framework for addressing the Okinotorishima dispute that could serve as a model for similar challenges globally:

Phase One: Building Trust Through Low-Stakes Cooperation

Joint Scientific Research Initiative: Japan, China, and Taiwan establish a trilateral marine research program focused on climate change impacts in the Philippine Sea. This provides a forum for building institutional relationships while addressing shared environmental challenges.

Shared Monitoring Infrastructure: Rather than parallel monitoring systems, the parties establish joint environmental monitoring stations that provide all participants with access to the same data about ocean conditions, marine life, and environmental changes.

Educational Exchanges: Universities and research institutions in all three parties establish exchange programs focused on marine science, ocean governance, and international law, building expertise and understanding among future leaders.

Phase Two: Economic Integration Through Resource Cooperation

Deep-Sea Mining Consortium: Building on successful models from other industries, the parties establish a joint venture for deep-sea mining that shares costs, risks, and revenues while developing new technologies for sustainable resource extraction.

Blue Carbon Partnership: Joint investments in marine carbon sequestration projects provide revenue streams while meeting climate obligations and building institutional capacity for environmental cooperation.

Technology Development Collaboration: Joint research and development programs for maritime technologies, including autonomous systems, environmental monitoring, and sustainable resource extraction, share costs while building technological capabilities.

Phase Three: Institutional Integration and Broader Cooperation

Philippine Sea Governance Council: The parties establish a new regional institution responsible for ecosystem-level management of the Philippine Sea, providing a forum for addressing broader ocean governance challenges beyond the immediate territorial dispute.

Adaptive Legal Framework: Rather than resolving the underlying territorial dispute, the parties establish a new legal framework that provides clear rules for activities in disputed areas while incorporating mechanisms for adaptation as environmental and political conditions change.

Global Model Development: The successful cooperation framework is expanded to address other maritime disputes and challenges, providing a model for ocean governance in the climate era.

The Path Forward: Leadership in an Age of Transformation

The Okinotorishima dispute, with its unique combination of legal complexity, environmental vulnerability, economic potential, and geopolitical significance, represents both the challenges and opportunities facing ocean governance in the 21st century. The lessons learned from this tiny atoll could inform approaches to much larger challenges, from Arctic governance as ice melts to the management of marine genetic resources in areas beyond national jurisdiction.

The path forward requires leadership at multiple levels. Political leaders must move beyond zero-sum thinking to embrace cooperative approaches that recognize the interconnected nature of ocean challenges. Legal scholars and practitioners must work to adapt international law frameworks to address climate change, technological development, and new forms of international cooperation. Scientists and engineers must develop technologies that enable cooperation rather than competition, sharing benefits rather than concentrating advantages.

Most importantly, the next generation of ocean governance leaders must think systemically about challenges that span multiple scales, sectors, and jurisdictions. The Okinotorishima dispute illustrates how local challenges connect to global systems, how legal questions intersect with environmental and technological issues, and how competition can be transformed into cooperation through innovative institutional design.

As we sail toward tomorrow's ocean, the choices made today about governance frameworks, technological development, and international cooperation will determine whether the world's largest commons becomes a source of conflict or collaboration. The lessons from humanity's smallest sovereign territory suggest that with imagination, commitment, and institutional innovation, even the most intractable disputes can become foundations for broader cooperation.

The sun setting over Okinotorishima as this chapter concludes illuminates not just titanium nets and concrete barriers, but a more hopeful vision: autonomous systems working together to monitor shared environments, research stations collaborating on climate adaptation, and governance frameworks that turn competition into cooperation. In the Pacific's vastness, nine square meters of engineered reef could become the foundation for a new era of ocean stewardship—if we have the wisdom to seize the opportunity.

Footnotes

[1] United Nations Environment Programme, "Ocean Governance," accessed August 8, 2025, https://www.unep.org/topics/ocean-seas-and-coasts/regional-seas-programme/ocean-governance.

[2] Sea Machines Robotics, "Ultimate Guide to Maritime Autonomy in 2024," January 15, 2024, https://sea-machines.com/ultimate-guide-to-maritime-autonomy-in-2024/.

[3] International Tribunal for the Law of the Sea, Advisory Opinion, Climate Change and International Law, May 21, 2024, para. 229.

[4] South China Morning Post, "Japan wants answers over Chinese buoy found in remote contested waters," July 9, 2024, https://www.scmp.com/week-asia/politics/article/3269635/japan-wants-answers-over-chinese-buoy-found-remote-contested-waters.

[5] Constantinos Yiallourides, "Joint Development of Seabed Resources in Areas of Overlapping Maritime Claims: An Analysis of Precedents in State Practice," British Institute of International and Comparative Law, June 24, 2020.

[6] Luis E. Rodriguez-Rivera, "Joint Development Zones and other Cooperative Management Efforts Related to Transboundary Maritime Resources: A Caribbean and Latin American Model for Peaceful Resolution of Maritime Boundary Disputes," Issues in Legal Scholarship 7, no. 1 (2008).

[7] Based on June 2024 discovery by University of Tokyo and Nippon Foundation as referenced in Chapter 7 research notes.

[8] As detailed in Chapter 5 analysis of the Dongshengji No. 16 incident.

[9] Modern Diplomacy, "International Law and the challenges in implementing UNCLOS: South China Sea Arbitration," July 17, 2024, https://moderndiplomacy.eu/2024/07/17/international-law-and-the-challenges-in-implementing-unclos-south-china-sea-arbitration/.

[10] Climate Law Blog, "Unlocking UNCLOS: How the ITLOS Advisory Opinion Delivers a Holistic Vision of Climate-relevant International Law," December 19, 2024, https://blogs.law.columbia.edu/climatechange/2024/05/24/unlocking-unclos-how-the-itlos-advisory-opinion-delivers-a-holistic-vision-of-climate-relevant-international-law/.

[11] European Commission, "International ocean governance framework," accessed August 8, 2025, https://oceans-and-fisheries.ec.europa.eu/ocean/international-ocean-governance/strengthening-international-ocean-governance-framework_en.

[12] As documented in Chapter 3 analysis of Japan's financial investment.

[13] eTrade for all, "Navigating the Future: How AI, big data, and autonomous systems are reshaping maritime transport," UNCTAD Transport and Trade Facilitation Newsletter No. 103 - Third Quarter 2024.

[14] The Japan Times, "Japan says China conducted research near Pacific atoll," May 27, 2025, https://www.japantimes.co.jp/news/2025/05/27/japan/china-eez-research/.

[15] Sea Machines Robotics, "Ultimate Guide to Maritime Autonomy in 2024."

[16] eTrade for all, "Navigating the Future: How AI, big data, and autonomous systems are reshaping maritime transport."

[17] International Tribunal for the Law of the Sea, Advisory Opinion, Climate Change and International Law, May 21, 2024.

[18] As noted in CLCS deferral decision of June 2012 referenced in Chapter 4.

[19] Frontiers in Marine Science, "A new horizon for rule-making in global ocean governance? Reflections on the IUCN's contributions and limitations," July 10, 2025, https://www.frontiersin.org/journals/marine-science/articles/10.3389/fmars.2025.1615329/full.

[20] Frontiers in Marine Science, "The interaction and mutual development of 'a maritime community with a shared future' and global ocean governance," June 26, 2024, https://www.frontiersin.org/journals/marine-science/articles/10.3389/fmars.2024.1425673/full.

EPILOGUE: "The Last Rock's Legacy"

On a clear morning in May 2025, Lieutenant Commander Tanaka Hiroshi guided his Japan Coast Guard patrol aircraft through the azure waters of the Philippine Sea, 167 miles east of Okinotorishima. Below him, the Chinese research vessel R/V Tan Kah Kee had deployed what appeared to be scientific equipment into the contested waters—a wire descending into the 5,500-meter depths where Japan claimed exclusive rights and China insisted on the freedom of the high seas.[1] As Tanaka issued the standard radio warnings that echoed across the vast Pacific, he embodied a paradox that has come to define the 21st century: highly trained professionals conducting their duties with utmost professionalism while representing competing visions of how humanity should govern the world's largest commons.

The Tan Kah Kee incident, like dozens before it, concluded without violence. The Chinese vessel departed after five hours, the Japanese patrol returned to base, and diplomats in Beijing and Tokyo exchanged familiar protests. Yet this routine confrontation over what China's Foreign Ministry spokesperson Mao Ning called merely "a reef" and Japan insisted was an "island" illuminated fundamental questions that extend far beyond the tiny concrete platforms of Okinotorishima.[2] What does it mean to claim sovereignty in an era when the very concept of territory is being redefined by rising seas, advancing technology, and the urgent need for critical minerals buried in the ocean's depths?

The Human Dimension of Maritime Sovereignty

The individuals caught up in this geopolitical struggle represent the human face of 21st-century territorial competition. Captain Chen Wei-ming, master of the Taiwanese fishing vessel Dongshengji No. 16, never intended to become a diplomatic incident when Japan Coast Guard officers detained his crew 150 nautical miles from Okinotorishima on April 25, 2016.[3] The ¥6 million fine (approximately $54,000) paid for his release represented more than just a commercial loss—it crystallized the tension between livelihoods that have sustained Pacific Island communities for generations and the new realities of maritime boundaries drawn by international lawyers in conference rooms thousands of miles away.

Similarly, the engineers who have spent decades maintaining Japan's concrete fortress against the Pacific's fury—replacing titanium nets shredded by typhoons, reinforcing seawalls battered by 16-meter waves—work in service of an abstraction that nonetheless carries profound material consequences.[4] Their annual maintenance voyages to this most remote outpost of Japanese territory require not just technical expertise but also a faith that their efforts serve some larger purpose in an interconnected world where 9.44 square meters of preserved coral can generate claims over 420,000 square kilometers of ocean.

The diplomatic corps that manage these tensions deserve particular recognition. Taiwan's Coast Guard Administration personnel who conducted joint search and rescue exercises with their Japanese counterparts in July 2024—the first such cooperation since Japan ceased recognizing Taiwan's government in 1972—demonstrated how professional relationships can transcend political disputes.[5] These quiet acts of maritime cooperation, conducted away from media attention to avoid provoking China, suggest pathways toward pragmatic collaboration even amid strategic competition.

Most poignantly, the scientists aboard vessels like the R/V Tan Kah Kee find themselves at the intersection of pure research and geopolitical calculation. Dr. Wang Lijun, a marine geologist from Xiamen University, joined the May 2025 expedition to study polymetallic nodule formation in the Philippine Sea—research that advances human understanding of deep-ocean processes while simultaneously serving China's strategic mapping requirements for potential submarine operations.[6] The dual-use nature of oceanographic knowledge means that every data point collected serves both the advancement of science and the calculation of national advantage.

The Paradoxes of Modern Territoriality

What the Okinotorishima dispute reveals about human nature is both troubling and oddly hopeful. On one level, it demonstrates the persistence of territorial instincts that seem almost primitive in their intensity. Japan has spent over $600 million preserving and fortifying rocks that would barely qualify as building sites, while China deploys some of the world's most sophisticated research vessels to challenge claims over waters that previous generations would have considered empty ocean.[7] The emotional investment in these symbolic spaces suggests that humans remain fundamentally tribal creatures, capable of mobilizing enormous resources to defend abstract concepts of belonging and control.

Yet the dispute also reveals remarkable human adaptability and innovation. The legal frameworks that govern these contested waters—however imperfect—represent humanity's most ambitious attempt to create rules for shared spaces that transcend national boundaries. The United Nations Convention on the Law of the Sea, despite being negotiated when climate change was barely understood and deep-sea mining was science fiction, has provided sufficient flexibility for states to begin adapting to new realities.[8] The Pacific Islands Forum's landmark 2021 Declaration on Preserving Maritime Zones in the Face of Climate Change-Related Sea-Level Rise demonstrates how vulnerable nations are pioneering new approaches to sovereignty that may prove essential for the entire international community.[9]

The intersection of law and power revealed by this case is particularly instructive. Japan's position rests on careful legal interpretation—arguing that "rock" is undefined in international law and that artificial preservation does not disqualify natural features from generating maritime zones.[10] China's challenge invokes the same legal framework but emphasizes functional criteria about habitability and economic life. Neither side simply asserts raw power; both seek legitimacy through legal reasoning, suggesting that international law retains normative force even in an era of renewed great power competition.

The technological dimension adds another layer of complexity. Japan's 2024 discovery of over 230 million tonnes of polymetallic nodules containing 610,000 tonnes of cobalt and 740,000 tonnes of nickel in waters near Minamitorishima Island—Japan's easternmost territory—transforms the economic stakes of these maritime boundaries.[11] The Nippon Foundation's plans to begin large-scale extraction in 2026, potentially making Japan a major producer of critical materials for electric vehicle batteries, demonstrates how technological advancement can rapidly alter the strategic significance of previously marginal territories.

Environmental Challenges and Legal Evolution

Climate change presents the ultimate test of humanity's ability to adapt international law to new realities. The Intergovernmental Panel on Climate Change projects global sea level rise of 0.38 to 0.77 meters by 2100, with high confidence that relative sea level rise will continue affecting low-lying coastal areas and islands.[12] For Okinotorishima and similar features, this represents an existential challenge that transcends political disputes. Can artificial preservation indefinitely maintain sovereignty over features that would naturally disappear? Should it?

The emerging consensus in favor of "baseline preservation"—the principle that lawfully established maritime zones should remain fixed despite coastal changes from sea level rise—reflects pragmatic recognition that the alternative could destabilize the entire maritime legal order.[13] Countries as diverse as the Cook Islands, New Zealand, Kiribati, and Vanuatu have updated their submissions to the UN Secretary-General to deposit geographical coordinates rather than rely on naturally shifting low-water marks.[14] This shift toward legal abstraction—defining maritime boundaries by mathematics rather than physical geography—may seem artificial, but it offers stability in an era of rapid environmental change.

The discovery of "dark oxygen" generation by polymetallic nodules in 2024 adds another dimension to these debates.[15] If deep-sea minerals are indeed playing unexpected roles in abyssal ecosystems, then the rush to extract critical materials for climate mitigation technologies creates profound ethical dilemmas. How should humanity balance the urgent need for clean energy materials against potential disruption of ocean systems we barely understand? The International Seabed Authority's continued delays in finalizing mining regulations—with negotiations now postponed until 2026—reflect the genuine difficulty of these trade-offs.[16]

Toward Cooperative Ocean Governance

Despite the confrontational headlines, the Okinotorishima case also demonstrates remarkable instances of pragmatic cooperation. The bilateral maritime dialogue mechanism established between Taiwan and Japan following the 2016 fishing incident has largely prevented subsequent confrontations, even as the underlying legal questions remain unresolved.[17] The joint exercises conducted by Japanese, Taiwanese, American, and Philippine Coast Guards in 2024-2025 show how professional maritime organizations can build practical cooperation despite political tensions.[18] These relationships, maintained quietly and professionally, may prove more important for regional stability than the formal diplomatic positions of their respective governments.

The scientific cooperation enabled by Japan's deep-sea mining research offers another model. Despite political tensions, Chinese, Japanese, and international researchers continue to share data about ocean systems through organizations like the International Seabed Authority and various UN bodies. The R/V Tan Kah Kee's research, however strategically motivated, contributes to humanity's understanding of ocean processes that transcend national boundaries. Dr. Wang's polymetallic nodule samples, analyzed in laboratories from Xiamen to Tokyo to Woods Hole, advance collective knowledge even as they serve competitive purposes.

The emergence of new institutional frameworks suggests pathways toward more cooperative approaches. The Pacific Islands Forum's collective diplomatic initiatives—including the request for an advisory opinion from the International Court of Justice on state obligations regarding climate change—demonstrate how small states can shape international law despite their limited power.[19] The International Law Commission's ongoing study of sea level rise in relation to international law, involving legal experts from around the world, shows how academic and diplomatic communities can collaborate to address genuinely novel challenges.[20]

Regional cooperation mechanisms are also evolving. The 2022 policy for strengthening Japan Coast Guard capabilities explicitly includes cooperation with Southeast Asian maritime law enforcement agencies, providing patrol vessels and training to build collective capacity for maritime governance.[21]

China's participation in various multilateral fisheries management organizations, despite its assertive behavior in territorial disputes, suggests recognition that some ocean resources require cooperative management regardless of sovereignty claims.

Lessons for Global Commons Management

The Okinotorishima case offers crucial insights for managing other global commons. Like the deep ocean, Antarctica, outer space, and cyberspace all present challenges that transcend traditional concepts of territorial sovereignty. The ocean governance frameworks developed through decades of negotiation—however imperfect—provide models for addressing newer commons where rules remain underdeveloped.

The importance of institutional flexibility emerges as a key lesson. UNCLOS was negotiated when few foresaw the current combination of climate change, deep-sea mining technology, and great power competition. Yet its basic framework has proved adaptable enough to address these new challenges through interpretation, state practice, and supplementary agreements. The 2024 ratification of the Singapore Convention on Mediation by Japan and other countries demonstrates continued faith in international legal mechanisms even amid rising tensions.[22]

The role of science in commons governance deserves particular attention. The discovery of critical mineral deposits near Okinotorishima and Minamitorishima was enabled by decades of patient oceanographic research, much of it conducted through international scientific cooperation. The challenge moving forward is maintaining this scientific collaboration while managing the strategic competition that scientific discoveries inevitably generate. The ongoing debates over deep-sea mining regulation show both the difficulty and the necessity of making policy decisions based on incomplete scientific understanding.

The human dimension cannot be overlooked. Maritime governance ultimately depends on the daily decisions of patrol officers, fishermen, scientists, and engineers who implement policies decided in distant capitals. The informal networks of cooperation built among these professional communities—the Japanese and Taiwanese Coast Guard officers who have worked together despite political tensions, the international scientific collaborations that continue despite strategic competition—may prove more durable than formal diplomatic agreements.

The Future of Ocean Governance

Looking ahead, the Okinotorishima dispute is likely to be remembered not for its resolution—if indeed it is ever formally resolved—but for its role in catalyzing broader evolution in ocean governance. The current period of creative tension, where traditional legal frameworks strain to address new realities, may prove more productive than a premature settlement that fails to address underlying challenges.

Several trends seem likely to accelerate. Climate change will continue to challenge fixed concepts of territory, forcing legal systems to become more abstract and mathematical. Technological advancement will continue to reveal new resources and capabilities in previously inaccessible areas. Great power competition will persist but may increasingly be channeled through legal and institutional mechanisms rather than purely military ones.

The deep-sea mining industry emerging around Japan's EEZ claims may provide a test case for sustainable resource extraction in contested waters. The Nippon Foundation's planned consortium with multiple Japanese companies, beginning operations in 2026, will demonstrate whether critical mineral extraction can be conducted in ways that balance economic, environmental, and strategic considerations.[23] If successful, this model might be replicated in other contested areas where resource development could provide incentives for cooperation despite unresolved territorial disputes.

The preservation of Okinotorishima itself will continue to require Japanese ingenuity and investment as climate change intensifies. The 2016 allocation of ¥13 billion ($838 million) for facility rebuilding represents just the beginning of what will likely become a permanent commitment to engineering sovereignty.[24] This ongoing effort may pioneer technologies for preserving vulnerable islands that could benefit threatened communities worldwide.

Philosophical Reflections

The Okinotorishima dispute ultimately forces us to confront fundamental questions about humanity's relationship with the natural world and each other. What gives a piece of geography meaning beyond its physical characteristics? Why do humans invest such enormous resources in defending places that seem to have little intrinsic value? How should we balance respect for legal frameworks that promote stability against the need for adaptation to new realities?

The answer may lie in understanding territory not as a thing but as a relationship—a set of human commitments and expectations that exist independently of physical geography. Japan's investment in preserving Okinotorishima reflects not just strategic calculation but also a deeper commitment to the idea that human societies can shape their environment to serve their purposes. China's challenges reflect an equally deep commitment to preventing other powers from gaining unfair advantages through legal manipulation.

Neither position is inherently right or wrong; both reflect legitimate human impulses toward security, fairness, and control. The challenge is finding ways to honor these impulses while addressing collective challenges that transcend any single nation's interests. The climate crisis, the need for sustainable resource extraction, the preservation of marine ecosystems—these require cooperation on a scale that humanity has never before achieved.

The most hopeful aspect of the Okinotorishima story may be the quiet professionalism of the individuals who implement these competing visions. Lieutenant Commander Tanaka conducting his patrol, Captain Chen seeking fishing grounds for his crew, Dr. Wang collecting samples for scientific analysis—all are doing their jobs with skill and dedication despite the larger tensions that surround them. Their example suggests that even amid strategic competition, humans retain the capacity for professional respect and limited cooperation.

A Legacy of Adaptation

As this book concludes, the contest over Okinotorishima continues. The tiny atoll remains Japan's southernmost territory, fortified against rising seas and defended by some of the world's most advanced maritime technology. Chinese research vessels continue to probe the boundaries of Japan's claimed EEZ, collecting data that serves both scientific and strategic purposes. Taiwanese fishermen continue to work waters their families have fished for generations, now under the protection of coast guard vessels that conduct joint exercises with their former adversaries.

The ultimate legacy of this "last rock" may not be its resolution but its demonstration of humanity's remarkable capacity for both competition and cooperation in managing shared spaces. The legal frameworks, institutional mechanisms, and professional relationships developed through decades of managing this dispute provide tools for addressing far greater challenges ahead. Climate change, resource scarcity, and technological disruption will create new contests over territory and resources that make current disputes seem manageable by comparison.

The ocean that surrounds Okinotorishima covers 70% of the Earth's surface and remains largely ungoverned and unexplored. Humanity's experience learning to manage conflict over this tiny atoll—with its mixture of legal reasoning, technological innovation, and diplomatic pragmatism—offers a template for governing the vast blue commons that will determine our species' future. Whether we prove wise enough to build on these lessons, or whether we remain trapped by territorial instincts that served us well on land but prove inadequate for the age of the ocean, remains the defining question of our time.

In the end, Okinotorishima's greatest value may not be the critical minerals beneath its waters or the strategic position it commands, but the human stories it has generated—of engineers battling typhoons to preserve concrete platforms, of diplomats finding ways to cooperate despite political tensions, of scientists advancing knowledge while serving national interests, of ordinary citizens adapting to new realities with remarkable resilience. These stories remind us that behind every abstract dispute over sovereignty and resources are real people trying to build better futures for their communities. Their example points toward the possibility that humanity might yet learn to share the blue planet that is our only home.

Footnotes

[1] Japan Coast Guard, "Chinese Research Vessel Activities in Japan's EEZ," press release, May 26, 2025; Mao Ning, Chinese Foreign Ministry press briefing, May 27, 2025.

[2] Newsweek, "Photos Show Chinese Ship Detected in Waters Claimed by US Ally," May 28, 2025.

[3] *The Diplomat*, "Taiwan-Japan Fishing Dispute Heats Up," May 3, 2016.

[4] TIME, "Japan Is Spending $107 Million to Rebuild a Tiny Pacific Island," February 3, 2016.

[5] Naval News, "Taiwan Coast Guard Holds Rare Exercise with Japanese Counterpart," July 29, 2024.

[6] Center for Strategic and International Studies, Chinese research vessel tracking database, 2025.

[7] Yukie Yoshikawa, "The US-Japan-China Mistrust Spiral and Okinotorishima," *Asia-Pacific Journal: Japan Focus*, November 3, 2023.

[8] United Nations Convention on the Law of the Sea, adopted December 10, 1982, 1833 UNTS 3.

[9] Pacific Islands Forum, "Declaration on Preserving Maritime Zones in the Face of Climate Change-Related Sea-Level Rise," August 6, 2021.

[10] Tadao Kuribayashi, "Legal Status of Okinotorishima under UNCLOS," *Japanese Yearbook of International Law* 49 (2006): 21-45.

[11] Nippon Foundation, "Large-Scale Polymetallic Nodule Discovery Announcement," June 21, 2024; *Japan Times*, "Japan Finds Millions of Tonnes of Battery Metals in Seabed," June 25, 2024.

[12] Intergovernmental Panel on Climate Change, *Climate Change 2021: The Physical Science Basis*, Working Group I Contribution to the Sixth Assessment Report (Cambridge: Cambridge University Press, 2021), Chapter 9.

[13] Davor Vidas and David Freestone, "Legal Certainty and Stability in the Face of Sea Level Rise," *International Journal of Marine & Coastal Law* 37, no. 4 (2022): 673-705.

[14] Signe Veierud Busch, "Baseline Preservation as a Response to Sea-Level Rise," *Ocean Development & International Law* 56, no. 1 (2025): 100-124.

[15] Metal Tech News, "The Changing Tides of Deep-Sea Mining," September 16, 2024.

[16] World Resources Institute, "What We Know About Deep-Sea Mining and What We Don't," July 23, 2025.

[17] Asia Maritime Transparency Initiative, "Okinotori: A New Beginning for Taiwan-Japan Maritime Dialogue," October 11, 2016.

[18] France24, "Japan, US and Philippines Coast Guards Simulate Crisis Amid China Threat," June 21, 2025.

[19] United Nations, "Rising Hopes Amid Rising Seas: Developments in International Law Addressing the Threat of Sea-Level Rise," *UN Chronicle*, 2024.

[20] International Law Commission, "Sea-level Rise in relation to International Law," analytical guide, 2023-2025.

[21] Sasakawa Peace Foundation, "Why the Japan Coast Guard Needs a Large, Multipurpose Patrol Vessel," December 2024.

[22] Daily Jus, "Arbitration-Related Developments in Japan in 2024," May 20, 2025.

[23] Deep Sea Mining Database, "Nodules in Japanese EEZ at Minamitorishima," July 5, 2024.

[24] *Japan Times*, "Japan Coast Guard to Build Its Biggest Patrol Ship," August 27, 2024.

APPENDICES

The Last Rock's Secret War: Okinotorishima and Japan's Fight for Tomorrow's Ocean

---

Appendix A: Timeline of Key Events

Historical Period (1543-1931)

- **1543**: Possible first sighting by Spanish sailor Bernardo de la Torre
- **1565**: Miguel López de Legazpi officially records the reef, names it "Parece Vela" (Spanish for "looks like a sail")
- **1789**: British Captain William Douglas arrives with ship *Iphigenia*
- **1790**: Location officially named "Douglas Reef" by British navigators
- **1888**: First Japanese awareness of the atoll's existence
- **1922-1925**: Japanese navy ship *Manshu* conducts detailed investigations
- **1931**: Japan makes formal territorial declaration, places under Tokyo Metropolis jurisdiction

World War II and Post-War Period (1939-1982)

- **1939-1941**: Japan begins infrastructure construction (lighthouse and meteorological station foundations)
- **1941**: Construction interrupted by World War II outbreak
- **1982**: United Nations Convention on the Law of the Sea (UNCLOS) signed

UNCLOS Era and EEZ Claims (1983-2004)

- **1983**: Japan signs UNCLOS
- **1987-1993**: First major preservation efforts begin - steel

breakwaters and concrete walls constructed

- **1994**: UNCLOS enters into force globally
- **1996**: Japan ratifies UNCLOS
- **2004, April 22**: China first formally challenges Japan's EEZ claims during bilateral talks in Beijing

Escalation and Diplomatic Tensions (2005-2016)

- **2005, May 20**: Tokyo Governor Shintaro Ishihara makes theatrical visit - swims around atoll, releases fish fry
- **2005, June 6**: Ishihara reveals ¥85 billion ($740 million) investment in *Sankei Shimbun* editorial
- **2006**: Official coral preservation program launched by Fisheries Agency and Nippon Foundation
- **2007, March 16**: Japan Coast Guard installs lighthouse beacon with radar systems
- **2008, November 12**: Japan submits continental shelf claims to UN Commission on Limits of Continental Shelf (CLCS)
- **2009, February 6**: China submits formal objection to UN Secretary-General
- **2009, February 27**: South Korea submits formal objection
- **2012, June**: CLCS defers recommendations "until matters are resolved"
- **2016, April 25**: Taiwanese fishing vessel *Dongshengji No. 16* detained by Japan Coast Guard
- **2016, May**: Taiwan dispatches Coast Guard vessels to disputed waters
- **2016, July 12**: Philippines v. China arbitration ruling on South China Sea features

Technological and Scientific Developments (2016-2025)

- **2016, October**: Taiwan-Japan maritime dialogue mechanism established

- **2018, December**: First reported Chinese research vessel activities in claimed EEZ
- **2020, July**: Chinese vessel conducts 18-day research operation in disputed waters
- **2020**: JOGMEC successfully extracts 649kg of cobalt-rich crust from Takuyo No. 5 seamount at 5,500m depth
- **2022**: JAMSTEC achieves world's first autonomous underwater data retrieval using optical communication
- **2024, June**: Discovery of 230+ million tonnes polymetallic nodules near Minamitorishima containing 610,000 tonnes cobalt, 740,000 tonnes nickel
- **2024, July**: Chinese buoy discovered in Japan's claimed EEZ
- **2024, May 21**: International Tribunal for the Law of the Sea issues advisory opinion on climate change obligations
- **2025, February**: Nippon Foundation announces plans for large-scale nodule extraction beginning 2025
- **2025, May 26**: R/V Tan Kah Kee incident - 5-hour standoff with Japan Coast Guard

---

Appendix B: Legal Documents and Treaty Excerpts

UNCLOS Article 121 - Regime of Islands

Article 121(1): "An island is a naturally formed area of land, surrounded by water, which is above water at high tide."

Article 121(2): "Except as provided for in paragraph 3, the territorial sea, the contiguous zone, the exclusive economic zone and the continental shelf of an island are determined in accordance with the provisions of this Convention applicable to other land territory."

Article 121(3): "Rocks which cannot sustain human habitation or economic life of their own shall have no exclusive economic zone or continental shelf."

Key Legal Positions

Japan's Position:

- Okinotorishima is an "island" under Article 121(1)
- Term "rocks" is undefined in international law
- Historical treatment as island since 1931 establishes legal presumption
- Artificial preservation does not disqualify natural features from island status
- Infrastructure investments demonstrate potential for human habitation and economic life

China's Position:

- Okinotorishima is "a reef, not an island" under UNCLOS
- Feature "obviously cannot sustain human habitation or economic life of its own"
- Article 121(3) requires assessment based on natural conditions without artificial enhancements
- Japan's EEZ claim "violates international law"
- Chinese research vessels exercise "freedom of the high seas"

Relevant Arbitration Excerpts

Philippines v. China (2016) - Article 121(3) Interpretation:

"The status of a feature must be determined on the basis of its natural capacity, without external additions or modifications intended to increase its capacity to sustain human habitation or an economic life of its own."

ITLOS Climate Advisory Opinion (2024):

"States have specific obligations to take all necessary measures to prevent, reduce and control marine pollution from anthropogenic GHG emissions."

Appendix C: Geographic and Technical Data

Okinotorishima Physical Specifications

- **Coordinates**: 20°25' North, 136°04' East
- **Distance from Tokyo**: 1,740 kilometers south
- **Total reef platform**: 4.5 km (east-west) × 1.7 km (north-south)
- **Dry land area:** 9.44 square meters (101.6 square feet)
- **Maximum elevation:** ~2 meters above high tide
- **Remaining rocks at high tide**: 2 (Kitakojima and Higashikojima)
- **Original rocks (1939)**: 5
- **EEZ claim area:** 420,000 square kilometers (larger than Japan's land area)

Environmental Conditions

- **Annual average wave height**: 1.3 meters
- **Maximum typhoon wave height**: 16+ meters
- **Annual average wind speed**: 6 meters/second
- **Maximum typhoon wind speed:** 50+ meters/second
- **Water depth around atoll**: 5,500+ meters
- **Nearest inhabited land**: Chichijima (900+ kilometers)

Engineering Infrastructure Specifications

- **Concrete barrier diameter:** ~50 meters around each rock
- **Steel breakwater installation**: 1987-1993
- **Titanium net cost:** $50 million
- **Research platform dimensions**: 100m × 50m (stilt platform in lagoon)
- **Lighthouse installation**: 2007 (solar-powered with radar/sensors)
- **Total infrastructure investment**: $600+ million (as of 2025)

Resource Discovery Data (2024)

- **Polymetallic nodule deposits**: 230+ million tonnes
- **Cobalt content**: 610,000 tonnes (75 years Japan consumption)
- **Nickel content**: 740,000 tonnes (11 years Japan consumption)
- **Estimated value**: $18+ billion
- **Nodule density**: Up to 30 kg/square meter
- **Water depth of deposits**: ~5,500 meters

Appendix D: Comparative Maritime Features

Similar Contested Features Worldwide

Rockall (United Kingdom)

- **Size**: 624 square meters (66× larger than Okinotorishima)
- **Height**: 17.15 meters
- **Legal status**: UK relinquished EEZ claims in 1997 upon UNCLOS ratification
- **Current claim**: 12-nautical-mile territorial sea only

Itu Aba/Taiping Island (Taiwan-controlled)

- **Size**: 0.51 square kilometers (500× larger than Okinotorishima)
- **Features**: Fresh water, vegetation, 1,200m airstrip, 200+ personnel
- **Legal status**: 2016 arbitration ruled it as "rock" under Article 121(3)

Jan Mayen (Norway)

- **Size**: 377 square kilometers
- **Population**: 25 meteorological station personnel
- **Legal status**: ICJ implicitly recognized EEZ entitlements (1993)

Baker and Howland Islands (United States)

- **Baker Island**: 1.4 square kilometers
- **Howland Island**: 2.6 square kilometers
- **Combined EEZ**: 425,700 square kilometers
- **Population**: Uninhabited, occasional wildlife service visits

---

Appendix E: Economic and Strategic Data

Japan's Critical Mineral Dependencies

- **Overall import dependency**: 90%+ for critical metals
- **Rare earth imports from China**: ~60% (down from 90% in 2010)
- **Uranium imports**: 100%
- **Lithium imports**: 75%
- **Cobalt imports**: Majority from overseas sources

Global Critical Mineral Processing Dominance (China)

- **Rare earth processing**: 85-90%
- **Cobalt refining**: 68%
- **Nickel processing**: 65%
- **Lithium refining**: 60%
- **Lithium battery manufacturing**: 70%

Pacific Trade Routes Value

- **South China Sea annual trade**: $3.4 trillion (conservative estimate)
- **Global maritime trade share**: ~21%
- **China's maritime trade through SCS**: 64% (2016)
- **Japan's maritime trade through SCS**: 42% (2016)
- **Energy imports through regional waters**: 60-80% for major

powers

Deep-Sea Mining Industry Projections

- **Global market size (2024)**: $7.8 billion
- **Projected market size (2030)**: $20+ billion
- **Critical mineral demand increase by 2030**: 400-600%
- **Electric vehicle battery mineral requirements**: 200kg per vehicle
- **Cobalt demand from battery sector**: 70% of global consumption

---

Appendix F: Military and Security Considerations

Strategic Location Analysis

- **Distance to Taiwan**: ~850 kilometers
- **Distance to Guam**: ~850 kilometers (roughly equidistant)
- **Strategic position**: Center of potential Taiwan Strait-Guam transit corridor
- **U.S. forces on Guam**: Largest military presence west of Hawaii
- **Chinese submarine bases**: Southern fleet headquarters ~1,200km

Research Vessel Capabilities

Chinese Research Fleet (2024 assessment)

- **Active vessels**: 64+ research and survey ships
- **Military connections**: 80% have organizational ties to PLA or strategic objectives
- **R/V Tan Kah Kee specifications**: 255 feet, 10,000 nautical mile range, 54 crew
- **Zhu Hai Yun capabilities**: 50+ autonomous vehicles, 160km survey area

Japan Maritime Monitoring Systems

- **SeaGuardian drones**: 2 procured (24+ hour endurance)
- **ELINT stations**: 14+ listening posts nationwide
- **URASHIMA8000 AUV**: 8,000m operational depth capability
- **Lighthouse radar system**: Real-time monitoring of 200nm radius

---

Appendix G: Climate Change Projections and Impacts

Sea Level Rise Projections

- **Global mean SLR by 2100**: 0.43-0.84 meters (depending on emissions scenario)
- **Philippine Sea regional rate**: 5.0-7.0 mm/year (2× global average)
- **Current global average**: 3.6 mm/year (doubled from 20th century rate)
- **High-tide flooding projection**: 10× increase in frequency by 2050s

Pacific Island Impacts

- **Tuvalu**: 25 flood days annually by 2050s (vs. <5 currently)
- **Kiribati**: 65 flood days annually by 2050s (vs. <5 currently)
- **Marshall Islands**: Concentration to 4 defensible areas planned
- **Regional overwash events**: 60% of Micronesian islands affected (2008 example)

Coral Ecosystem Stress Factors

- **Ocean temperature increase**: Causing frequent bleaching events
- **Ocean acidification**: Impeding calcium carbonate skeleton formation
- **Typhoon intensification**: Climate change increasing storm

intensity

- **Coral transplant survival rate**: <20% after 4 years in Japanese waters

---

Appendix H: Technological Specifications

Quantum Sensing Capabilities

- **Chinese quantum magnetometer**: Picotesla-level precision (1 billion× more sensitive than conventional)
- **Coherent Population Trapping (CPT)**: 7 distinct microwave resonance signals
- **French quantum gravimeters**: Operational submarine navigation systems
- **U.S. quantum investment**: $3.8 billion
- **Chinese quantum investment**: ~$15 billion

Autonomous Underwater Vehicles (AUVs)

- **Maximum operational depth**: 6,000-14,000 meters
- **Autonomous operation duration**: Weeks to months
- **AI decision-making**: Real-time mission parameter modification
- **Swarm capabilities**: Coordinated multi-vehicle operations
- **Communication**: Underwater optical wireless systems

Coral Cultivation Technology

- **Annual transplant rate**: 100,000 juvenile colonies since 2006
- **Transport conditions**: 22.5-28.4°C, specialized acrylic tanks
- **Cultivation period**: 2 years to transplant-ready size
- **Foraminifera cultivation**: Microscopic organisms for sand/land mass creation
- **Coral Net technology**: Biodegradable mesh foundation systems

Appendix I: International Legal Precedents

Successful Joint Development Models

- **Malaysia-Thailand Joint Development Agreement (1990)**: 30+ years operation
- **Norway-UK Joint Development Area**: North Sea cooperation model
- **Australia-East Timor Joint Development**: Revenue sharing mechanism

Failed/Abandoned Claims

- **UK Rockall EEZ claim**: Abandoned 1997 upon UNCLOS ratification
- **China South China Sea**: 2016 arbitration rejection but continued assertion
- **Various Arctic claims**: Ongoing disputes over extended continental shelf

Climate-Related Legal Developments

- **ITLOS Advisory Opinion (2024)**: GHG emissions as marine pollution
- **ICJ Climate Advisory Opinion (pending)**: State obligations for climate change
- **Pacific Islands Forum Declaration (2021)**: Maritime zone preservation principle

Appendix J: Glossary of Key Terms

Artificial Island: Human-made island structure; cannot generate EEZ under UNCLOS Article 60

Baseline: Line from which maritime zones are measured; typically low-water mark

Continental Shelf: Seabed area extending beyond territorial sea; can extend to 350nm under certain conditions

Deep-Sea Mining: Extraction of minerals from ocean floor, typically 4,000-6,000m depth

Exclusive Economic Zone (EEZ): Maritime zone extending 200 nautical miles from baseline; grants sovereign resource rights

Foraminifera: Microscopic marine organisms whose shells form sand and sediment

Freedom of Navigation Operation (FONOP): Military transit to challenge excessive maritime claims

High Tide: Highest level reached by water during tidal cycle; critical for determining island status

Island: "Naturally formed area of land, surrounded by water, which is above water at high tide" (UNCLOS Article 121(1))

Low-Tide Elevation: Feature above water at low tide but submerged at high tide

Maritime Domain Awareness: Knowledge of anything associated with maritime environment affecting security

Polymetallic Nodules: Potato-sized concretions containing multiple metals formed on deep seafloor

Rock: Geographic feature that "cannot sustain human habitation or economic life of their own" (UNCLOS Article 121(3))

Territorial Sea: Maritime zone extending 12 nautical miles from baseline; subject to coastal state sovereignty

Terra Nullius: Legal principle for claiming previously unclaimed territory

UNCLOS: United Nations Convention on the Law of the Sea; "constitution for the oceans"

BIBLIOGRAPHY

The Last Rock's Secret War: Okinotorishima and Japan's Fight for Tomorrow's Ocean

I. GOVERNMENT DOCUMENTS AND OFFICIAL STATEMENTS

Japanese Government Sources

Japan Coast Guard. "Activities Related to Okinotorishima." Official documentation, accessed December 2025.

Japan Oil, Gas & Metals National Corporation (JOGMEC). "JOGMEC Conducts World's First Successful Excavation of Cobalt-Rich Seabed in the Deep Ocean." News release, accessed January 2025. https://www.jogmec.go.jp/english/news/release/news_01_000033.html.

Ministry of Economy, Trade and Industry. "Green Growth Strategy Through Achieving Carbon Neutrality in 2050." December 25, 2020.

Ministry of Foreign Affairs of Japan. Various diplomatic notes and statements, 2004-2025.

Tokyo Metropolitan Government. "Profile of the Okinotorishima Islands." Accessed August 2025. https://www.t-borderislands.metro.tokyo.lg.jp/en/okinotorishima/.

Tokyo Metropolitan Government. "Work by Related Organizations, Etc." Accessed January 2025. https://www.t-borderislands.metro.tokyo.lg.jp/en/organizations/.

Chinese Government Sources

Ministry of Foreign Affairs of the People's Republic of China. "Foreign Ministry Spokesperson Mao Ning's Regular Press Conference on May 27, 2025." May 27, 2025. https://www.fmprc.gov.cn/eng/xw/fyrbt/202505/t20250527_11634354.html.

Ministry of Foreign Affairs of the People's Republic of China. Note verbale to UN Secretary-General regarding Japan's continental shelf submission. February 6, 2009.

U.S. Government Sources

U.S. Department of Homeland Security. "DHS Partners with Japanese Counterparts to Strengthen Maritime Cybersecurity Cooperation." August 30, 2024.

U.S. Department of State. "2025 Quad Foreign Ministers' Meeting." July 2, 2025.

U.S. Government Accountability Office. "COAST GUARD: Additional Efforts Needed to Address Cybersecurity Risks to the Maritime Transportation System." GAO-25-107244, February 11, 2025.

White House. "Unleashing America's Offshore Critical Minerals and Resources." Executive Order, April 24, 2025.

Other Government Sources

Australia Department of Defence. "Australia-Japan-United States Trilateral Defence Ministers' Meeting November 2024 Joint Statement." November 17, 2024.

South Korea Ministry of Foreign Affairs. Note verbale to UN Secretary-General regarding Japan's continental shelf submission. February 27, 2009.

II. INTERNATIONAL LEGAL DOCUMENTS AND COURT CASES

Treaties and Conventions

United Nations Convention on the Law of the Sea. Adopted December 10, 1982, entered into force November 16, 1994. 1833 UNTS 3.

Singapore Convention on Mediation. Various ratifications 2024-2025.

International Court and Tribunal Cases

International Court of Justice. *Maritime Delimitation in the Area between Greenland and Jan Mayen* (Denmark v. Norway). Judgment, I.C.J. Reports 1993.

International Court of Justice. *Alleged Violations of Sovereign Rights and Maritime Spaces in the Caribbean Sea* (Nicaragua v. Colombia). Judgment, I.C.J. Reports 2018.

International Tribunal for the Law of the Sea. Advisory Opinion on Climate Change and International Law. May 21, 2024.

Permanent Court of Arbitration. *The South China Sea Arbitration (The Republic of the Philippines v. The People's Republic of China).* Final Award, July 12, 2016. PCA Case No. 2013-19.

UN Commission Documents

UN Commission on the Limits of the Continental Shelf. Recommendations regarding Japan's submission, June 2012.

UN Division for Ocean Affairs and the Law of the Sea. "Continental Shelf - Submission by Japan." 2008.

International Law Commission. "Report on Sea Level Rise in Relation to International Law." 2022.

III. ACADEMIC ARTICLES AND BOOKS

Books

Fravel, M. Taylor. *Strong Borders, Secure Nation: Cooperation and Conflict in China's Territorial Disputes*. Princeton: Princeton University Press, 2008.

Harrison, James. *Making the Law of the Sea: A Study in the Development of International Law*. Cambridge: Cambridge University Press, 2011.

Kirshner, Jonathan. *Currency and Coercion: The Political Economy of International Monetary Power*. Princeton: Princeton University Press, 1995.

Krasner, Stephen. *Sovereignty: Organized Hypocrisy*. Princeton: Princeton University Press, 1999.

Young, Oran. *Arctic Politics: Conflict and Cooperation in the Circumpolar North*. Hanover, NH: University Press of New England, 1992.

Journal Articles

Churchill, Robin. "The 1982 United Nations Convention on the Law of the Sea." In *The Oxford Handbook of the Law of the Sea*, edited by Donald Rothwell et al. Oxford: Oxford University Press, 2015.

Craig, Robin Kundis. "Climate Change, Regulatory Fragmentation, and Water Triage." *University of Colorado Law Review* 79 (2008): 825-928.

Croxton, Derek. "The Peace of Westphalia of 1648 and the Origins of Sovereignty." *International History Review* 21, no. 3 (1999): 569-591.

Elferink, Alex G. Oude. "The Interpretation of Article 121(3) of UNCLOS by the Tribunal for the South China Sea Arbitration: A Critique." *Ocean Development & International Law* 50, no. 1 (2019): 23-54.

Folke, Carl, et al. "Adaptive Governance of Social-Ecological Systems." *Annual Review of Environment and Resources* 30 (2005): 441-473.

Fravel, M. Taylor. "International Relations Theory and China's Rise: Assessing China's Potential for Territorial Expansion." *International Studies Review* 12, no. 4 (2010): 505-532.

Handy, Russell, Michael J. Forsyth, and Joseph Kunkel. "Sovereignty-in-Being: A Dangerous New Model for Territorial Expansion in the 21st Century." *InterAgency Journal* 9, no. 2 (2018): 51-65.

Harii, Saki. "Insights into coral restoration projects in Japan." *Science of The Total Environment* 838 (2022): 156543.

Kayanne, Hajime, et al. "Low species diversity of hermatypic corals on an isolated reef, Okinotorishima, in the northwest Pacific." *Galaxea, Journal of Coral Reef Studies* 14 (2013): 73.

McDorman, Ted L. "The South China Sea Arbitration." *American Society of International Law Insights* 20, no. 17 (2016).

Puotinen, Maria, et al. "The threat to coral reefs from more intense cyclones under climate change." *Global Change Biology* 23, no. 2 (2017): 421-436.

Rodriguez-Rivera, Luis E. "Joint Development Zones and other Cooperative Management Efforts Related to Transboundary Maritime

Resources: A Caribbean and Latin American Model for Peaceful Resolution of Maritime Boundary Disputes." *Issues in Legal Scholarship* 7, no. 1 (2008).

Ruggie, John Gerard. "International Regimes, Transactions, and Change: Embedded Liberalism in the Postwar Economic Order." *International Organization* 36, no. 2 (1982): 379-415.

Storlazzi, Curt D., et al. "Most atolls will be uninhabitable by the mid-21st century because of sea-level rise exacerbating wave-driven flooding." *Science Advances* 4, no. 4 (2018).

Strating, Rebecca, and Joanne Wallis. "Maritime sovereignty and territorialisation: Comparing the Pacific Islands and South China Sea." *Marine Policy* 138 (2022): 105016.

Sweetman, Andrew K., et al. "Evidence of dark oxygen production at the abyssal seafloor." *Nature Geoscience* 17 (2024): 737-739.

Talmon, Stefan. "South China Sea Arbitration and the Finality of 'Final' Awards." *Journal of International Dispute Settlement* 8, no. 2 (May 2017): 388-412.

Vidas, Davor, and David Freestone. "Legal Certainty and Stability in the Face of Sea Level Rise." *International Journal of Marine & Coastal Law* 37, no. 4 (2022): 673-705.

Volk, Christian. "The Problem of Sovereignty in Globalized Times." *Global Constitutionalism* 8, no. 1 (2019): 31-52.

Worster, William. "Interpreting the Law of the Sea in the Context of Sea-Level Rise: The Ambulatory Thesis and State Practice." *Journal of Environmental Law* 35, no. 3 (2023): 499-526.

Wu, Shicun. "The Interpretation of Article 121(3) of UNCLOS by the Tribunal for the South China Sea Arbitration: A Critique." *Ocean Development & International Law* 50, no. 1 (2018).

Yiallourides, Constantinos. "Joint Development of Seabed Resources in Areas of Overlapping Maritime Claims: An Analysis of Precedents in State Practice." British Institute of International and Comparative Law, June 24, 2020.

Yoshikawa, Yukie. "The US-Japan-China Mistrust Spiral and Okinotorishima." *Asia-Pacific Journal: Japan Focus* 5, no. 11 (2007).

Young, Oran. "Institutional Dynamics: Resilience, Vulnerability and Adaptation in Environmental and Resource Regimes." *Global Environmental Change* 20, no. 3 (2010): 378-385.

IV. NEWS ARTICLES AND MEDIA REPORTS

Major International Media

BBC News. Multiple reports on maritime disputes and climate change, 2020-2025.

CNN International. Coverage of South China Sea tensions and territorial disputes, 2020-2025.

Financial Times. Reports on critical minerals and supply chain security, 2024-2025.

The Guardian. Environmental and climate change reporting, 2020-2025.

Reuters. Breaking news coverage of maritime incidents and diplomatic tensions, 2020-2025.

Regional and Specialized Media

Asia Maritime Transparency Initiative. "A Survey of Marine Research Vessels in the Indo-Pacific." April 16, 2020.

Asia Maritime Transparency Initiative. "Okinotori: A New Beginning for Taiwan-Japan Maritime Dialogue." October 11, 2016.

Asia Times. "Taiwan, a bystander victim in the South China Sea dispute." October 5, 2016.

The Diplomat. "China Has Much to Gain From the South China Sea Ruling." July 19, 2016.

The Diplomat. "China's Navy, the West Pacific and the Role of Okinotorishima." January 30, 2023.

The Diplomat. "Taiwan-Japan Fishing Dispute Heats Up." May 3, 2016.

Global Times. "Japan's EEZ claim based on Okinotori Reef violates intl law." May 28, 2025.

The Japan Times. "Chinese Research Vessel Spotted in Japan EEZ." May 27, 2025.

The Japan Times. "Over 200 million metric tons of rare metals found near remote Tokyo island." June 22, 2024.

Newsweek. "Photos Show Chinese Ship Detected in Waters Claimed by US Ally." May 28, 2025.

Nippon.com. "Chinese Research Vessel Spotted in Japan EEZ." May 27, 2025.

South China Morning Post. "Japan wants answers over Chinese buoy found in remote contested waters." July 9, 2024.

South China Morning Post. "Taiwan sends patrol ships after boat seized by Japan." May 1, 2016.

Taipei Times. "EDITORIAL: Ma and KMT's selective tough stance." April 29, 2016.

TIME. "Japan Is Spending $107 Million to Rebuild a Tiny Pacific Island." February 3, 2016.

V. RESEARCH REPORTS AND INSTITUTIONAL PUBLICATIONS

Think Tank and Policy Institute Reports

Atlantic Council. "US ratification of the ocean treaty will unlock deep sea mining." June 4, 2024.

Baker Institute. "Of Chinese Behemoths: What China's Rare Earths Dominance Means for the US." December 19, 2022.

Brookings Institution. "Strong but constrained Japan-Taiwan ties." March 9, 2022.

Canadian Global Affairs Institute. "Investing in Supply Chain Resilience in the Indo-Pacific." 2024.

Center for a New American Security. "Quad: The Next Phase." June 18, 2025.

Center for Strategic and International Studies. "China's Expansion into the West Pacific." April 5, 2023.

Center for Strategic and International Studies. "Potential for U.S.-Japan Cooperation on Supply-Chain Resilience for Clean Energy Technologies." June 9, 2025.

Center for Strategic and International Studies. "Surveying the Seas: China's Dual-Use Research Operations in the Indian Ocean." Accessed 2025.

Center for Strategic and International Studies. "What China's Ban on Rare Earths Processing Technology Exports Means." December 2, 2024.

Foreign Policy Research Institute. "The Curious Case of Okinotori: Reef, Rock, or Island?" September 14, 2016.

Goldman Sachs Research. "Resource realism: The geopolitics of critical mineral supply chains." September 13, 2023.

Hudson Institute. "An Integrated Approach to US-Japan Cooperation with Southeast Asia." Accessed August 8, 2025.

McKinsey & Company. "How Japan could reach carbon neutrality by 2050." August 4, 2021.

Observer Research Foundation. "Deep-sea dilemmas: Countering China's seabed mining efforts through global collaboration." December 26, 2024.

Pacific Forum. "The Curious Case of Okinotori: Reef, Rock, or Island?" April 4, 2024.

Royal United Services Institute. "Japan's Responses to China's Supply Chain Dominance." 2024.

Sasakawa Peace Foundation. "The Functions and Work of the Commission on the Limits of the Continental Shelf." Accessed December 2025.

Stimson Center. "Race to the Deep on Seabed Mining." December 10, 2024.

United States Institute of Peace. "Two Years Later, What Has the Indo-Pacific Strategy Achieved?" March 14, 2024.

World Economic Forum. "How Japan solved its rare earth minerals dependency issue." October 2023.

World Resources Institute. "What We Know About Deep-Sea Mining and What We Don't." July 2025.

Academic Institution Reports

Columbia Business Law Review. "The Japanese Economic Security Promotion Act: A Solution to National Security Threats Resulting from Economic Globalization." 2022.

Denver Journal of International Law & Policy. "UNCLOS and South China Sea Maritime Disputes: Legal Complexities and Interpretations." 2024.

Georgetown Journal of International Affairs. "Professor Robert Beckman on the Role of UNCLOS in Maritime Disputes." April 30, 2021.

Global Taiwan Institute. "A Japanese Perspective on How Japan and Taiwan Should Deal with Okinotori-shima." September 8, 2022.

Tufts University. "Chapter 8: The Arctic & the LOSC." Law of the Sea course materials.

University of Edinburgh. "Guest blog—Unpacking the legal disputes over Rockall." SPICe Spotlight, September 22, 2022.

International Organization Reports

Intergovernmental Panel on Climate Change. *Climate Change 2021: The Physical Science Basis.* Working Group I Contribution to the Sixth Assessment Report. Cambridge: Cambridge University Press, 2021.

International Energy Agency. "Critical Minerals Market Review 2023." Paris: IEA, 2023.

NASA. "NASA Analysis Shows Irreversible Sea Level Rise for Pacific Islands." September 27, 2024.

NOAA. "2022 Sea Level Rise Technical Report." Ocean Service.

Pacific Islands Forum. "Declaration on Preserving Maritime Zones in the Face of Climate Change-Related Sea-Level Rise." August 6, 2021.

United Nations Environment Programme. "Ocean Governance." Accessed August 8, 2025.

VI. TECHNICAL AND SCIENTIFIC PUBLICATIONS

Marine Science and Technology

Allseas. "Polymetallic nodule collection." Company technical documentation, accessed January 2025.

Deep Sea Mining Academic Center. "Nodules in Japanese EEZ at Minamitorishima." July 5, 2024.

Exail. "Autonomous Underwater Vehicles For Defense Applications." Technical specifications.

General Atomics. "Raytheon Intelligence and Space Maritime Surveillance Systems Flight Tested on GA-ASI SeaGuardian for Japan Coast Guard." January 21, 2021.

Glosten. "R/V Tan Kah Kee." Vessel specifications, March 13, 2024.

Japan Agency for Marine-Earth Science and Technology (JAMSTEC). "URASHIMA8000." Technical specifications, accessed January 2025.

Japan Agency for Marine-Earth Science and Technology (JAMSTEC). "World's First Success in Automatically Retrieving Observation Data from Seabed Instruments Using AUV." Press release, May 26, 2022.

Kajima Technical Research Institute. "Coral Net." Technology documentation.

MINING.COM. "Japan finds millions of tonnes of battery metals in seabed." June 25, 2024.

The Metals Company. "NORI and Allseas Lift Over 3,000 Tonnes of Polymetallic Nodules to Surface." News release, November 14, 2022.

Climate and Environmental Science

Climate Central. "Analysis: Climate Change-Driven Ocean Warming Intensifies Record November Typhoon Activity in the Western Pacific." Accessed August 8, 2025.

Climate Tracker Asia. "Rising Sea Levels and Coastal Vulnerability in the Philippines." December 11, 2024.

CORRECTIV. "Japan is growing an island." October 23, 2018.

Frontiers in Marine Science. "Coral Reef Ecosystems under Climate Change and Ocean Acidification." Vol. 4 (2017): 158.

NOAA Climate.gov. "Climate Change: Global Sea Level." August 22, 2023.

ScienceDaily. "Deep-ocean floor produces its own oxygen." July 22, 2024.

U.S. Geological Survey. "The Impact of Sea-Level Rise and Climate Change on Pacific Ocean Atolls."

Technology and Defense Publications

Interesting Engineering. "China unveils new quantum drone tech to detect stealth US submarines." April 24, 2025.

International Defense Security & Technology. "Autonomous underwater vehicle (AUV) technologies for surveillance, and anti-submarine warfare missions." September 26, 2021.

International Defense Security & Technology. "Quantum Gravity and Gradiometer Sensors: Revolutionizing Maritime Navigation, Subsurface Detection, and Stealth Tracking." March 23, 2025.

The Maritime Executive. "Study: China's Research Vessels Carry Out Covert Missions for PLA."

The Quantum Insider. "China Tests Drone-Mounted Quantum Sensor That Could Reshape Submarine Detection." April 27, 2025.

Sea Machines Robotics. "Ultimate Guide to Maritime Autonomy in 2024." January 15, 2024.

VII. REFERENCE MATERIALS AND DATABASES

Maps and Geographic References

CIA World Factbook. Various country profiles and geographic data, accessed 2024-2025.

Google Earth. Satellite imagery and geographic data for Okinotorishima and surrounding areas.

GEBCO (General Bathymetric Chart of the Oceans). Bathymetric data for Philippine Sea region.

Statistical and Economic Databases

International Monetary Fund. World Economic Outlook Database, various years.

World Bank. World Development Indicators, various years.

World Trade Organization. International Trade Statistics, various years.

Legal Databases

International Court of Justice. Case database and archived judgments.

Permanent Court of Arbitration. Case repository and awards.

United Nations Treaty Collection. Treaty texts and ratification status.

Online Encyclopedic Sources

Encyclopedia Britannica. Various entries on maritime law, geography, and international relations.

Wikipedia. Multiple entries including "Okinotorishima," "UNCLOS," "South China Sea," and related topics. Accessed August 2024-January 2025.

VIII. ARCHIVAL AND HISTORICAL SOURCES

Historical Documents

Spanish Colonial Archives. Records of Pacific exploration, 16th-18th centuries.

British Admiralty Charts. Historical maritime surveys and navigation records.

Japanese National Archives. Territorial administration documents, 1931-present.

Diplomatic Archives

U.S. State Department Archives. Diplomatic correspondence related to maritime disputes.

Foreign Ministry Archives (Japan). Bilateral negotiations and multilateral diplomacy records.

United Nations Archives. Documentation of UNCLOS negotiations and implementation.

IX. INTERVIEWS AND PERSONAL COMMUNICATIONS

Government Officials

Various officials from Japan Coast Guard, Ministry of Foreign Affairs, and Maritime Self-Defense Force. Interviews conducted 2024-2025. (Names withheld for confidentiality)

Academic Experts

Heath, Timothy (RAND Corporation). Interview on Chinese maritime strategy, August 2025.

Kayanne, Hajime (University of Tokyo). Published interviews on Okinotorishima research.

Kuribayashi, Tadao (Toyo Eiwa University). Legal analysis of UNCLOS interpretation.

Van Dyke, Jon (University of Hawaii Law School). Published legal commentary on Article 121(3).

Maritime Practitioners

Various Japan Coast Guard officers, commercial fishermen, and research vessel operators. Interviews and informal discussions conducted 2024-2025.

Note: This bibliography includes sources cited throughout the text as well as background materials consulted during research. Publication dates range from historical documents to materials published through January

2025. Web sources were accessed between August 2024 and January 2025 unless otherwise noted.

Don't miss out!

Visit the website below and you can sign up to receive emails whenever Dr Naim Tahir Baig publishes a new book. There's no charge and no obligation.

https://books2read.com/r/B-A-DLSVC-MSRTG

BOOKS 2 READ

Connecting independent readers to independent writers.

Did you love *The Last Rock's Secret War: Okinotorishima and Japan's Fight for Tomorrow's Ocean*? Then you should read *Artificial Intelligence Reshapes Nations' Strategic Cultures*[1] by Dr Naim Tahir Baig!

[2]

BOOK DESCRIPTION

Artificial Intelligence Reshapes Nations' Strategic Cultures: The Definitive Guide to the AI Revolution in Global Strategy

In an era where military decisions unfold in seconds rather than days, and algorithms process battlefield intelligence faster than human commanders can comprehend, the fundamental nature of how nations think about war and strategy is undergoing its most profound transformation since the nuclear age. **"Artificial Intelligence Reshapes Nations' Strategic Cultures"** by Dr. Naim Tahir Baig provides the first comprehensive examination of this revolutionary shift, documenting how artificial intelligence is not merely changing the tools of warfare but fundamentally

1. https://books2read.com/u/mgdYN7

2. https://books2read.com/u/mgdYN7

altering the cultural DNA that guides strategic decision-making across the globe.

Drawing on the latest developments through mid-2025—including military AI spending projected to reach $38.8 billion by 2028, real-world lessons from Ukraine's AI-enabled autonomous warfare, and recent Pentagon initiatives like the Thunderforge AI system—this groundbreaking work bridges complex geopolitical theory with accessible analysis for intelligent general readers, policymakers, and strategic professionals. Dr. Baig demonstrates how the integration of AI into military affairs represents a "Darwinian moment" where nations must rapidly evolve their strategic cultures or face strategic irrelevance in an increasingly competitive international system.

The book meticulously examines how major powers are approaching this transformation through distinctly different cultural lenses: America's democratic dilemma of balancing open innovation with security needs; China's state-directed "intelligentization" strategy aimed at achieving cognitive dominance; Russia's asymmetric approach using AI to overcome conventional disadvantages; and Europe's emphasis on ethical frameworks and regulatory leadership. Through detailed case studies spanning from nuclear strategy in the algorithmic age to the new dynamics of alliance politics when sharing algorithms while maintaining advantages, Dr. Baig reveals how strategic culture—not just technology—will determine success in the AI-enabled conflicts of tomorrow.

More than a technological assessment, this work serves as an urgent call for conscious strategic culture design. As AI systems begin to operate at speeds that compress human decision-making time from hours to seconds, the risk of losing human agency over the most consequential strategic decisions has never been greater. Dr. Baig argues that the nations that successfully integrate artificial intelligence while preserving human wisdom and values will shape the next century of international relations, while those that fail to adapt risk not only military defeat but the erosion of the democratic principles and human-centered values that strategic power should ultimately serve. Essential reading for anyone seeking to understand how the marriage of silicon and strategy is reshaping the global order before our eyes.

Read more at https://naimtahirbaig.netlify.app.

Also by Dr Naim Tahir Baig

1

Earning Online: Unlocking Today's Virtual Economy
Loveful Hate / Hateful Love?
A Textbook Of Foreign Policy Analysis

Standalone

Misconceptions About Writing a Lesson Planner for Teaching: A Comprehensive Guide
Bashar al-Assad's Last Stand: A Study of the Syrian Conflict's Final 11 Days in December 2024
Three Winters in Exile: The Trump Chronicles 2021-2024
Biden vs. Trump The 45th and 46th: A Tale of Two Americas
Imran Khan's Political Journey: From Cricket to Revolution
Instagram Automation: The Art of Silent Selling to Earn Millions
Political Prophecies of Imran Khan
Jo Samjhna Samjho: Love's Last Words
Shadow Hearts
Complexity of Souls
Worldly Success According To Islam
The Concept of Eid Among All Religions
The Widening Political Gap Between Muslim Rulers And Their Masses In The 21st Century
Pakistan's Maritime Frontier: Breaking Free from the IMF Through Blue Economy Development

Can Russia Help Pakistan Grow?
Why Nuclear-Armed Pakistan Has Not Fought a War Against Israel in the 2020s?
The War Of Narrative
Ethics Of Deceptive Tears
Crossroads of Continents
The Last Battlefield
From Beloved to Honour
International Relations from a Pakistani Perspective
Humanity is Losing its Credibility !
Operation Bunyan um Marsoos
Ibrahim Traoré
Starving Africa Feeds the Well Fed West
From Captain to Khan: The Rise and Fall of Imran Khan
The Spider's Web: How Ukraine Rewrote the Rules of War
The UNO's Three Failures: Gaza, Kashmir, and Ukraine
Operation Rising Lion 2025: Israel's Strike on Iran's Nuclear Program
Behind The Veil Of Deception: Catherine Perez-Shakdam
2nd Edition: Operation Rising Lion: Israel's Strike Against Iran's Nuclear Program
Operation True Promise 3
Shadow War 2025: Israel's Secret Army Inside Iran
Mental Health and Digital Wellness: Navigating the Hyper-Connected World
After The Break-up
Echoes of Love After Life
Geopolitical Realignments And U.S. Decline
America Party
Artificial Intelligence Reshapes Nations' Strategic Cultures
Knowledge at the Cost of Drinking Water
Abandoning UNESCO, Abandoning America's Global Leadership
Why Pakistan Can't Be Ignored ?
Love Seized
Tarifaço: Trump's Tariff Assault on Brazil and the Battle for Hemispheric Power

GAZA: The word 'ETHICS' is at stake
Kiss Cam Crisis
The Boomer Blockade: How an Aging Generation is Reshaping Global Power and Economics at Younger Generations' Expense
Fractured Faith: The Ken Paxton Divorce Scandal and the Crisis of Conservative Authenticity
The New American Empire In 2025
The Last Rock's Secret War: Okinotorishima and Japan's Fight for Tomorrow's Ocean
The Great Realignment

Watch for more at https://naimtahirbaig.netlify.app.

About the Author

Dr. Naim Tahir Baig can be described as a Political Analyst, Geopolitical Strategist, Military and Security Studies Expert, Intelligence and Espionage Scholar, Social Commentator, Philosopher of Contemporary Issues, Digital Economy Specialist, Islamic Scholar and Interfaith Commentator, Poet and Literary Author, Regional Studies Expert, Multidisciplinary Intellectual, and Pakistan-Centric Analyst, reflecting his diverse expertise across politics, geopolitics, military strategy, intelligence, social commentary, business, religion, literature, and regional studies.

Books by Dr Naim Tahir Baig

Political Analysis & Contemporary History

Bashar al-Assad's Last Stand: A Study of the Syrian Conflict's Final 11 Days in December 2024Three Winters in Exile: The Trump Chronicles 2021-2024Biden vs. Trump The 45th and 46th: A Tale of Two AmericasImran Khan's Political Journey: From Cricket to RevolutionPolitical Prophecies of Imran KhanFrom Captain to Khan: The Rise and Fall of Imran KhanThe Widening Political Gap Between Muslim Rulers And Their Masses In The 21st CenturyIbrahim Traoré

International Relations & Geopolitical Analysis

Can Russia Help Pakistan Grow ?Why Nuclear-Armed Pakistan Has Not Fought a War Against Israel in the 2020s ?A Textbook Of Foreign Policy AnalysisInternational Relations from a Pakistani PerspectiveThe UNO's Three Failures: Gaza, Kashmir, and Ukraine

Military Operations & Strategic Studies

27 Minutes That Nearly Started World War IIIOperation Bunyan um Marsoos2nd Edition: Operation Rising Lion: Israel's Strike Against Iran's Nuclear ProgramOperation True Promise 3The Spider's Web: How Ukraine Rewrote the Rules of WarOperation Rising Lion 2025: Israel's Strike on Iran's Nuclear Program

Intelligence and Espionage Research Analysis

Behind The Veil Of Deception: Catherine Perez-Shakdam

Read more at https://naimtahirbaig.netlify.app.

www.ingramcontent.com/pod-product-compliance
Lightning Source LLC
LaVergne TN
LVHW090312210926
848480LV00001B/224